"Kunze Up Front!"

A Private's Perceptions from the Bottom Up
The Infantry in World War II

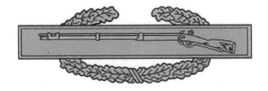

Otto R. Kunze,

38701724 Private First Class

Third Army European Theater of Operations (ETO)

ISBN 978-1-64458-181-0 (paperback)
ISBN 978-1-64458-182-7 (digital)

Christian Faith Publishing, Inc.
832 Park Avenue
Meadville, PA 16335
www.christianfaithpublishing.com

Every effort has been made to identify and credit copyright holders. Any omissions are unintentional. The author should be notified in writing immediately for full acknowledgement of such omissions in future editions.

No copyright is claimed for materials in the references cited or in the appendices. The author will appreciate receiving any corrective comments, omissions or additions that will further authenticate and enhance the manuscript.

Cover illustration: The background map is from the Taschen Atlas by Moes (undated) cited in the book's references. The author's approximate path of activity is indicated by the heavy black line.

Printed in the United States of America

This memoir is dedicated to:

My parents, John and Hermine (Moerbe) Kunze, who firmly believed that their children deserved the opportunity to get a high school education even if this commitment increased and intensified their labors and reduced the farm's net income. Their faith in us and their morals, patience, persistence and untiring dedication to work served as an inspiration to all their children.

and to

My wife, Alice (Eifert) Kunze, who passed away on July 25, 2015, and children Glenn, Allen, Charles and Karen (Kunze) Gerdes for their unwavering support and help to get the manuscript written and rewritten numerous times before it evolved as a publication that realistically reflects the training for and the battleground environment of World War II.

Contents

List of Figures

Acknowledgments

More than seventy years have passed since the actions that are reported. During this period, the activities were recalled, rethought, reexamined, re-dreamed and rerun through the author's mind many, many times. The activities did not change, but the rationale for them has continued to evolve to give reason for the actions. The events all happened, but they may not be remembered in a precise chronological order. The first day of battle remains vividly clear, but the subsequent days of battle may be only in approximate order.

Throughout the manuscript, references are made to my squad, my platoon, my company and my battalion. These are not at all mine, but instead I was a private in them. They are the units in which I served. I had no command of them but was being commanded. I in no way want to imply that I was in charge.

That which is written is what the memory recalls. Other individuals in the conflicts probably saw the battles a little differently; they may have a different and deeper perspective of them. The author will appreciate corrective or related aspects as well as specific observations. Officers at any level probably saw the battles differently. They had much more information than what was available to a private. The manuscript reports that which the author sensed, saw, felt, heard and has remembered.

With each excursion and with each reading of a related manuscript, the author has gained new insights about how, why and when things happened. Usually these can be related to the author's experiences. Others do not fit because they were written from another's perspective. Any additional information that the reader can add to the actions reported will be appreciated. The author has become much more knowledgeable about the activities with the passing of the years than what he was while the actions were evolving.

The author wishes to thank all those who encouraged him to write these memoirs. The Sterling C. Evans Library Personnel at Texas A&M University suggested that the manuscript be written as if "you are writing it for your family." This has been a guideline. The author thanks them for their interest, suggestions, inspiration and encouragement.

"How did it feel?" or "How did you feel?" are questions that are often asked. The emotions can hardly be put into words, but this manuscript is an attempt to do so.

This memoir takes the reader to the front lines and into the actions in which the author was engaged. The combat is real; the decisions are tough and the results are usually final and irreversible. The soldier's life is on the line. Other veterans have attempted to describe the combat environment, and many have concluded "I cannot tell you how it was, but those of you who were there remember." *A Veterans Presentation* (Anonymous, 2004). In this text, the author makes the attempt once more to describe the combat environment. You, the reader, must decide how well he was able to capture the spirit and the realities of the moments.

Let me wish for you some hours of interesting reading.

—The Author

1

Kunze Family History

Otto R. Kunze, US Army serial number 38701724, was reared on a diversified farm in Warda, Fayette County, Texas, in the United States of America. My Father, John P. Kunze, was an infantryman in World War I. He had received his basic training before he was shipped to France. En route to the front lines, he contracted pneumonia. The war came to an end before he regained his health. My Grandmothers were born in the States, but both of their Mothers were born in Germany. One of my Grandfathers came from Prussia. He migrated to the United States at the age of sixteen. My other Grandfather came from the Kingdom of Saxony in Germany. He migrated to the United States in 1869 at the age of twelve years.

The John Kunze Family consisted of my Father, John; my Mother, Hermine; two brothers, George and Raymond; one sister, Doris; and myself. George served in the Pacific area during World War II. He was a gunner on a B-24 bomber. Raymond was underage for World War II but later served in the Korean War.

My Father grew corn, cotton, peanuts and ensilage for a feed silo. The farm had milk cows, hogs and chickens. In my teen years, my Father operated a farm dairy and sold milk to a nearby Carnation plant. All the siblings had the responsibility of hand milking three or four cows before breakfast. Thereafter, they had the privilege to drive twelve miles to a high school in La Grange, Texas. Our grammar grades were in a local public school as well as in a parochial school of the Lutheran Church, Missouri Synod. The public school teacher drove from La Grange to Warda. Her vehicle was a sedan automobile that also served as a school bus. She picked up children en route and brought them to the Warda schools.

Children of families in the rural area went through four to six grades of grammar school before they became farm workers. My Mother walked four miles, one way, to attend the parochial school and completed only the first four grades. The beginning of school in the fall was often delayed for a week or two because there was still cotton in the fields to be picked. Six grades were taught in the parochial school while the public school taught seven. The latter qualified a student to go on to high school.

The public school teacher, a woman, convinced my Father that brother George (a farm boy) should go to high school. This was unheard of in the community. Her family in La Grange offered to board George for five days a week during the school season. She had a good argument, and George was the first country boy in the community to have the privilege to attend high school. The procedure required two trips to La Grange every week. Before any commitment was made, my Father set forth the ground rules or the game plan: "You fail one course, and you will become a full-time farm worker. I am not sending you to high school to fail courses." I am happy to report that the game plan worked and none of the siblings became full-time farm workers. All three sons continued their education through PhD degrees while the daughter proceeded on to graduate from a business college.

After George had boarded in La Grange for one year, he drove to school the following year. Three additional trips per week would take him to high school and bring him back home every day for the farm chores. Then Doris graduated from the public school and became a candidate for high school. There was no further boarding. Instead, the run to La Grange was made every day.

The next year, I graduated from public school and joined my brother and sister in the daily trip. A 1928 Model A Ford was the school bus. Now our vehicle could pick up other children and take them to high school in La Grange. George drove the Model A Ford for three years before he graduated. Then I drove it for three years before graduating. Thereafter, Raymond drove it for another three years. The Model A Ford was the Warda school bus for nine years. As I remember, gasoline sold for thirteen to seventeen cents per gallon.

Highway 77 led to La Grange. It was a graveled road and continuous improvements were being made. These caused us to detour on some of the worst washboard roads on which I have ever driven. It was highway traffic on a country road that received no extra maintenance.

2

The United States Enters World War II

The Japanese bombed Pearl Harbor on December 7, 1941. This infamous attack caused the United States to declare war and enter the conflict against Japan, Germany and Italy. I was in the tenth grade in high school. Young men were required to register for military service when they reached the age of eighteen years. High school grades were from eight through eleven.

During my senior year, the war had reached into the high schools. A course in aeronautics was taught. It made use of algebra, trigonometry and physics. I remember problems relating to an aircraft carrier and its planes. With the carrier at an initial position, its planes would take off toward a target. With a given wind, what direction would the planes have to fly? At a given speed and the wind, how long would they have to fly to reach the target? After reaching the target, what direction would the planes have to fly with the wind still blowing? How long would they have to fly to get back to the carrier which was also moving? The planes had to find the carrier before they could land. The course was new, interesting and challenging. It demonstrated the application of mathematics in a very practical way.

My senior year was soon over. I turned eighteen years of age on May 27, 1943, and graduated from high school on May 28 with a class of sixty-four students. I was on track to be called into the service.

Brother George and his entire class at Texas A&M University had already been called into the service. My life was on hold as I helped at home with the farm chores.

The morning routine was for my Father to get up at about 5:30 a.m. to prepare for the cow milking chores. During the winter, his first job was to build a fire in the kitchen cook stove and another one in a wood-burning heater in the dining room. We all slept upstairs in the central part of the home. It was not heated. While doing these early tasks, he would listen to the morning news. After getting the fires going and before leaving for the dairy barn, which was not heated, he would stop off at the bottom of the stairs and announce the latest news from the radio. For instance: the Germans invasion of Africa, Rommel and his escapades, General Montgomery and his battles made my Father's announcements quite regularly. The seesaw battles were announced to us each morning; the fall of France and the early air strikes by the British and the Germans were news worthy items. Then one morning the announcement was "The German battleship, Bismarck, has sunk the British battleship, Hood." We always had the latest news in a nutshell before we got up.

Then one winter morning, he announced, "The Japanese have attacked Pearl Harbor!" A morning or so later, the announcement was that the United States has declared war on Germany, Italy and Japan. These announcements concerned the United States and other Allied countries at war; but more particularly, they concerned my older brother, George, who was in college and myself still in high school. We were on track to become involved in these actions that were occurring on other continents. Both of us could look ahead and see ourselves in these historic events.

The Kunze Family was touched in many ways: sugar rationing, fuel rationing, tire rationing, good used tires had to be recapped, goods and services became scarce. The reality that the United States was at war touched us at every turn.

The young folks (fourteen years or older) in our church community had a Walther League (named after the church's founder). This group met perhaps once a month on a Sunday evening. Other Lutheran churches in the area had similar groups. To make the meetings more interesting, a competition was organized for individual arts and crafts. These efforts were to culminate in a Walther League Talent Festival. How could I become involved? How should I become involved? Individual youths were encouraged to put their talents to work. Categories for participation were in the areas of poetry, handicrafts and hobbies.

Our home was in the line of single engine air force plane training flights between Austin and Houston. On certain flight days, one plane was not yet out of sight when the next one could be seen approaching. Their flights were no more than 1,500 to 2,000 feet high. The pilots were easily visible, but they would pay no attention to us. During one afternoon, twenty to thirty planes would fly over. After two or three planes had flown over, we would start counting to see how many would come over that day. After about two hours, they would come flying back. The insignia of a US plane (as I remember it) was a navy blue star on a white field in the shape of a rectangle that had a blue border around it.

I had seen so many of these insignia that I decided to make a rug with that pattern. It would be beautiful to hang on a wall. I made such a rug with a sewing machine, some canvas and purple and gold yarns (my high school colors). The star and edge trim could be gold, and the background field could be purple. Also the tips of the star, or the whole star, were enclosed in a thin golden circle.

While writing this document, I described the rug to my wife. She was able to dig through some storage boxes and find it (Fig. 1). I do not remember how it was rated at the Walther League Talent Festival, but the project is an indication of my subconscious thoughts at the time.

Fig. 1. A rug sewn in the pattern of United States Air Force plane insignia. Purple and gold were the La Grange High School colors. The rug was entered in a Walther League Talent Festival competition. Evaluation sheets from the judges are not available.

Since we were in the flight line of the planes, single planes would also fly by from time to time. We more or less became used to them. Highway 77 runs from north to south between Giddings and La Grange. The flight line and our home were about half way between the towns.

One day a local young man from La Grange was making the flight back from Houston to Austin. He was familiar with the country roads. On his flight he deviated from his flight plan and followed Highway 290 into Giddings. Then he followed Highway 77 from Giddings to La Grange (his old stomping grounds). He did not stay at his designated flight elevation but descended to about 150- to 200-feet elevation. Our dairy barn was adjacent to the highway. I was at the barn when he buzzed by. He scared the life out of me. In La Grange (his home town), he did several maneuvers over the city; enough to get a write-up in the local newspaper, the *Fayette County Record*. The community was impressed. I never heard whether the deviation from his flight path was reported to his superiors. He did excite the local communities.

Another category of the contest was "Poetry." Individuals were challenged to write a poem on a subject of their choice. The radios and newspapers were filled with war stories. Such stories made the headlines. Some of our local young men were in the service and made the news. A young man from La Grange had flown twenty-five bombing missions and was on furlough at his home. After his furlough, he returned to Europe and flew two or three more missions before his plane and crew were shot down. He did not survive. Such stories were very real. I could project them into my future.

After living with such news for month after month, a poem relating to it seemed to be an appropriate challenge. After thinking about the prospect, I accepted the challenge and wrote the poem "The American Soldier." I feel that it captures the sense, spirit and my vision of the time. The poem participation certificate and the judges' evaluations of the poem are shown in Figures 2 and 3.

The American Soldier

Leaving home and church behind him,
Leaving friends without dismay,
He has joined the greatest army
Fighting for the U. S. A.

Training with his Christian buddies,
Learning of the enemy,
Bombing, blasting, shooting, stabbing,
Which his future days may see.

Sailing over the vast waters,
Hearing the great oceans moan,
Crowded in a small compartment
Which he cannot call his own.

Then one day his ship is anchored
In a land so far away;
He is in the combat area,
There the tyrant hordes to slay.

He is always in the battle,
Gaining ground from tree to tree;
Never fearful of the foe there
Knowing God his refuge be.

Fighting day and night unceasing,
In the air or on the land;
You will always find him battling
Under God's almighty hand.

Then someday he may be wounded
In the battle's bloody storm;
Lonely tired and forsaken,
Resting in his Savior's arm.

He can no longer fight the battle;
He can no longer run the lathe;
His heart is happy and unbroken,
He still can fight the fight of faith.

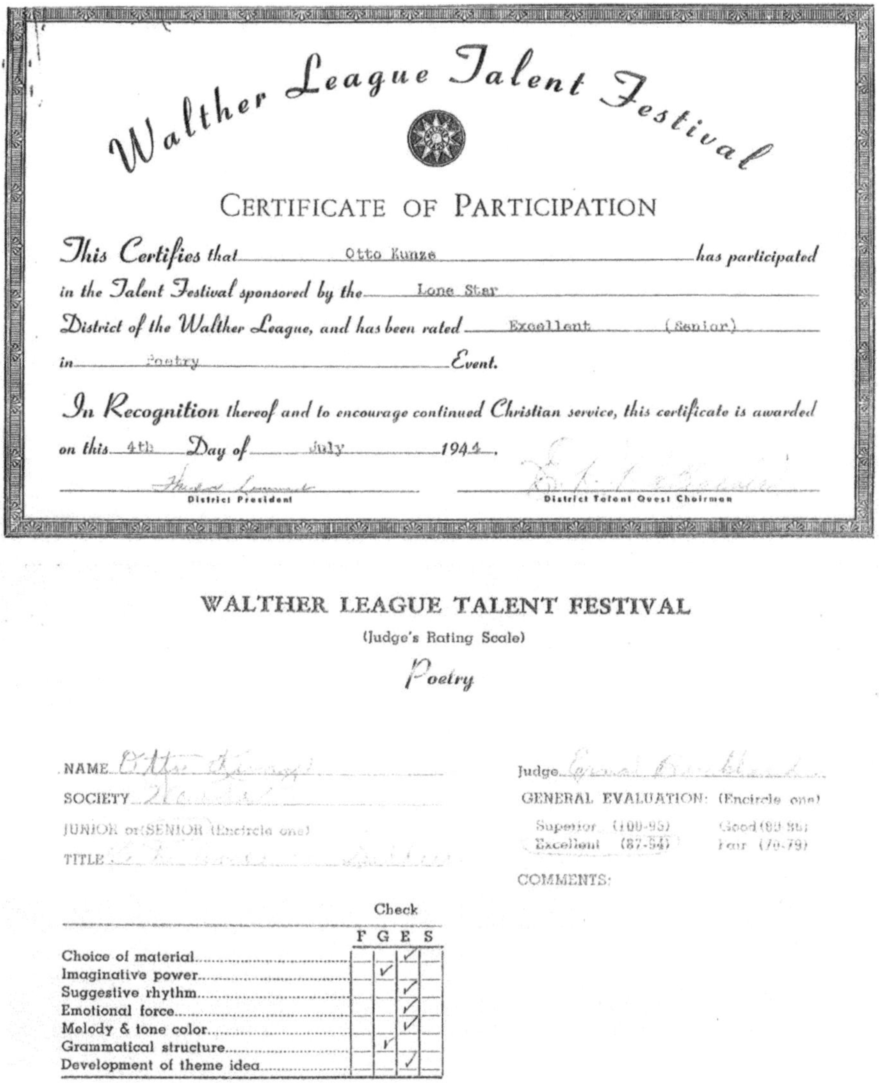

Fig. 2. The Certificate of Participation in the Walther
League Talent Festival competition (Poetry) held in July
1944. The rating sheet of one judge is also shown.

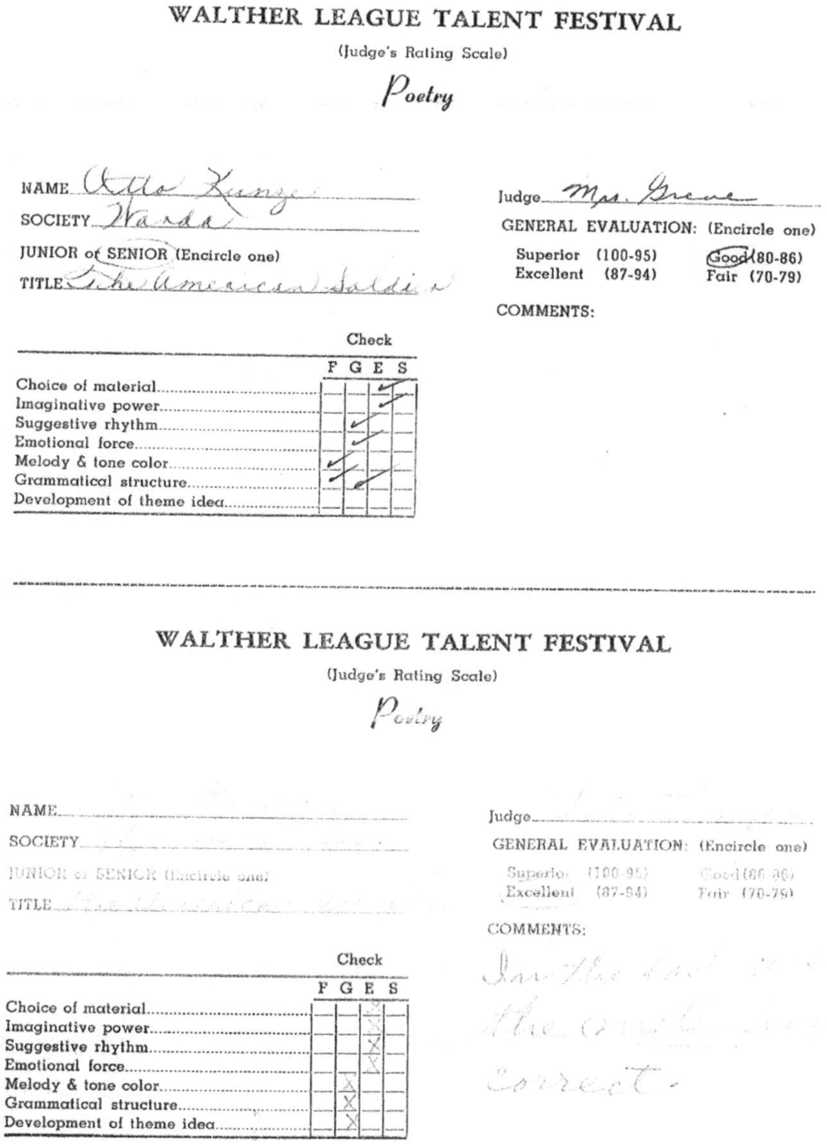

WALTHER LEAGUE TALENT FESTIVAL

(Judge's Rating Scale)

Poetry

NAME _Otto Kunze_
SOCIETY _Warda_
JUNIOR or SENIOR (Encircle one)
TITLE _The American Soldier_

Judge _Mrs. Greve_

GENERAL EVALUATION: (Encircle one)

Superior (100-95)   (Good) (80-86)
Excellent (87-94)   Fair (70-79)

COMMENTS:

Check	F	G	E	S
Choice of material			✓	
Imaginative power		✓		
Suggestive rhythm		✓		
Emotional force		✓		
Melody & tone color	✓			
Grammatical structure	✓	✓		
Development of theme idea				

WALTHER LEAGUE TALENT FESTIVAL

(Judge's Rating Scale)

Poetry

NAME
SOCIETY
JUNIOR or SENIOR (Encircle one)
TITLE

Judge

GENERAL EVALUATION: (Encircle one)

Superior (100-95)   Good (86-86)
Excellent (87-94)   Fair (70-79)

COMMENTS:

In the last
the oral
correct.

Check	F	G	E	S
Choice of material			✓	
Imaginative power			✗	
Suggestive rhythm			✗	
Emotional force			✗	
Melody & tone color		✗		
Grammatical structure		✗		
Development of theme idea		✗		

Fig. 3. The rating sheets of two judges who evaluated
the poem entitled "The American Soldier" at the
Walther League Talent Festival in July 1944.

Another section for the talent festival was concerned with handicrafts and hobbies. An older cousin of mine had given our family a sitting monkey carved out of a peach stone. I looked at it and decided that I could do that also. Subsequently, I carved five such monkeys and mounted them on a small platform. They are shown in Figure 4. Figures 5 and 6 show the Certificate of Participation and the evaluation sheets of the judges.

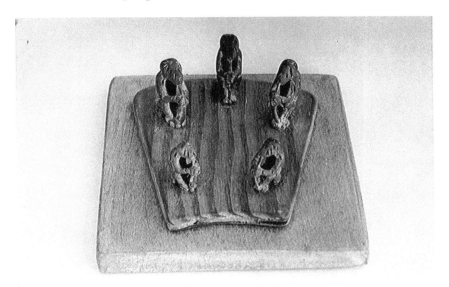

Fig. 4. Sitting monkeys carved out of peach stones, which were entered in the Walther League Talent Festival competition held in July 1944.

Fig. 5. The Certificate of Participation in the
Handicraft and Hobbies Division of the Walther
League Talent Festival competition, July 1944. The
evaluation sheet of one judge is also shown.

WALTHER LEAGUE TALENT FESTIVAL

(Judge's Rating Scale)

Handicraft & Hobbies

NAME _(handwritten)_   Judge _(handwritten)_

SOCIETY _(handwritten)_   GENERAL EVALUATION: (Encircle one)

JUNIOR or (SENIOR) (Encircle one)   (Superior) (100-95)   Good (80-86)
                                        Excellent (87-94)   Fair (70-79)

TITLE _(handwritten)_   COMMENTS:

	Check			
	F	G	E	S
Craftsmanship				✓
Handling of medium				✓
Fidelity & sensitivity of rendering				✓
Design				✓
Balance & placement				✓
Attractiveness & fitness				✓

WALTHER LEAGUE TALENT FESTIVAL

(Judge's Rating Scale)

Handicraft & Hobbies

NAME _(handwritten)_   Judge _(handwritten) V. E._

SOCIETY _(handwritten)_   GENERAL EVALUATION: (Encircle one)

JUNIOR or SENIOR (Encircle one)   Superior (100-95)   Good (80-86)
                                        Excellent (87-94)   Fair (70-79)

TITLE _(handwritten)_   COMMENTS:

                                        (handwritten)

	Check			
	F	G	E	S
Craftsmanship				X
Handling of medium				X
Fidelity & sensitivity of rendering				X
Design				X
Balance & placement				X
Attractiveness & fitness				X

Fig. 6. The evaluation sheets of two judges who rated the monkeys carved out of peach stones in the Walther League Talent Festival competition held in July 1944.

With the passage of time, the number of young men in the service from my home congregation increased. Early volunteers and inductees were already overseas engaged in battle; others were in training while young men like myself were looking forward to be called.

The Warda Community was originally settled by Wends (1854) who immigrated from Eastern Germany to the United States and Texas. They left their homes in order to preserve their religious beliefs, their Wendish heritage and language. Another issue was the continuous warfare in their area.

Earlier migrations from the area had been made to Australia. After some years a few immigrants elected to migrate to Texas. They entered through the port of Galveston and then migrated westward to what is known today as Serbin. There they built the first Lutheran Church in Texas. After some years, the church divided and a small group started another congregation near the Lee County line close to Fayette County. After a few more years, this new congregation moved across the county line. A small church building was constructed and used for a few years before a larger church was built on the location where the Lutheran Church is today.

During World War I, the Warda area was still very much German and stories abound about how these people were expected to buy war bonds with their savings. Their allegiance was watched and challenged. My Father and his brother (Otto) were both inducted into service and served their country with gallantry and honor.

During this time, both the German and the Wendish languages were depressed but the German language prevailed. The area newspaper, first published in Wendish, soon became a German publication. Children going to school learned to read and write German. True Germans had settled in the area before the Wendish-Germans arrived. The Wends soon lost their identity and began to speak German.

The Wendish language declined. The Wendish newspaper was replaced by a German one, *Das Duetsches Volksblatt* (*The German People's Page*). German-speaking children went to school to learn English. This environment prevailed until World War II.

The second World War put pressure on the area to use the English language, and the German language was largely depressed. The author of this book learned English in the public school but also learned to read and write German in the parochial school. When war was declared by the United States on Germany, Italy and Japan, the English language quickly became the preferred means of communication. The Wendish language was essentially gone and lost and the German language was greatly subdued. The name of my church was "Die Evangelisch-Lutherische Kreuz Gemeinde Ungeaenderter Augsburgischer Confession am Rabbs Creek bei Serbin, Lee County, Texas" (Evangelical Lutheran Church of the Unaltered Augsburg Confession on Rabbs Creek, Lee County, Texas). After some years, the church was moved across the county line into Fayette County near Warda.

The congregation kept its German name until after World War II. On August 17, 1947, the current English name of "Holy Cross Evangelical Lutheran Church– Unaltered Augsburg Confession" was adopted.

World War I broke the lines of communication between the Texas immigrants and their relatives in Germany. As a child, I remember that the Kunze Grandparents had a shoe box full of old letters that had been received from Germany. I do not remember that such letters were received during my early childhood years. The adult immigrants died, and their children were not motivated to continue the communications. Few, if any, immigrants made return visits to Germany.

After the turn of the century (2000), there has been a lively interest to find long-lost relatives back in Germany. A surprising number of lost relationships have been reestablished. Several immigrant descendants still have an old picture of a home or business structure that is still in the family back in Germany.

The current generation of descendants has established a Wendish museum at the church in Serbin. Many old pictures, stories, official documents and artifacts are on display there. The museum has a library with many interesting books and historic manuscripts. The reader is advised to contact the museum for further information concerning the history of the area. The environment in the community is still changing from that which it had in World War II. At that time there were no communications with relatives in Germany. The community was fully involved in the war and the current friends were foes.

My notice to report for duty soon arrived. The day before my induction, September 19, 1944, I put in a day's work by helping my Father thresh peanuts in our field. Many people were surprised. They thought that I should have gone out on the town for a real booze bust. I did not imbibe then and have never enjoyed booze that much.

On September 20, 1944, my Father and I got up at 4:00 a.m. to have breakfast. Once more we used the Model A Ford for a trip to La Grange. A bus was loading new inductees and left at about 6:00 a.m. en route to Fort Sam Houston in San Antonio, Texas. I was destined to repeat my Father's adventure in World War I. His call to duty was just twenty-eight years earlier. His parting words to me were: "Otto, remember, it is a whole lot easier to get into trouble than it is to get out of it." His words served as an excellent guideline for my ethics while I was in the military service.

Now more than seventy years have passed. Minute details have faded into oblivion, but there are snapshots of occasions that are still very clear. This treatise attempts to recall the snapshots, what led up to them and what happened thereafter.

3

Otto Kunze Becomes Private Kunze

There were twenty-eight young men in my high school graduating class of 1943. None were on the bus with me. Upon arrival at Fort Sam Houston, we were introduced to life in the military. We were marching before we had military clothes. After some routine paper work, we, along with others, were marched off to a clothing depot. There we formed a single line and proceeded to get our army clothes. All my life I had been trying on clothing and shoes to get an appropriate fit. This time a non-com (non-commissioned officer) behind the counter took one quick glance at me and, all of a sudden, shirts, pants, underwear and socks were literally flying at me. They were mine to wear; shoes were at least a half size larger than anything I had ever worn. Thereafter, we packaged up our civilian garb and sent it home.

During my senior year in high school, I weighed in at 128 pounds for the varsity football team roster. The army clothes did not exactly fit me, but I had no problem getting into them.

The first night was spent in a little wooden hut just big enough for a squad. It was square and more permanent than a fabric tent. Its roof came to a point over the center of the room. High up in the point was a single electric light, perhaps sixty or seventy-five watts. After visiting and getting acquainted with each other, we decided to go to bed. The beds were cots for individual men. Everyone was retiring, but when the last GI was ready to tuck-in, we found that there was no switch for the light. If there was a pull-string or chain, it had been pulled off. So we faced our first challenge. The hut was covered with wooden shingles. There were lathes across the rafters with spaces between the lathes. The openings were big enough to put your fingers through and grab the rafters. After debating the dilemma, a couple of GIs offered to hoist me up to a rafter if I could then shimmy myself up the rafter with hands and arms to unscrew the bulb. I took on the offer and succeeded. We were not around for the next night when the light was again needed. Maybe some new recruit shimmied up the rafter to turn the light back on. The next day, I, along with others, was put on a passenger train en route to Camp Crowder, Missouri.

I had an Uncle Otto after whom I was named. He had a clothing store in Elgin, Texas, and was also a veteran of World War I. I was informed that we were going through Elgin and somehow was able to get word to him that I was coming through. The train did stop in Elgin, and my Uncle was there. I was not allowed to de-board, but we were able to exchange greetings by waving our hands at each other.

The train then continued its journey through Texas and soon the villages and towns became unknown to me. We traveled all night and into the afternoon of the next day. The train then stopped, perhaps on a side railing, out in the country. The conductor announced, "All those who have Camp Crowder as their destination will de-board here." I, with others, left the train and an army two-and-a-half-ton truck soon picked us up for our ride to the camp.

4

Another Clem Chowder
from Camp Crowder

The Camp and Its Facilities

After being checked in, one of the first pieces of literature that we received was a little booklet entitled *Clem Chowder from Camp Crowder*. It told us where the camp was and what facilities it had, i.e. PX (post exchange) stores, barber shops, churches and so on. Neosho was a small town nearby, while Joplin and Springfield were larger towns more distant from the camp.

Camp Crowder was a training facility for the Signal Corps. The Signal Corps sounded good to me. I had taken typing in high school and had become sufficiently proficient in the skill to pass the course. It seemed like the war could actually give me the opportunity to increase my skills in typing and other forms of communication. I really appreciated the opportunity and became an enthusiastic, happy and spirited soldier.

I went to Fort Sam Houston with no one that I knew. I shipped out of Fort Sam Houston with no one that I knew and was now at Camp Crowder with no one that I knew. I had to pick my friends and associates as I became acquainted. Who might such friends be? I grew up in the Lutheran Church, Missouri Synod, so someone in that religious group would have a common background and would appeal to me.

The Church and Home Connection

My Minister back home stayed in touch with all the young men from his congregation who were in the service. He would send an occasional common letter to all the young service men. These letters would tell who was where and what the individuals were doing. In these letters he would let the young men know if there was a Lutheran church in the area. Such a letter informed me that the closest Lutheran church was in Neosho, a nearby town. Soon thereafter I requested a Sunday pass and attended the church. It made me feel at home. The Pastor and his Family invited me out for lunch. I met no other GIs at the church service, but it was a thread that connected me to home.

The church was not in town but rather in its outskirts in the foothills of the Ozarks. The congregation was small, but the church was in a beautiful setting. The service was a traditional one, and I enjoyed it. During my stay at Camp Crowder, I was able to attend only one church service.

Introduction to Military Training

At the camp, we lost no time getting started into basic training. The routine of the day included close order drills, physical exercises (push-ups, sit-ups, running in place, knee bends, jumps and claps, sitting toe touches and many others). The instructor (a Corporal) would demonstrate the exercise, and then we would practice and do it. With just one or two practice runs, everyone was able to do them. After loosening up, we usually had a distance run of four hundred to six hundred yards. This was quite a challenge with those big army shoes.

The day usually included an hour of instruction in how to shoot a rifle, hand-to-hand combat, shooting positions, infiltration maneuvers and others. After six weeks, the training began to include pole climbing, typing and other specialized battlefield exercises for the Signal Corps. We did not go on maneuvers, forced hikes, night patrols or compass directed hikes. We spent little time in disassembling and reassembling the Springfield 1903 rifle. We had no bayonet practice, fired no mortars and were not exposed to mortar or artillery fire. We did not heave hand grenades over a dam and feel the subsequent concussion and hear the explosion. We were in the Signal Corps.

Each day there was something new, interesting and challenging. Everyone was eager and in good spirits. What we were learning could possibly carry over into our private lives after the war.

We were housed in wooden, two-story barracks. Nearly immediately we were issued bolt-action Springfield 1903 rifles and were soon practicing close order drills. We learned the commands and the activities and positions for them.

The bulletin board became the standard means for communications. Individual duties such as KP, guard and fireman were posted there. A person could request a pass; if approved, the list appeared on the bulletin board. If a private did not pass inspection, i.e. his shoes were not polished, his bed was not properly made up, his rifle was not clean, he was not cleanly shaven or any of a dozen other little things, he did not have to apply for a pass as it would not be approved. Other activities, such as barrack scrub-downs, barrack inspections and the uniform for tomorrow were posted there. The bulletin board was a primary source of communication; it was to be checked at least twice a day. The system quickly developed where your fellow soldiers informed you when your name was on the bulletin board. Perhaps your request for an evening pass was approved.

Generally, no one was excused from the barrack floor scrub-down. This occurred about once a month. The floor must have been double wood with tongue and groove edges. Additionally, there must have been tarpaper between the wood layers. There was no leakage from the second story floor to the first story ceiling. The non-commissioned officers were around to assure that the floor did indeed get scrubbed and that we did not get too much water on the floor or leave it there too long.

During cold weather the barrack was heated with a coal-burning furnace. A "fireman" was designated to keep the fire going throughout the night. This assignment was posted on the bulletin board. I was assigned to that duty at least once during my stay in Camp Crowder. Back in Texas, we always burned wood to warm our homes in cold weather. Both fuel sources provided good heat but the smoke smelled a little different.

One of my pleasant memories of the training at Camp Crowder was a Corporal White in our platoon. He must have been a professional soldier. He was probably old enough to retire but loved his work so much that he would not quit. Corporal White taught us the commands and the moves for close order drill. He just loved to drill us. Seemingly he had done the drills for so long that they were effortless for him. He could march a platoon of privates down the street and be the happiest man in the world. His vocation was also his avocation. I feel that we enjoyed him just as much as he enjoyed us. His movements or steps were in a gait rather than in a march.

After the first six weeks, we had acquired the basic skills and demeanor for a soldier. We had learned to march, count cadence, salute officers and were able to respond to drill commands. We had been on the rifle range, learned the shooting positions and were recognized for our shooting skills with an appropriate medal. The physical conditioning continued but we then began to spend time to further develop our communication skills such as using the typewriter. Additionally, we learned other skills in the trade, such as climbing poles with the traditional leg brace and gaff. We did not get to work on top of the poles. For me this was a new and interesting experience. Prior to army life, I had just climbed post oak and pin oak trees with no particular equipment. Play ground ventures and squirrel hunting trips provided such climbing opportunities.

The training activities soon became routine with daily practices. The morale of the men was excellent. Everyone was putting forth his best effort. But after six weeks of basic and another six weeks of specialized training, our routine suddenly ended.

On December 16, 1944, Hitler's armies launched the Battle of the Bulge. Abruptly and suddenly without warning or explanation, our Signal Corps training ceased. We were shipped out of Camp Crowder, Missouri, to Camp Maxey near Paris, Texas, for Infantry training. We no longer needed the Springfield 1903 rifles. When we arrived at Camp Maxey, we were issued the Garand M-1 rifle. I had been in the military service for less than three months.

5

Rifles of World War II

The Springfield 1903 rifle was a manually activated bolt-action weapon that fired one shot at a time. The expended shell then had to be ejected by manually operating the bolt and injecting a new loaded shell into the firing chamber. The bullets came in clips of five shells. The clip was set above the open magazine and then with thumb pressure, the loaded shells were pressed out of the clip into the rifle magazine. The bolt-action in its rearward movement ejected the expended shell and with its forward movement picked up a loaded shell and inserted it into the firing chamber. These rifle mechanics were interesting and acceptable on the rifle range but were hardly what the soldier needed in battle where his life was on the line. Generally, the Springfield 1903 rifle was a precision and refined weapon. A person was really challenged to shoot well with it. I did.

The Garand M-1 rifle was less refined and was a more rugged weapon. It could be disassembled and reassembled in the field without any particular tools. The rifle was semi-automatic in that the user could get a shot with every pull of the trigger. The burst of the exploding gunpowder in the shell was used to eject the expended shell and to insert a loaded one into the firing chamber. To obtain this action, a small hole was necessary between the gun barrel and a gas chamber that could automatically initiate the bolt action. This was a wonderful idea. It was particularly great when it worked. When did it not work? Such incidents will be related later. For the work of a sniper, I would have preferred the Springfield 1903 rifle. As a battle-field weapon, the advantages of the Garand M-1 rifle far outweighed its disadvantages.

The M-1 rifle was loaded with a clip of eight shells. The entire clip with the shells was inserted into the rifle's magazine. After the eighth shot, the empty shell along with the empty clip were both ejected from the rifle and the bolt locked in the open position until another loaded clip was inserted. After the loaded clip was inserted, it locked in position. Then a slight pull to the rear on the bolt lever released the bolt and allowed it to slam forward with a loaded shell. The firing chamber was now closed and the rifle was ready to fire. This automatic action was an excellent feature when a person was engaged in combat.

6

Infantry Training at Camp Maxey, Texas

The drill and exercise activities at Camp Maxey were similar to those at Camp Crowder. The focus of the training was very different, however. Man-to-man combat was emphasized. How is that done with a rifle and bayonet? How does a person do close combat? The bayonet was attached to the discharge end of the rifle barrel. We had bayonet practice on stuffed human dummies. We charged across open fields where the dummy enemy would suddenly pop-up out of the ground. Instead of shooting, we would stab the dummy. We watched a light machine gun being fired with its tracer bullets. About every fifth round was a tracer bullet. The gun was fired in bursts while we were seated in an earthen bleacher. After being fired for sometime, a Lieutenant lectured us about its capability. Suddenly there was another shot. The machine gun barrel had become so hot that the shell inserted in the chamber fired on its own.

A common battlefield explosive was primacord. This is an explosive formed into a cord. It can be used to connect explosive charges that are set apart in numerous places in a structure. We were told how fast the cord burns or explodes. This rate is fast enough to ignite charges separated some distance from each other in a building, bridge, or other structure. The demonstration was impressive. The cord was strung like a fence barbwire around several wood posts set

41

into the ground before us. We watched the cord explode without any additional charges along its length. I never saw such cord used in our battles. No one carried it; there was no need for it since the infantryman did not carry explosives that needed primacord for ignition. The cord could have been useful for our troops as they were battling through the pillboxes in the Siegfried line.

The Lieutenant's lecture on close combat continued. A soldier does not make a sustained advance with his rifle butt against his shoulder. Rather, the rifle is carried with both hands ready to raise it to the shoulder. If the enemy suddenly appears there may not be time to raise the rifle. How good is shooting from the hip? This shot can be made very quickly, but how good is its accuracy? Then it just so happened that a dummy Kraut erected himself about thirty-five or forty yards before us. The Lieutenant asked who would volunteer to engage this Kraut with "shots from the hip." The Lieutenant made several calls, but there were no volunteers. Well, Private Kunze finally raised his hand and stepped forward. An M-1 rifle was loaded with a clip of tracer shells and I was given the order to "fire at will." The first shot was well to the left of the dummy; the second shot was closer but still to the left. The third shot was near but still to the left. Then I overcorrected with two shots to the right. The last three shots were all around the dummy, but I had no hits. The elevations of all the shots were good, but laterally the shots missed the mark. If I could have had another clip of ammunition, I may have scored a hit. As it was, I convinced myself and others that shooting from the hip could be fast, but the accuracy was not very good. I did not distinguish myself that day even though I was brave enough to step forward.

Thereafter we were exposed to dummy mortar fire or, more accurately, to mortar fire with dummy shells. The mortar rounds were real but they were not loaded with gunpowder. We could hear the blast which sent the mortar shell on its way and moments later could see the mortar shell drop from the sky in front and to the right of us. To make the experience more memorable and complete, we had to dig the mortar rounds out of the ground after the demonstration. Our bayonets were the best digging tool that we had. The afternoon was not complete until we had retrieved all of the mortar rounds. The finned back end of the mortar shell was perhaps eight or ten inches below ground level.

The infiltration course was one to be remembered. We had to cradle the M-1 rifle in our arms while moving forward on our elbows and knees. There was a webbing of barbwire above us and there was machine gun fire with tracer bullets above the barbwire. We probably had less than two feet of clear space in which to crawl. Within the crawling space there were holes in the ground about three feet in diameter and perhaps eight to ten feet deep. Each of these had been loaded with about one foot of mud, water and an explosive charge. As we approached the holes, the charges were set off. These blasted out the mud and water, which rained all over us. The whole exercise was realistic. However, all of us were confident that we would survive the course. We did.

Everyone took the opportunity to pull the pin and lob a hand grenade over an earth embankment. Everyone experienced the feel of the concussion wave from the resulting explosion. The hand grenade is heavy enough to where a person needs to know about how far he can throw it.

We had a mock battle exercise set up for one night. Each of us received a clip of blank ammunition shells. We marched out to the mock battle ground during the early evening hours. There we deployed into a battle line. We were told to fire our clip of ammunition and then to retrieve our empty ejected clip.

The battle line was formed in a wooded area. At a given command we began to fire at an imagined enemy. I was surprised that I had fired my eight rounds so quickly. The last pull of the trigger was just a click. Then I could not find my ejected clip in the darkness. I searched and searched with my hands, but there was no clip to be found.

Finally, the mock battle was over and we reassembled. Soon we were on the march back to our barracks. I did not have my empty clip and I could not explain why! I had looked or felt for it a long time. The thought finally came to me, if the rifle chamber is closed, the clip should still be in it. If the gun chamber is open, then the clip was ejected and I lost it. So when we get back to our barrack, I need to check the gun chamber. There should have been no rifle click when the trigger was pulled if the gun chamber was open.

We marched in formation back to camp. At our barracks, there were street lights. We soon returned to our quarters; our platoon came to a halt, and the First Sergeant dismissed us. I immediately brought my rifle up; the gun chamber was closed. I opened it and there was the clip in my rifle with two unexpended blank shells. I removed both the clip and the two blank rounds of ammunition. The First Sergeant saw that I did not break formation with the rest of the men and also saw what I retrieved from my M-1 rifle. He immediately called the platoon back into formation. After the necessary preliminary commands, he gave the command "Prepare to fire" followed by the command "Fire." Within the platoon, there were at least two shots. Other soldiers had the same problem. They had not solved the mystery either.

The blank shells, which we fired, produced sufficient gun barrel pressure to eject the empty shell but not enough for the bolt to pick up the next loaded round. Perhaps another eighth-inch retraction was required to insert the next round. In this case the bolt moved backward far enough to cock the gun, then moved forward without a loaded shell, closed the gun chamber and allowed the trigger to be pulled. The M-1 rifle was semi-automatic most of the time! I remembered the lesson well.

The infantry consists of foot soldiers, and if we did not know it before, we learned it at Camp Maxey. We took short hikes, long hikes, double time hikes, night hikes, day hikes and hikes with full battle gear and backpack. We hiked until we were tired, and then we hiked some more. We had one or more "forced marches." In these we had to reach a location in a limited time. (The exercises were a good "snap shot" of things to come, but I did not know it.)

I was probably the smallest man in the platoon but managed to compete well with my fellow soldiers. I was never last in any competitive activity; neither was I first. But I was easily in the top quarter and was challenging the best. Long hikes with a full pack were a real challenge, but I completed every one of them. The weight of the full pack, ammunition and other gear was more than one-half of my body weight. These successful completions caused me to become a fully qualified infantryman.

After completing our training exercises, we went out on bivouac for several days. Bivouac consisted of living away from the conveniences of the camp. We spent several days out in the field. We did not try very hard to simulate battle field conditions. There was no real enemy around. I do not remember digging a foxhole. We did not deploy as if there was an enemy before us. We had our activities on one side of the ridge of a long hill. The "rear" was over the ridge on the backside. Ammunition and other supplies were in the rear. After several days on the front, I was sent to the rear for some detail. I did what was necessary and proceeded back to the front. It must have been a long day, and I was dragging a little. (After a day's work on the farm, I was used to dragging home). I met a Lieutenant who was going to the rear. I saluted the officer and he returned the salute. After a few more paces, the Lieutenant had decided that I did not look exuberant enough. He did an about face and called, "Soldier, come back here!" I obeyed and did an about face. After a few steps, I saluted him once more, and he returned the salute while I stood at attention. Then he proceeded to do his exercise for the day by chewing me out. "Soldier, look lively! Put a spring into your step! Where is your combat spirit!? We are in a war!..." After completing his chewing exercise, I said, "Yes Sir!" I saluted him, did an about face and was back on my way. If I was not fully awake when we first met, he did wake me up. For me, that has been the most memorable part of the bivouac. I remember it; he got my attention. Otherwise, we occupied our slope of the hill under battlefield conditions, but there was never an enemy before us.

After only six weeks of intensive training, we were pronounced to be qualified infantrymen. I think that the Battle of the Bulge influenced how much training we needed. Without any fanfare, we were given a furlough home. Our return ticket was to Fort Meade, Maryland.

7

Preparation to Ship Overseas

There were no close friends who shipped out with me from Camp Crowder, Missouri, to Camp Maxey, Texas. At Camp Maxey, I do not remember ever taking a pass. The closest town was Paris, Texas. Bonds that were beginning to develop at Camp Crowder were shattered as we were shipped out from there. We did not ship out as a platoon, company or battalion. We were shipped out as individuals.

The Battle of the Bulge in Europe seemingly set the schedule for our training. Many GIs gave their lives in this battle; there were open empty slots in the ranks that needed to be filled. We were the ones who would fill them.

After completing my furlough to Texas, I was on the train to Fort Meade, Maryland. En route I met a fellow soldier from the Rio Grande Valley of Texas. He seemingly had the same schedule as I did. He had spent more than a half day to get to Central Texas where I boarded the train, and we spent another half day together to get to the northern border of Texas. Thereafter, we spent another day before we reached Fort Meade, Maryland. My fellow Texan spent as much time getting out of Texas as he did to get from Texas to Maryland. At Fort Meade, we were separated and did not see each other again.

At Fort Meade, we were allowed to take a pass into Washington D.C. I took the opportunity but really had nothing in particular to see. Of course there was the Capitol Building, the White House and many other places. But what could a foot soldier (a stranger to the city) see in one or two days? I was not familiar with the city. Toward evening, I found a USO (United Service Organization) station. There I met another GI, perhaps a Sergeant, who was stationed there but did not live on a base or in a camp. He had his own private quarters. He invited me to spend the night at his place. I have never figured out how he related to the big picture. After leaving the USO, we had to walk several blocks to a bus stop. There were a lot of soldiers in the city, also officers. When meeting such brass, I saluted as I was supposed to. My new friend never saluted any officer. After two or three salutes by me, we stopped, and he told me, "Quit saluting the officers. You are going to get me into trouble when you salute and I do not!" So I (we) saluted nothing more the rest of the evening. I was very uncomfortable because now I was not giving the officers the respect that they deserved. My companion appeared to be completely comfortable while I was on the opposite end of the comfort zone.

We caught a bus that took us across the Potomac river and after a short walk, we were at his apartment, which had a bedroom and a kitchenette. I was uncomfortable that night because I really did not understand the status of my host companion. In the morning, we got up; he fixed us breakfast and I caught a bus back into the city where I found transportation back to Fort Meade.

My visit to the nation's capital was short and less than a memorable one. I went to visit because I had the opportunity; the trip was unplanned, and I had no goals for the visit.

We were in a waiting mode at Fort Meade. My new friend from Texas was somewhere around but well removed from me. While waiting, I recall only one activity. We were asked to fall out with all of our equipment (backpack and duffel bag). We were then formed into squads and platoons. After a short march with our equipment, we reached a drill field. There we were subjected to a field inspection. Members of the platoon were dispersed so we could lay out all of our clothing and equipment. Two Lieutenants inspected our possessions. They made sure that every soldier had the required equipment and materials and no more. Standard equipment that we did not have was (1) a rifle, (2) ammunition, (3) bayonet, (4) hand grenades and

(5) a shovel. All other items were required. In those days, the army personnel were not integrated. But on this occasion, one of the two inspecting officers was a black Lieutenant. Otherwise, there were no blacks who trained with us in the Signal Corps or the Infantry.

We were in a holding or waiting mode. After another day, there were no more passes. Then within another day, we were loaded on a troop train and shipped to Boston, Massachusetts. There we unboarded the train and boarded the USS *America* whose name had been changed to the USS *West Point*. The name change was for security reasons. In peace time, the United States had no USS *West Point*.

8

Voyage Across the Atlantic Ocean

We boarded the ship around midafternoon by the use of several covered ramps. The boarding area was covered and concealed so that nothing on the outside was visible to us and certainly we were not visible to anyone on the outside. Each GI carried his duffel bag and backpack but no rifle, shovel or bayonet. The boarding went smoothly. The procedure was well organized indicating that the ship had been loaded with troops before. Movement of the GIs led directly to the room where we had our bunks. As we checked in, our names were called, and we received our bunk assignments. The top of my room was close to the waterline with the floor being below the water level. There was a porthole in the area that was in and out of the water. The bunks consisted of heavy sheets of canvas hung at four corners and stacked about six high. There were no mattresses or springs. My bunk was perhaps the fourth one up. The distance between the bunks was eighteen inches or less.

Initially we were restricted to the compartment with our bunks. This restriction continued until we had a roll call. Evening was setting in and the view out of our porthole disappeared into the darkness. We shuffled and stacked our duffel bags and backpacks to clear the aisle. We had dim lights—just enough to see each other. After a while, we were ushered out for the evening meal. The route included going up several flights of stairs and down on others. In the hallways, we turned several corners, but we arrived there. The food seemed to be regular army chow. After the meal, we retraced our path to our quarters. There being nothing else to do, we soon crawled into our bunks.

I could not jack up my knee without making contact with the bunkmate above. The closeness was particularly noticeable when the bunks were occupied. I would often get a nudge on my bottom from the bunkmate below and the GI above me would get nudged by me because a person could not twist or turn without making contact. This was an awakening reminder that I was now on ship.

Most everyone was trying to envision that which was before us. No one talked about it. We were about to leave a secure environment and move into a dangerous and unpredictable one. Everything was calm and quiet. The days ahead would not be that way. How different would they be?

Whatever was done outside the ship was handled very well. I never felt any bumps, jolts, or tremors. We were not aware that ramps were being drawn up or otherwise moved away. There were no generators starting up, no flickering lights, no engines cranking and we could feel no ship movement. Yet when morning came, we were out somewhere on the Atlantic Ocean. All that we could see was water.

The USS *West Point* was a large, proud, magnificent ship that could easily qualify to be at the top of the list of enemy targets. The GIs were in a somber mood. We had no drills or inspections. At best a Sergeant may have had an occasional roll call. We could wander about the ship into areas that were not restricted or off limits.

From my point of view, the GIs were a mix. There seemed to be no groups that had trained together. There was no unit, outfit or bond. There were few if any familiar faces. If there were officers aboard, we were not quartered with them. Non-coms were new. Some bonding developed among the passengers during the voyage. This, however, was short lived. Faces that became familiar and friendly were lost as we landed. Yet we started our service together in Europe with essentially the same qualifications, served together through the same period, accumulated go-home points at the same rate and a few of us were finally reunited on the little victory ship on our voyage back to the States.

Going up on deck of the USS *West Point* became one of our favorite pastimes. For a landlubber, the Atlantic Ocean was a magnificent sight, something new and special. I had never seen a large body of water that was so blue, clear, crisp and clean. The weather was generally fair, cold and calm, but there was always a change from one morning to the next. Perhaps there was a little more wind or a little less, bigger or smaller waves, more or less overcast. There may have been birds or there were no birds. The sites were always new and interesting. The water may just have heaved and waned; where was the next heave going to be? Why was it not just flat? But regardless of the sights, the ship was plowing on toward a definite destination.

On the second day, we could occasionally see a B-24 bomber that seemed to be escorting us by circling the ship and exploring the waters before us. Undoubtedly it had the latest radar equipment on board to detect enemy submarines in the area. I never saw it attack anything, and neither did I see anything attack it. The bomber was just a pleasant, friendly and assuring sight to see. Someone else knew where we were in the wide-open spaces of the Atlantic Ocean.

The B-24 bomber continued to escort us on the third day. The weather was cold, but in general, the atmosphere was clammy and damp. Everything was half-wet from the continuous dampness. We slept in our clothes, and after several days, a bath seemed to be in order. I found a shower room and got myself a towel. The water was refreshingly cold and tasted salty. I tried my best to get the soap to lather, but that was impossible. I made the mistake of trying to wash my hair. The soap rubbed into the hair and became wax. Any amount of rubbing or scrubbing did not change the soap. More soap just made more wax. I finished taking my shower and finally had to use some limited and precious drinking water from my canteen to get the soap out. Needless to say, I had only one bath during the trip. No one else faired any better, and we could foresee no baths in the future. So this last bath was probably still the best bath that I had within the weeks and months before me.

In the morning of the fourth day, there were two destroyers escorting us. These were easily visible and perhaps a mile or so before us. They were something new, and the B-24 bomber of the previous days had seemingly completed its mission. Toward evening, a dark blue low haze emerged in the distance ahead and to the right of us. It was land! The coast of Ireland! The news quickly spread, and everyone rushed to the ship's deck. The two destroyers were leading the way and were taking us on in. Somewhat routinely there were signal flashes of light from the destroyers to the USS *West Point*. But these latest flashes set off sirens, bells, horns and every other alarm system on the ship. Sailors were running triple time to their battle stations while also ordering us to clear the aisles by sitting up against the immediate walls. The ship itself began to turn and swerve at top speed while everyone was helplessly trying to hold on or hang on to something. What was going on? What was happening? Where is the enemy or what is the enemy? Everything that was not tied down was swinging, screeching and clanging. Life boats were like a child's swing rocking to and fro. Then there were a series of terrific explosions in the near distance ahead of us. These made the USS *West Point* shudder, shake and tremble. What is happening? What can I do? What should I do? I do not even have a rifle. Our training was to stay calm, and this we did. Every GI had visions of his own about what was going on. The destroyers had dropped depth charges in an attempt to sink submarines that were lying in wait for us in the waters between Scotland and Ireland. The explosions were friendly fire, but they were directed at the real enemy; the enemy was now here with us and not over there somewhere. The enemy was no longer an imagined one. The action was genuine, focused, determined and directed to achieve specific results. Can the news of recent years be related to the activities described above? In about 2015, Ocean researchers discovered something on the Atlantic Ocean floor between Ireland and Scotland. Divers went down to investigate and found the object to be a sunken German submarine. The USS *West Point* passed through that area on about February 14, 1945. Did the depth charges dropped by our escorting destroyers sink the submarine that is now resting on that ocean floor? We silently and helplessly sat on the cold clammy ship's deck with all of our energy, eager to help, wanting to engage the enemy but could do nothing but hold on and sit tight. We were just precious cargo. We had visions of what was ahead and realized that there would be no more practice or dry runs. We were in the war; everyone was playing for keeps. After an hour or more and when darkness hit, we returned to the ship's bosom and had an anxious but quiet and peaceful night. The next morning as we saw the sunrise we were safely anchored in Glasgow Bay, Scotland.

9

Glasgow, Scotland
to Weymouth, England

The Scottish sun did not shine on us very long before we debarked from the USS *West Point* and bade the ship good-bye with thanks for an eventful but safe voyage. As I remember, the debarkation was simultaneous with the embarkation onto a troop train. This movement was short and within the port enclosure. We saw no Scotsmen, and essentially no Scotsmen saw us. Personnel were all military or otherwise official. We experienced no taste of Scotland, its people, food or culture. The train we boarded had passenger suites instead of passenger seats. Each suite was shrouded and enclosed. The intent was to keep the cargo of the train a total secret. Was the train empty or full? Were troops moving north or south? We were not to do so much as to peek out of a window. Hence, we did not get to see the Scottish country side nor any of the lands of England. I do not know any towns or villages through which we passed. Our only sensation was to be aware if the train was moving or not moving. I do not know if we had the right-of-way and other trains side-tracked for us; or if we may have side-tracked for other trains that may have had more important cargo. Chow on the train consisted of army rations. The train never traveled very fast but it was very persistent in traveling. Since no one was allowed to get off or on the train at stops, the engineer at the throttle did not have to worry about giving the "all aboard" signal to his conductors. There were none.

The demeanor of the troops was that of being quiet and resolved while conserving all the adrenaline for that surprising moment when all our adrenaline flow would be needed. The trip was peaceful and quiet. We heard no gunfire, the roar of no planes and the pounding of no bombs. The train tracks were apparently in acceptable condition. Occasionally there may have been noises which indicated that the tracks were being repaired. Everything happened slowly but with deep resolve. The next sight we saw was Weymouth, England. I really never saw a sign that said so, but that is what the rumor was. The train stopped in an enclosed compound where all personnel were military and official. We de-boarded the train and boarded a small victory ship that was in port along with similar other victory ships. Our small ship seemed to be loaded and was perhaps ready to sail while other of such ships at some distance from us were still being loaded. Possibly a convoy of ships was gathering to make the run across the English Channel to France. There was no concentration of these ships that could possibly become an enemy target. Our ship was at a pier by itself and other individual ships were visible at piers along the waterfront.

10

The Next Challenge:
The English Channel

The small victory ship was our home for about two days. Our movement was restricted to a small compound. The area had essentially no signs of the war's devastation. Facilities were minimally adequate with nothing elaborate. Systems were functional and operating. There were no passes and we never were allowed to mingle with any English countrymen.

I did not smoke, drink, roll dice, play cards or gamble by other means. So on occasions I had free time while others were engaged in their favorite pastimes. On such occasions, I usually wrote letters to friends and family and possibly to a prospective girl friend. Prior to entering the army, I was reluctant to even date my best girl friends because I did not want to have someone committed to me when the prospect was very good that I might not come back or that I might come back in such a condition that the girl friend might regret her commitment. I left home uncommitted and really did not pursue the finding of a mate until after the war. So writing letters was an acceptable pastime.

Most of the young ladies who considered me as a candidate for a potential husband were being courted by other young men and were firmly and happily committed to their betrothed mates by the time that I was discharged from military service.

Perhaps once a day towards evening, we were called into formation for a roll call. For such occasions there were always some adventurous GIs who would answer "here" for a newly acquired buddy who was not there. It seemed to me that this deception was obvious and that the Sergeant was aware of it. Now the time had come when we were about to cross the English Channel. The Sergeant took notice of the deception and reprimanded those who responded with the false "here". He told the guilty ones "one of these days we are going to walk up the ramp from British soil onto the victory ship for the last time and all those who answered "here" had better be on board."

The ship was shrouded so that we could see nothing and no one could see us. On about the third evening we boarded the ship as usual and disappeared into its bosom. The next morning our ship was anchored next to a sturdy but simple pier in the area of Le Havre, France. The vicinity was open with a small clear and relatively clean debarkation area. A road led up to the docking area which allowed trucks to drive up. There were no other piers or ships immediately around us. This was a small pier which together with the victory ship made a very small target to bomb or strafe. There was no activity in the sky by either friend or foe. The area in itself was an isolated small functional target of which there were many.

We had crossed the English Channel during the night. I do not know if our victory ship crossed by itself or if it was in a convoy. Our delayed departure would indicate that we probably moved in a convoy—small ships and a large number of them. The Germans really would have had to consider whether any given target was worthy of a torpedo. The trip across the channel was smooth and without incident. I slept through it all.

An interesting observation can be made about these days of travel. A person really rested whenever he became tired enough or whenever the opportunity really presented itself. While crossing England on the train, we had no bunks or beds. All resting was in the sitting position. All night long there was starting, stopping, jerking, braking, going, waiting and voices on the outside along with other distractions. The victory ship was so small and the quarters were so tight that few GIs spent their time on board during the day.

There was no need to go on deck because a person could see everything from the pier. Inside quarters of the ship were shared by everyone. Your only space was the bunk. The ship's bosom was designed to deliver troops over short runs. I do not remember that it had a kitchen. After de-boarding the USS *West Point*, our meals consisted of army rations. Our biological systems were out of schedule by six hours from Boston, USA time. So it was not surprising to need and get a night of sound sleep when such an opportunity presented itself. Departing from England and crossing the English Channel to Le Havre, France provided such an opportunity. The little ships engines may have roared and the waves may have rocked and rolled the ship, but whatever happened was just right for me to get a night of good sound sleep. I still thank the Lord for such occasional nights.

11

Le Havre to Metz, France Via "Forty or Eight" Railway Cars

We disembarked from the victory ship and loaded onto two-and-a-half-ton army trucks for a short ride to a railway siding. There we boarded a "forty or eight" boxcar train and started eastward toward Germany. The "forty or eight" boxcar received its name in World War I, at which time it was designated to be adequate for forty soldiers or eight mules. The car is much smaller than railway cars in the United States.

We were now on the European Continental mainland and were beginning to see what we had heard and read about for years. Damaged sections of the railway had been restored and bridges had been reconstructed to temporarily serve the purpose, but much of the devastation of the invasion and war was still as it was left after the last battle. There were very few cattle in the pastures and the fields had not been plowed for some time. Each site presented an imaginary image of what it was before, what it was now and what actions of devastation were necessary to bring about the change. Everyone was somber, quiet and resolved. We had a job to do, and we were on our way to do it.

Travel was slow but continuous. We never officially de-boarded the train but gained relief as needed when the locomotive had to be serviced. The railway cars were old but new to me. I inspected the bridge housing between the pairs of wheels on a single track and happened to find the names of "Knorr und Kunze" cast into the housings as they were poured. The latter family name was spelled just like mine. The boxcars must have been built in Germany. Shortly after the sound of the whistle, the train commenced to move. Our movement was no longer secret. We could see some French people going about their tasks. Automobile and truck traffic was negligible; instead there was an occasional army truck or jeep. Humans pushed or pulled their carts, and occasionally there was a horse-drawn wagon. The people did not hail us, and we did not hail them. Our ride was not comfortable, but no one complained; much more danger and discomfort were envisioned before us. We were thankful for every moment of clear sky with no enemy planes above us. The course of our bombers from Great Britain was well north and perhaps parallel to the path that we were taking.

After a day of chugging along, the evening came, and the train pulled into the passenger station in Metz, France. The building superstructure was still intact. The station was essentially a super-sized Quonset hut enclosed with thousands of small windowpanes. It needed no artificial light during the day. We detrained with our duffel bag, backpack and blanket roll and then waited. After a few moments of wonderment, a challenge presented itself: find an unbroken windowpane! After much searching, I found none.

Metz, a military bastion, is located in northern France just south of Luxembourg and the Maginot Line. It served as a hub in the supply route of men who manned the line and of materials that were used in the line to defend France. Many battles were fought to take the city. However, after the city fell, our military was able to repair and rebuild vital military facilities so they could be conveniently used by our troops. We used such facilities extensively to convert the paraphernalia of our incoming troops from travel regalia to battlefield gear on the front lines.

We were picked up by truck and transported to an army depot. There we received rifles, bayonets and shovels that were not new. Every soldier was ordered to fire his weapon several times. Mine would fire and eject the empty shell but would then fail to inject the next live one. The result was only a click when the trigger was pulled. With some concerted effort, I managed to get the faulty weapon exchanged. I did not get to fire any practice rounds with the exchanged rifle.

We exchanged our duffel bags for cartridge belts, clips of ammunition, bandoliers of ammunition and hand grenades. The immediate task ahead was going to be different. A change of clothes would no longer be necessary. We would need no more money. There would be little if anything to buy. We could make a final arrangement to invest our monthly pay in savings bonds that would be sent home. I elected to be paid a minimum and let most of my earnings be invested for future years. Thereafter, we boarded two-and-a-half-ton army trucks and began our ride northward.

Late in the war, we were billeted in a home. There on a dresser was a little Pocket Atlas (*Taschen Atlas*). I liberated it and it is still mine (Figs. 7, 8). There was a swastika on its cover that I immediately defaced. Its cost of twenty pfennig (approximately twenty cents) is printed on the cover. Additionally, there are the comments "*Kraft durch Freude*" (Power through Pleasure). It was published by the Bureau for Travels, Excursions and Vacations (*Amt für Reisen, Wandern und Urlaub*). In it I traced my path through Germany (Fig. 8). The heavy line approximates my journey from Metz, France, through Germany to the Czechoslovakia border (near Chemnitz) and then back to Metz, France.

Fig. 7. The Pocket Atlas (*Taschen Atlas*), which
I liberated from a German home in which we were
billeted late in the war. The cover contained the imprint
of a swastika. It was removed from the area that now
appears white in the gear wheel, (Moes, undated).

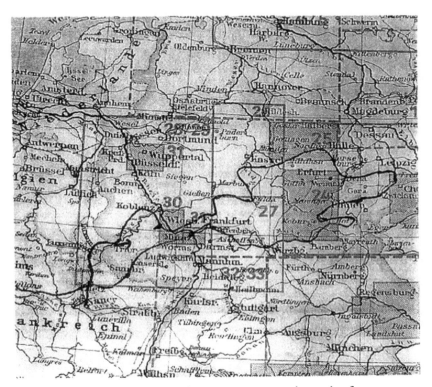

Fig. 8. The heavy line approximates the path of
I Company, Third Battalion, 417th Infantry Regiment,
Seventy Sixth Division, Third Army across Germany
during World War II, (Moes, undated).

12

Metz, France to Luxembourg Via Army Trucks

The trucks moved through the darkness without light to a destination unknown to us. Maybe the driver did not even know where he was going; the routine was to follow-the-leader. Progress was slow; the roads were hardly passable. The start, stop and wait routine became standard operational procedure (SOP). We carried our backpacks and blanket rolls with the shear optimism that we might get to use them sometime. After a number of hours on the road, we reached a farmer's animal courtyard in what seemed to be a small village. Where? In Luxembourg! We unloaded and moved into the courtyard as inconspicuously as possible. In the quieter moments, a person could feel the tremors and hear the thunderous exchange of artillery barrages in the distance.

At that time, farm courtyards were still a common necessity. The farmer kept his draft animals and equipment in this enclosure at night. The area also served as a pen for cattle, hogs and chickens. The space was so configured that the farmer's barn and home provided a section of the wall, which otherwise was eight or ten feet high. Usually there was only one wall entrance which consisted of solid heavy double doors each of which was five or six feet wide. When closed, they were heavily barred on the inside. On the street side, the residence and barn had no windows on the first floor, only a single heavy entrance door. The combination of the courtyard wall, barn and residence was in itself a little independent enclosed fortress. This type of construction had evolved over the centuries when crusades, wars, raids and invasions were common occurrences. To further resist these intrusions, the area farmers built these little fortresses together in clusters to form a dorf, burg or little town. Farmers did not live out on their land but rather in a little dorf. In the morning, they would take their draft animals and go to work their fields and in the evening come back home to the security of their dorf. Animals were fed and watered in the courtyard, while the wagon and other equipment was stored on the inside for the night. In 1945, there were few animals left that had not in some way been taken and used or otherwise were consumed by the war effort. The farm family still occupied the home. I tried to acquaint myself with the surroundings and walked through a hayloft and barn to a door. It led into a room with a narrow walk beside a pen of hogs and on to another door. I tried the next door; it led into the kitchen-dining area of the home. Three older people, two old women and one old man, along with a preteen girl were having dinner by a dim single candle. The kitchen-dining area was on the ground floor and had no windows. They were startled and speechless and so was I. After quickly and gently shutting the door, I returned to the hayloft and courtyard. The GIs and I slept in the hayloft that night.

In the quietness of the night, the exchanges of the artillery barrages and the tremors of the explosions could be distinctly heard and felt. My prayers became more fervent. I needed to memorize my prayers because the moment might be near when I could not read my prayers. One prayer in the *Service Prayer Book* (Weber, 1941) that seemed appropriate and that I remember to this day follows:

> Who knows how near my end may be?
> Time speeds away and death comes on.
> How quickly, ah! how suddenly,
> May death be here and life be gone.
> My God for Jesus sake I pray
> Thy peace may bless my dying day.

The next day a soldier was standing guard under a small shed extending from the wall in the courtyard. Harnesses and plows were in the area. The situation looked odd. I inquired about the purpose of his duty. His reply was "I am guarding the hen on this nest. Whenever she gets that egg laid, it will be mine." At dusk in the evening, a few of us were called forward out of the courtyard. We moved out on foot in the direction of the artillery pounding.

13

Luxembourg to Front Lines Via by Foot

March by Night

All of the group were replacements. After several hours of hiking into the night, we were on the front lines. There on February 20, I joined the Second Platoon of I Company, Third Battalion, 417th Infantry Regiment of the Seventy-Sixth Division in General George S. Patton's Third Army.

The Seventy-Sixth Division had been committed into combat only thirteen days before, February 7. Their assignment was to attack the Siegfried line by crossing the wintery, cold, swollen Sauer River at Echternach in Luxembourg on the German border. The attack did not go well and the resulting casualties were heavy. Many attempts were made to get some type of bridge across the Sauer River, but these attempts failed because of enemy fire of all types. Our group of replacements was plugging holes left by the fallen. Just ten days before, I had boarded the USS *West Point* and sailed out of Boston harbor (February 10, 1945).

The artillery pounding was no longer in the distance. We were under the arch of the shells. I met my Sergeant, Corporal and perhaps the GI before and after me in the squad. The new group of recruits disappeared into the GIs on the line. Without delay or further introductions, my platoon began to move in single file. I did not know where we were going but felt certain that we were within range of most any type of enemy fire. Suddenly there was a thunderous rumble of explosions and I hit the dirt. The buddies before and after me remained on foot and must have chuckled. I tried to raise my head to use my M-1 rifle but was unable to do so because I had a blanket role over my backpack. I really needed to lengthen the harness on my pack to carry it lower. Meanwhile there was a wafting noise high in the sky as our 105mm shells were headed for their target. Then there was the tremendous rumble of explosions as the shells hit. I stood up and looked at my buddies and noticed that they carried no blanket rolls. I promptly discarded mine. Shortly thereafter the thunderous noise came from the other side as the Germans sent a barrage of their whining 88mm shells over us followed by the explosions as they hit. Then a fellow soldier in the squad gave me a lesson in frontline acoustics. If you hear the whine of a shell, it has already passed you. Hitting the dirt is not necessary. If the shell is coming at you, the whine of the shell and the impact of the explosion are nearly simultaneous. There is little time to hit the dirt. The advice was very useful. I proceeded with my backpack but observed that the veterans had already relieved themselves of theirs. The favored uniform became a field jacket, raincoat or poncho, shovel, gloves, hand grenades, a cartridge belt full of ammunition, two extra bandoliers of ammunition, bayonet, rifle, a canteen of water and some rations. In all cases the advice was to stay mobile.

Attacking the Enemy through Trier

When morning came we were approaching Trier from inside of Germany. Trier is about five kilometers (three miles) from the Luxembourg border. The Seventy-Sixth Division had crossed the Sauer River and had fought through the Siegfried Line when General Patton ordered it to change course and attack the Siegfried Line from the rear in the direction of Trier. The section of the city through which we passed had been seized the day before I joined I Company. I do not believe that I Company was involved, but apparently it was in reserve. We crossed over the Moselle River bridge which had been captured intact and pressed onward. We cautiously walked through Trier in single file, on each side of the street, spaced ten to twenty paces apart. There was no opposition; the city was quiet and seemed deserted. There was little evidence of heavy artillery bombardment or other types of combat.

We left the city in single file through an opening in a massive stone wall; apparently at one time a city gate during the Roman era. Just beyond this opening was one of our large, most up-to-date tank destroyers (TD). It had been knocked out and the canvas and camouflage materials carried behind its turret were still burning and smoldering. I noticed no physical damage but also could not afford to look for any. There were no bomb craters or obvious indications of shell bursts. A "Molotov cocktail" could have been the culprit. My understanding of a "Molotov cocktail" is that it consists of a tightly closed glass bottle or jar filled with gasoline to which is attached a burning candle or a small burning torch. When this home-made bomb is thrown and strikes an object, the container breaks and the gasoline explodes. If this was thrown behind the TD against the turret, the resulting explosion of flaming gasoline would have fallen into the air intake of the TD engines and thereby would have cut off the air supply and smothered the engines. The TD would then have become an ideal stationary target. This scenario also would have set the camouflage canvases on fire. A German bazooka or panzerfaust then could have knocked it out. A bazooka is a hand carried weapon. One or more bazooka men could usually be found within a company. Similarly, there was usually a man in each platoon that carried one or more rifle grenades. Within the company there were also men who carried Browning automatic rifles. These were usually referred to as BARs.

A German panzerfaust could have knocked out our TD. A bazooka hit would melt steel armor that was five or six inches thick and with the blast splatter the molten metal over the inside of the TD. Otherwise the TD seemed unharmed. I saw such a knocked-out TD in a later battle.

The knocked-out TD carried a 90mm cannon instead of a 75mm gun as was used by our earlier tanks. This moving fortress was much larger and heavier. Yet this mobile bastion was still vulnerable to bombs, bazookas, land mines, artillery and homemade weapons.

A crew member had tried to escape but was gunned down. His body lay perpendicular to the tank tracks. Our squad, along with others before and after us, passed through the wall gate and used the tank for cover. (Was it good cover, or was it about to explode?). What a staunching odor of burning cloth and flesh!! We stepped over the GIs dead body with hardly a glimpse, silently said our prayers more fervently; this was the enemy's goal for me; tightened the grips on our M-1 rifles. Everyone raised his level of vision to the highest level. We were wanting to see into and beyond the trees and brush lines before us. If anything moved, what was it? What is my destiny today? There are many others with me. This is my first day of combat and I really cannot tell when the day started (at least thirty hours ago). We had just hiked out of Luxembourg last evening. War is no longer a distant thing. It is right here. This is it. When I step over dead bodies, how much closer can I get?

We advanced several hundred yards over an open meadow. This was in single file in broad daylight with ten to fifteen paces between individuals. A single shot from the enemy would expose their position at the price of possibly one of us. We came to a small swollen country stream. This was still February, and the winter snows were melting. One by one our platoon waded through the icy, cold water that was deep enough to fill our hip pockets. No one hesitated, no one complained, no one spoke; life itself had become much more important than warmth and comfort.

We made contact with the enemy and soon found that it consisted of foot soldiers, one or more machine guns and a motorized 88mm support cannon, mounted on something like a half-track. We advanced through most of the woods in single file but deployed into a lateral spread formation as we approached another clearing. As we reached the wood's edge, the enemy had retreated over the crest of a ridge before us. The Captain of our company caught up with us and was operating in the area of our squad. He carried only a forty-five-caliber pistol and some terrain maps, which he and individual Lieutenants would momentarily study. This was then repeated with another Lieutenant. These officers would then disappear but would soon be back. They never did huddle together so as to form a target for a machine gun or a well-placed mortar round or an artillery shell. The Lieutenants carried carbines. I was impressed. The Captain and his Officers were on the front line with us. Was he wanting to see his replacements in action? Was he himself a replacement? Did he just want to be up there with his men? In training, the Captain and his Lieutenants were never on the cutting edge of the line as I was seeing here. A scout was sent to the ridge to observe where the enemy was beyond. He drew some rifle fire but came back to report that there were enemy foot soldiers and a mobile cannon waiting for us.

The company brass momentarily huddled together and synchronized their watches. The Lieutenants repeated the procedure with their platoon Sergeants. Then at a prearranged time, the company was to attack over the crest of the hill. The company was dispersed into a single line along the edge of the woods and essentially parallel to the crest of the ridge. The advance was made in double time, and the Captain was not leading the charge but he was making the charge with us. I was not double-timing it any faster than the Captain. Apparently this was not fast enough because my Corporal (whom I had just met hours before) commanded me to get abreast with the front of the charge. The Captain and his Officers were gradually left behind. I never saw them again.

This was my first charge on the real live enemy. All previous attacks (in training) were interesting challenges performed with complete confidence that the attack was safe and we would prevail over the mock gunfire and explosions. How different this was!!! The enemy gunfire was directed and aimed to hit, and their explosions were meant to achieve. The harmless enemy silhouettes were gone; the figures before us were alive, could move and had deadly firepower, just as we had. The enemy was looking for us just as we were looking for them. Until the foot soldier takes the turf, the land is not ours. We were taking the turf from the enemy at the foot soldier's pace. As we moved over the crest, there was sporadic gunfire, but the enemy had not imbedded itself. As we approached the woods, the gunfire ceased. The enemy had disappeared and cleverly ceased to disclose its position by firing at us. Were they running?? Or not? Were they waiting to see the "whites of our eyes" before they would let us know where they were?

The Captain and his Lieutenants obviously were not far behind us because there was no protection on the enemy side of the ridge. The Sergeants were working and directing their squads. We were in pursuit of an enemy of which we had lost sight. Where were the enemy foot soldiers, the machine guns and the mobile 88mm canon? We very slowly and cautiously moved into the woods which contained trees, underbrush and other wild growth. We were as quiet as we could be and the enemy seemed to be even quieter. Not a word was spoken or even whispered. Step by step, I moved forward while keeping in visual contact with the GI on either side. The hunt continued for perhaps an hour during which time we may have advanced a hundred yards. The silence became more deadly with each passing step. What is that little noise that the enemy could accidentally make? From where might that little noise come?

Suddenly there was machine gun and rifle fire along with the burst of the cannon and the explosion of the shell. The armored vehicle with the 88mm cannon was only thirty or forty meters before me and to my left. Only about twenty meters behind me and to my left was the explosion of the shell. The pressure waves of the double concussion were staggering; my knees buckled; strength was gone, my vision wavered between that of seeing light to the verge of darkness. Seemingly I was behind the cone of shrapnel produced by the bursting shell. It was a real, real struggle to remain conscious and on foot.

With each consecutive cannon blast and shell explosion, the pupils in my eyes contracted from the pressure waves until only a tiny opening remained. I tried hard to keep on seeing. The action in my eyes was much like closing the aperture in a camera lens. If the normal pupil area was equivalent to an aperture opening of eleven, the pressure wave closed it to an opening of thirty-two or smaller. I saw darkness with only a tiny pinhole of light. What would have been the consequence of a complete closure? Would it have been fatal, or would there have been only a temporary blackout? I do not know!

Consecutive bursts of the cannon and the exploding shells continued as fast as their gunner could reload. Simultaneously with the first blast, the driver of the armored vehicle hit the starter and the engine started with the first turnover. That was a noise that I heard and remember. The engine fired on the first compression stroke. Maybe it was a diesel engine. Gasoline engines never did start that way for me on the farm. In cool weather, they would test our patience every day. Sometimes we had to jack up the rear wheel on our T-model Ford truck and put it into gear. The wheel produced a flywheel effect when the engine fired. The wheel then carried the engine through the next compression stroke and caused the next cylinder to fire. The enemy had a much better and more reliable starting system.

Then a small segment of the panorama in the underbrush came to life and started to retreat further into the woods. It was the armored vehicle that had been ingeniously camouflaged with native growth. It possibly fired three or four rounds before disappearing out of sight along with the foot soldiers.

The time fuses on the 88mm shells obviously had been set to a minimum to explode the shell after it was fired from the cannon. With each shot there was the one-two punch of the cannon blast and the exploding shell. There was no time for recovery between the two blasts. The two together delivered knockout punches.

The GIs on either side of me were less than forty or fifty feet away. We, as individuals, did not attract the cannon and machine gun fire. Apparently the shots were fired into a better concentration of our troops behind us. The GIs on both sides of me survived. I saw no casualties and heard no cries for medics. But we were totally stunned for several minutes before regaining any measure of composure.

We advanced no further and neither did we retreat. We held our position for perhaps an hour while the battle continued with rifle and machine gun fire from the enemy. We listened intently and returned our rifle fire in the direction from which the enemy fire came.

Our company had casualties but they were not our immediate and primary concern. We just held our ground. The enemy repositioned itself and the battle continued. Our squad was shocked, stunned and emotionally unstable. I had not yet made the acquaintance of my squad members. My Corporal and Sergeant knew me, and I was just beginning to know them. I had not yet been in formation with my platoon and did not know who my Lieutenant was. After regaining our senses, emotions and strength, we cautiously returned to the edge of the woods from which we had earlier launched the attack. Enemy machine gun and rifle fire continued in our direction and we returned rifle fire in the direction from which the enemy bursts came. I was lying behind the trunk of the biggest tree (they were all small) that I could find. Enemy machine gun bullets were clipping off the twigs and leaves from the lower branches. My immediate reaction was "I am reasonably safe as long as he does not lower his sights." The orders soon came to dig in and hold our position through the night. It had been a long day.

We had walked out of Luxembourg about thirty-six hours before and had engaged the enemy for the last twelve hours. My feelings were "I need to shoot but how much should I shoot? What is before me for tonight and tomorrow? How much ammunition must or should I conserve? When can I get more ammunition? The more I shoot, the more I expose my position. During the battle, (to my knowledge) nothing had come forward from the rear. Where was the supply line?" Everyone had to answer these questions for himself. Food was a secondary concern. In general, my answers were "Listen intently and well, take calculated and well aimed shots at the target that I could not see, conceal my position by letting others shoot after I have taken a shot and be conservative with my ammunition until there is a visible target."

After getting my foxhole dug that evening, I watched intently along the wood's edge. I was so shocked, stunned and beside myself that I could see German soldiers walk by between me and the woods when all the time I knew they were not there. We dug in individually but well within sight of each other. The order was to take a good look at the adjacent foxholes before darkness set in so that I would know where they were when night came.

During my earlier teens, my Grandfather had given me a pocketknife (a good one). During my free moments (in my teens), I had used it to carve sitting monkeys out of peach stones. I had carried it with me throughout my basic training. It slipped out of my pocket that night as I was squatting in that hole. Unknowingly I left it behind when I left that first foxhole in combat.

I Company did not attack through the woods again. Instead we moved out in another direction. I never saw the Captain and Lieutenants again. Why did the enemy focus its attack on an area behind our most forward troops? GIs on the line were well dispersed and any rifle shot, machine gun burst, or even an 88mm shell explosion may have knocked out only one or two men. The enemy found itself a better more lucrative target immediately behind the most advanced troops.

Subsequently the word spread that the company ended the previous day under the command of a non-commissioned officer. Did the Captain and his Lieutenants walk directly into the muzzle of the German mobile 88mm cannon? There probably were some GI casualties among the infantrymen directly in front of the cannon and machine guns. However, I heard no cries for medics and never saw any wounded GIs. The casualties and dead were evidently removed while we held the line immediately after we had walked into the enemy's ambush.

Within a couple of days, we had a new, eager and tough platoon Lieutenant. I thanked the good Lord for bringing me through the battle safely. On second thought, I should have thanked my Corporal for urging me forward with the foremost men in the line. Company headquarters with its staff proved to be a very fatal and unsafe place. How fortunate I was to survive my first twenty-four hours on the front line.

What Did I Know?

As we walked out of Luxembourg under the cover of night, I did not know that there was a Seventy-Sixth Division that had been committed into combat on February 7, 1945. Its objective was to cross the Sauer River at Echternach and establish a bridgehead through the Siegfried line on German soil. The details of this battle are vividly recorded in *We Ripened Fast: the Unofficial History of the*

76ᵗʰ Division, compiled by First Lieutenant Joseph Hutnik (1946). The crossing was a costly but successful one. The division pushed across the Sauer River and then proceeded to crack the Siegfried Line wide open. After penetrating into Germany for perhaps six to eight miles, General Patton commanded the division to change course and attack the Siegfried Line from the rear in the direction of Trier. Trier was not taken by an attack from Luxembourg, but rather by an attack from Germany. I did not know that I had walked onto German soil during the night and then proceeded through Trier to push the enemy back toward Luxembourg. So as the enemy retreated before us, it was retreating into our front lines advancing from Luxembourg. It may well be that the enemy group which we were battling disintegrated into nothing or that they retreated into US troops that were behind them. Higher headquarters probably knew exactly what happened so that we did not have to pursue the enemy before us any further.

14

Life on the Front Lines

Leaving Trier Behind

After leaving our foxholes, we did not return as we had come through Trier. Instead we proceeded along country roads, combed wooded areas and perhaps passed through a dorf (village) or two. We were in Germany and I felt confident that I could talk enough German to communicate with any people that I saw. The rule, however, was "do not fraternize" with Germans or any other people. Our movements on foot were slow, sporadic and unpredictable. Someone at the head of the column was cautiously searching out the area even if it had been proclaimed as safe and occupied by the Allies. Occasionally a civilian could be seen out somewhere or perhaps a woman with a cart and a child might be on the road heading in the direction from which we came.

When approaching a small dorf or village, we were never sure whether it had been taken, whether we had to take it or if the German army had just pulled out. I am sure that the officers and non-coms had more information but it had not reached us. Could there be an ambush set up for us? The higher command obviously knew more. Even the Battalion and Company Commanders probably knew if the situation was under control, but such communication did not trickle down to the privates in the ranks. The situations were very fluid, dynamic and uncertain. Most of my squad members, as well as I, lived without much information and less communication. But I could speak German and hence had the potential to be an information source at the bottom end of the information line. So if there was a little kid out in the street just looking us over (they had not yet learned the words "gum" or "cigarette"), I did not pass up the opportunity to try my American German: "When were the last German soldiers here? Were they walking or riding in trucks? How many trucks? How big were the trucks? What else was on the trucks? Which way did they go? Were any panzers with them?" And so on. This of course was observed by my squad members and subsequently passed up the line to the Sergeant, platoon Lieutenant, company Captain, battalion Major and perhaps even further. The first reprimand was by my Sergeant, but my ability to communicate in German soon became common knowledge among the troops. So if we reached a dorf in the late afternoon or evening, it became somewhat routine to have the command come down "Kunze up front!" Some officer perhaps had found someone he wished to interrogate, he wanted to communicate with the Bürgermeister, or perhaps we were going to stay in the dorf that night and two or three families needed to evacuate their homes because we were going to stay in them. This was an interesting but not necessarily pleasant experience. Often their first reaction was something like "No speak English." To which I would reply *"Was? Sie sprechen nicht Deutsch?"* (What? You do not speak German?) This would bring out the white of their eyes to see in dismay and unbelief such German coming out of a GI uniform. They would take another look at me and then at each other. But we got down to business fast.

All my life, I had been taught to respect other people and their property and particularly the elderly. My Grandpas had made sure that I understood what "respect" was. I accepted that philosophy to be good. Now the only folks left in these homes were very old and very young. To go up and knock on the door and tell them *"Rouse in zehn minuten. Wir bleiben hier für die nacht."* (Get out in ten minutes. We are staying here for the night.) was contrary to everything that I had ever been taught. Of course there was pleading: "Where can we go? Can we stay in our barn? What can we take with us? How long will you be here?" But the bottom line was "Out in ten minutes." There usually was no great problem! Some of our soldiers then spent much of the night pilfering the house and searching for small collectables that they could carry with them. I had no problems living with my morals and learned to live, with mixed emotions, with the morals and activities of some others. Theirs were vastly different from mine. I had too many enemies on the other side of the front line and did not need any on my side.

A Visit to Battalion Headquarters:
It's All in a Day's Work

One morning we proceeded down a cobblestone road to a little village bigger than a "dorf." It could have been classified as a "burg." The distance from the center of town to its outskirts was perhaps five or six blocks in any given direction. It had a few obvious signs of combat destruction. The streets were deserted, and the window shutters were generally closed. Occasionally there was a partially opened shutter with perhaps someone peeking through. What was behind these walls? Hopefully unarmed civilians. The burg must have been old. The buildings (perhaps homes and businesses) adjoined each other such that they formed a solid street-front wall. A person on the street could not get to the back of a building because there were no openings between the buildings. The history of the area probably caused the burg to evolve in this manner. Previous wars and perhaps ethnic raids may have dictated such construction to make the town more capable of defending itself. Homes and businesses could be in the same area and from the street could hardly be distinguished if there were no signs.

Where was the enemy? There was occasional gunfire in the outskirts of town. What was the objective of our platoon and company today? Such information normally did not reach down into the ranks of a private first class. Progress was slow, cautious and uncertain. GIs were perhaps ten paces apart in the country, but in town this was reduced to four or five paces. Also in town, we normally moved on both sides of the street. We had advanced essentially to the center of town without opposition. The lead group was probably through town. There was occasional gunfire and artillery bombardment, but we were not the target. The enemy was near. A church stood close to the center of town, and its steeple had been hit by an artillery shell. This was a common sight. Any tall structures such as churches and water towers usually showed one or more artillery hits. Why? As we or any other unit advanced on a town, the enemy probably had observation posts in these tall structures. The shelling was probably done as our forces approached the town. When these tall structures first appeared on the horizon, they were targets for our artillery.

On the front lines, good sleep becomes a desired goal that is nearly impossible and very improbable. After a day or two on the line, every foot soldier is ready to snatch a few short moments of peaceful rest and relaxation if possible. Our forward movement had essentially reached a standstill. After a short wait in the exposed street, we were given permission to enter the immediate building to which we had advanced. This was prudent. If the enemy was in them, we needed to know. However, we were not commanded to search the place. Four of us entered the building to which we had advanced. The door was not locked and led into a short hallway with some doors and a stairway. The inside was not elegant; it was old and much used, but clean. A coat of paint could have done wonders for it. There were no lights, only that which filtered through the windows. This structure gave us some protection. We could see no one on the outside and no one could see us on the inside.

We cautiously proceeded by opening doors and checking the rooms. Our immediate ambition was to find a bed and get some rest. A few moments would be just wonderful. We did find a bedroom and then a kitchen. To our surprise, there were three old women and an old man in it. A candle was burning on the table. This was my first encounter with German civilians without higher-ranking supervision. It proved to be an interesting engagement because I could speak and understand German, but these German civilians did not know it. I did not let them know of my ability to comprehend the language. Without a doubt, their heart rates were way up; they were afraid and did not know where to run or how to react. There was the expression of total fright and "What should we do?" Here were four grimy soldiers with steel helmets, grenades, bandoliers of ammunition, shovels, some backpacks, bayonets, canteens and M-1 rifles in their kitchen. All were wearing clothes that had been worn in foxholes a night or two before. We probably had several days of whiskers on our faces and must have been a frightening sight.

We had our guns in the rifle ready position and had to ask ourselves the question: "Are they friendly, or are they as mean as we have been told they are? Do they have enemy instincts or intents?" Undoubtedly we had tired but piercing eyes. Possibly, just a few hours ago, they were housing and hosting German soldiers. After exchanging our dull and tired but piercing stares with their tensioned and frightful ones, one of the women anxiously spoke in a low and frightful voice to another, "*Sollen wir sie kaffee machen?*" (Shall we make them coffee?). The others quickly nodded in agreement and the wall of tension broke down as they put the coffee pot on. The fire was probably on because this was still winter. The kitchen may have been the only heated room. We said nothing but knew what was going on. We stared at ourselves with the questions: "Are we doing the right thing? What is right for this occasion? Can we trust them?" Yet "fresh coffee" was the best news we had heard in some time. They set out some well-used cups or mugs and soon poured "kaffee." We keenly watched their actions to determine if they should merit our trust. After the coffee was poured, we continued our dull stare without grabbing the cups. We did not trust them. They soon surmised our misgivings. I motioned to them, "You drink first." This first startled them but they soon caught on and one said to another, "*Ach die wollen das wir erst trinken!*" (Oh, they want us to drink first!).

They were about to show us just how good their "kaffee" was when there was a commotion out in the street. We released our adrenaline and with rifle ready, rushed to the door and cautiously out into the street. Here was an elderly civilian male running down the street shouting, "*Die panzer kommen! Die panzer kommen!*" (German tanks are coming! German tanks are coming!). While running and shouting, he rolled his hands over each other to imitate the treads on a tank. We took the best positions we could find (mostly doorways) and glued our eyes on the street from where he came, sharpened our ears to hear the anticipated sound and stood firmly on the ground to sense the tremors of their approach. Meanwhile, the man disappeared behind us down the street into nowhere. Our vigilance was up with adrenaline flowing for perhaps fifteen or twenty minutes before we convinced ourselves that no panzers were coming. We let our guard down a little while keeping one eye on the street—wondering if the "kaffee" was getting cold? The tactic achieved its goal by instilling fear of a potential attack. We ratcheted up our concern for safety and security by several notches.

We returned into the home but did not see the elderly civilians or the "kaffee" any more. The civilians probably took refuge in a more secure location in their home. The alarm had scared both of us. With both the "kaffee" and the civilians gone, the choice was now an easy one in a somewhat uneasy environment. Find the bedroom and snatch up a few quick moments of rest. We had no more than put ourselves at ease, when another disturbance developed outside. Again an elderly man came running down the street with the same warning shouts, "*Die panzer kommen! Die panzer kommen!*" He rolled his hands in a similar manner to indicate the treads on a tank. Once more everyone scrambled into a combat position and raised his level of awareness to the "ready for combat level." We waited for the panzers to arrive, but nothing happened.

After some wait for the anticipated attack, a third man came running down the street with the same message. Once more our troops rallied to meet the enemy but none appeared. By this time the higher command had made the decision to move up the street and meet the enemy. We were hardly panzer fighters with only M-1 rifles, hand grenades and perhaps a couple of rifle grenades. But if we could find them, we could let others know where they were. We were not ready to take on the panzers and in order for the panzers to take us on, they would need ground support. Such support was probably not available in substantial force. We slowly and cautiously moved up the street all the way out of town. The enemy was not there. The alarm exercises were simply a harassment technique for the devoted Nazis to use on us when the conditions were right. The tactic worked. We never did enjoy our cup of "kaffee" and neither were we able to snatch up any moments of rest on a nice clean bed.

The determination was soon made that there was no enemy in the suspected area and the street was at least neutral even if it was not secure. We did an about face and slowly walked back into town with a much greater sense of security and relief. As we approached the point of our previous advance, the notice came back "Kunze up front!" Some Sergeant was waiting on me. He took charge and we proceeded on foot to Battalion Headquarters. We headed down the street toward the big church that had been blasted on its steeple with an artillery shell burst. In the shadow of this church was a nice old home in which the Priest for the church was living.

I was told that the Battalion Commander (a Major) had selected the Priest's residence for Battalion Headquarters. The problem was a Priest in the house. It was my job to get the Priest out!!! I had received twelve weeks of signal corps training and then six more weeks of basic infantry training. With all that training, it was now my job to evict the Priest from his home. Undoubtedly, others had tried to get the message across to him before I arrived, but no one had yet physically thrown him out. The Battalion Commander must have given some thought to the public relations involved. If we harm the Priest, we could well array the whole town of civilian or non-military folks against us in addition to the German army.

I do not know what had gone on before, but when I arrived, the Major (Major Moe, as we knew him) had taken over the Priest's office and posted a guard outside the door. The Priest (an old man perhaps sixty or seventy years old) was wandering from room to room looking for what he wanted to take along but could not find what he was looking for. I told the Priest, *"Du muszt rouse!!"* (You must get out!!). He mumbled to himself and then told me he had to get something out of his office. We approached the guard, and I explained what the request was. The Priest was allowed in to pick up the needed item and then was promptly ushered out. Without a doubt, he was in disarray and subsequently wandered from room to room looking for things that he could not find. Soon he came up with another very good reason to get back into his office. I was also in disarray. I had been brought up in a home and in a church where respect for the elders was impressed on me at a very young age. Also, the Ministers of our Lord and that of the church were to be revered and held in highest esteem. This old gentleman had all the qualifications for respect as I knew them. I had never ventured so far as to think that I could tell my Grandpas how to run their businesses. Yet here I suddenly found myself telling an old Priest (a servant of God) to get out!! And don't ask me any questions. I weighed his request to get back into his office a second time with some misgiving but finally proceeded with his plea. The guard let us in. The Major was doing his thing with maps all over the Priest's office. I finally got the Priest out and turned him loose in the street. I do not know where he went. I finished the job and still had respect for myself. In retrospect, if I would have grabbed the Priest by the collar and dragged him out into the street, kicked him in the pants and told him to go, I might have earned myself a new job in Battalion Headquarters. That kind of treatment was not what I was fighting for over there.

My job was done, and I was ready to return to I Company. We proceeded to return, when word arrived that I Company had moved out and was no longer in town. Here I was at Battalion Headquarters, and my company was gone!! Evening had come. The noise of battle was intensifying on the outskirts of town opposite from where we had entered. Since I was now an "extra" in Battalion Headquarters, they immediately found a job for me. "You will guard the battalion ammunition dump tonight in increments of two hours," I was told. This dump was perhaps a hundred or more yards from Battalion Headquarters (the Priest's residence). I was shown a room where others had left their packs and where they would lodge for the night. Here is where I could leave my pack and get some rest when not on guard duty. I dropped my pack and other items not necessary for guard duty (including my gloves) and was promptly marched off to stand guard. The dump contained mostly ammunition, hand grenades, some bazooka rounds and other things that could explode. Additionally, there was a little bit of a lot of other things. In my own mind I was hoping that I would not be around if mortar rounds should begin to drop or if the enemy's artillery should get word of the location. The dump was in town, but I never saw a civilian or anyone else close by.

Darkness had set in, and the noise of battle increased on the outskirts of town. The engagements were primarily with rifle and machine gun fire. I did my two-hour tour before being relieved on schedule. During my off period, I got some much-needed rest, before being called on for my second shift. Nothing had changed at the dump, but the noises of battle had escalated. Every few moments, there was a rifle flare somewhere in the sky. These seemed bright and close enough to light up the dump area. They could have been less than a half-mile away. The gunfire continued and intensified, but there was little artillery involved. Things were quiet where I was, and I was praying that they would stay that way. The only backup I had was the man who would relieve me when my tour was over. During my hours of duty, no one ever came to the dump to get supplies. It was not a very popular or safe place. Guard duty was a lonely vigil. Yet two guards at the dump would have attracted more attention than one. I did nothing to attract attention but silently watched.

After my two hours, I was relieved. I walked with the Sergeant, who posted the guard, back to Battalion Headquarters and to my night quarters. To my surprise, the room was empty; it had been evacuated. My pack was gone. All I had was my guard duty battle gear. What had happened? At that time all I knew was that a battle was raging on the outskirts of town. Some days later, the scenario of the night was related to me. I will get back to that story after telling my own. The immediate story was that during the night the battle-field situation deteriorated to the point that the safety and security of Battalion Headquarters became doubtful. Subsequently Battalion Headquarters packed up and made a strategic retreat. Some rear-guard GIs remained to take care of details. I was one of them. The next day they implanted me into another company. I think it was M Company, but this is without certainty.

M Company moved out of town and onto some wooded high ground, a plateau that had evidently just been cleared or perhaps we cleared it without opposition. The tree population was heavy enough to limit the undergrowth. We moved to the very edge of the plateau and then were told to dig in. On our left, at the bottom of the plateau, were a few houses. Not enough to be a dorf although they could have been on the outskirts of one. Among the buildings was a barn that had been used as an ammunition dump by the Germans. The barn had been hit and set on fire. There was the intermittent crackle of exploding shells and then the stronger blast of perhaps a grenade. From time to time the smoke drifted our way and there was that odor of burning hair, cloth, flesh, leather, ammunition and whatever else. What a disgusting, offensive, disagreeable odor. It was not one of dead or decaying flesh. It was not an odor of something fermenting or rotting. This was fresh flesh, hide and hair burning with all the other things in a barn. The odor was one that a person abhorred but remembered with the thought: *I hope that I will never have to smell it again.* In war, that was at best a wishful thought.

Shortly after I started to dig in, a couple of non-coms came by and said there would be a patrol leaving shortly and they wanted me to join it. I said okay and kept on digging with the assumption that someone would come and get me or the patrol would come by to pick me up. Well, no one ever came. I was reprimanded for not making it. Here I was in the wrong company, I had missed a patrol and was getting into trouble fast while trying to be a good soldier. I was ready to go back home to my company.

We spent the night and most of the next day holding the rim of the plateau. Toward afternoon, there were human noises before us at the bottom of the plateau. There were really no words, instead just intermittent yells and yelps. We looked hard and finally saw two German soldiers dancing from side to side with their hands up. They were gradually moving toward us. Obviously they were trying to get our attention and appeared to be unarmed. Or were they just trying to locate our positions for a maneuver of their own? Since they did not have guns in hand, we did not open fire. The dancing was with the hope that if we fired we would not hit them and they would run. After we really saw them and they saw us, we waved them to come on in. As they neared, I yelled *"Die hande in die höhe! Kommt rauf!"* (Hands up! Come on up!). They were taken prisoners without incident. After another day or so we moved out and somehow I was sent back home to I Company. There are sometimes good reasons to want to get back to your own outfit.

I Company had been on the front lines for several days. It now moved back into reserve, perhaps a few miles behind the front lines. On the front line or near the front the soldier is always ready. Our Corporal's advice was to "always stay mobile." As a squad member, a soldier seldom knew his exact status. If you were massed together and sleeping in some sort of building with only guard duty, the company was probably in reserve.

Now in reserve, one morning our First Sergeant ordered us to fall out and into formation. This we did. After a few moments a Second Lieutenant appeared out of the building. He was limping and hardly walking, just dragging. With one hand he held his back as he approached his platoon in formation. We were called to attention and gave him the necessary salute which he returned. He came to address the platoon. With some effort, he brought forth the words, "You are the damndest bunch of fighting men that I have ever seen. All that we need is a little more cooperation." After a few sentences, he saluted the platoon Sergeant, and the platoon returned the salute. He did an about face and limped back into the building, and the Sergeant dismissed us. I do not know if we ever saw the Lieutenant again.

Now what happened when I Company pulled out of town that night while I was extracting the Priest from his office and home? The outskirts of town were wooded, and I Company was attacking the enemy outside of the town and driving them into the woods. Our attack in the woods was in single file with one GI following another. Darkness of the night determined if there was any space or how much space there was between individuals. On really dark nights in a forest, we made advances by holding hands. This, however, now was not a kindergarten game. On this night, the attack proceeded; and after some time, the word was passed forward: "We have lost contact." This meant that the chain was broken somewhere. The message reached the leaders up front, and the advance was stopped. The Lieutenant told those with him to assume their best battle positions and sit tight. "I am going back down the line to see where the contact was lost and reestablish the line." The Lieutenant immediately disappeared into the darkness as he moved down the line. Those up front watched and waited… and waited some more while rifle and machine gun fire, with occasional rifle flares, continued in the near distance before them. Finally, there was some noise ahead of them. It came closer and closer towards them. Soon the breaking twigs were right in their midst. They jumped the intruder, stripped him of his gun, wrestled him to the ground and then used his gun to beat him into submission. All the while the victim was screaming "*Ich geb auf, kamerad, Ich geb auf!*" (I give up, comrade, I give up!). But as the tussle continued, the captured victim also knew some English by screaming "I give up, I surrender!" It was good English. Then there was the sudden realization that the club which they were using was a carbine and the victim's apparel was GI clothes. The victim they had beat into submission and captured was their own platoon Lieutenant. Hence the Lieutenant's comments when he addressed his platoon, "You are the damndest bunch of fighting men I have ever seen. All we need is a little more cooperation." During all this time, I was guarding an ammunition dump, losing my pack and being injected into another company. After a few days, we had a brand new, eager and tough Second Lieutenant commanding our platoon.

The Road to the Rhine River

Attack, Advance and Ride: Rest When You Can

The battles and skirmishes described so far were in the Trier area near the German border. This area was on the southern flank of the Battle of the Bulge as well as on the southern flank of the Ardennes. The Ardennes consists of rolling and forested lands. The Allied territorial losses experienced during the Bulge had been recaptured, and the Seventy-Sixth Division in the Third Army was now advancing into Germany. The French language had been left behind, and the prevalent language had become German. The rule was "*no fraternization,*" and this rule was strictly enforced. The more interesting aspect was now the change of dialect that could occur within a region of thirty or forty miles. In one town, I was perhaps quite at ease in translating and understanding what the Germans were trying to convey, whereas, in the next town several kilometers away, it was quite a challenge to understand. This was because the individuals seemed to use another dialect with which I was less familiar. Of course the information that I conveyed to them was always in my Americanized German, which was difficult for them to understand regardless of what their dialect was. When I did not know the needed German word, I would slip in the English one, which was not always understood.

I had not used or practiced my German for more than eight years. My native language was German. I learned to read and write the German language while in parochial school. Thereafter, the emphasis was to master the English language. In high school we spoke only English and were encouraged to also make it the language used at home. When the United States went to war, use of the German language was further suppressed. Now suddenly there was not only the opportunity but also the need to speak German again. At first this was difficult because I had not used it for so long. But with a little practice I soon became proficient at speaking the language. Since I could speak it better than anyone else, poor German was better than no German at all.

It was always most interesting to see the shock of surprise and amazement on the faces of the German listeners when they heard German coming out of a GI uniform. This was not possible; they could not possibly understand what was being said. Hence their first comments without any thought were *"nichts verstehe"* (don't understand). To which I would come back rather forcefully in good German with the words *"Was? Sie sprechen nicht Deutsch?"* (What? You do not speak German?). This would catch their attention and instead of wanting to leave or withdraw, they suddenly perked up their ears and were not only willing but eager to talk. They had never heard such Americanized German before.

After such an official conversation, there were always bystanders eager to ask the question *"Wo hast du dein deutsch gelernt?"* (Where did you learn your German?). Others, who had listened intently, would want to tap me on the shoulder and say *"Nach deiner sprache miessen deine fore-eltern von eine bestempte gegend von Deutschland sein.*" (According to your accent and dialect, your forefathers must have come from this or that area of Germany). These conversations were usually very short and on the run. Comments from the Germans meant little to me then. But in 1989, I was back in Germany attending a scientific meeting in Rostock, East Germany. Before the meeting, I had some opportunity to practice my German and was able to converse quite well with the German scientists. When my proficiency in using the German language became a matter for discussion, one German scientist from a University in Dresden spoke up and said "*Du komst nach Dresden für 30 tage und dan weis niemand das du nicht ein Deutscher bist.*" (You come to Dresden for thirty days and no one will know that you are not a native German). My Grandfather was baptized at Hochkirch which is about seventy-five kilometers (forty-five miles) east and a little north of Dresden. He was born in Lauske.

In one little burg, our platoon was given the task to destroy all the weapons (mostly civilian hunting rifles) that the inhabitants still had in their possession. Evidently the commander of previous US troops that had taken the burg had put out this order. When we arrived all the rifles, shotguns, etc. had been collected at a central location. It was then our task to make them unusable. There were some beautiful high-powered hunting rifles that must have been the pride and joy of some hunters. Some could have been of historical significance. They could have been passed down through several generations. However, that was not a matter for discussion. What did we do? We took them by the stock and wrapped the barrel around a tree or light post. They were beautiful souvenirs, but we could not carry them and our order was to destroy them. In a sense, we were angry and at war with the German people, and it did not hurt our feelings to disarm the burg. There was always the prospect that such rifles could be used by some loyal Nazi civilian sniper and anyone of us could be the target. I do not know what provoked the command. The task was done with mixed emotions, but we did it. If the burg's inhabitants were glad to see us come, they were probably also happy to see us go. We probably made no friends there. This only happened once, and I do not know what the circumstances were that provoked it.

The next Major natural obstacle before us was the Rhine River. Survivors of the Sauer River crossing at Echternach did not look forward to another similar experience. Yet, if that was to be our task, everyone was ready to take it on. The prevailing and deep-rooted sentiment was "Let's get on with the war and get it over with." After breaking through the Siegfried line, we were seventy-five to eighty kilometers from the Rhine. All of that territory was still in enemy hands and also in the enemy's homeland. The engagements were now on German soil. The battleground tactics by the German soldiers seemed to change as our forces progressed from enemy held foreign lands to the enemy's homeland. In the former, every structure was used as a fortress or shield and was relinquished only after a battle forced the enemy out. Every town was a bastion to hold. The enemy would hold until the town was literally destroyed.

As the 417th Infantry Regiment advanced into Germany, most engagements were no longer in town or in a burg. Instead the battles were fought in the outskirts and in the woods or forests. There were exceptions of course and these will be related later. Because of this change in tactics, we had to comb through all the wooded and forested areas before they were ours. This is the kind of activity in which we engaged for much of the month of March 1945.

We had the German army on the run. General George S. Patton had the philosophy "If you have them on the run, keep them (the enemy) running." To keep the enemy on the run, meant that we had to be persistent and diligent in our pursuit in chasing them. Being chased and chasing are both very exhausting maneuvers. The only difference is that those who are running are losing ground while those engaged in the chase are gaining it. Neither the chasers nor the chased have an easy time. Both become very exhausted.

The early advances that we made were on foot. They were seemingly long and endless. To keep the Germans running, we often walked all day and into the night before being able to take a break. After such advances we were usually told to dig in and hold. Often we were on the cutting edge of the front line and perhaps even moving it. Undoubtedly other units were given the opportunity to catch up and then advance beyond us. Also while holding, we were usually able to replenish our ammunition and rations.

These maneuvers were still stressful because the hold periods were often quite short. A person did not yet have an adequate foxhole dug when the order would come to move on. A person could not afford not to dig-in because the enemy could attack at any time. "Digging in" provided a measure of security that was not present while advances were being made.

We experienced some memorable times during these periods. I had lost my pack including my gloves when Battalion Headquarters evacuated while I was standing guard at the ammunition dump. So after getting back to I Company, I put in a requisition for another pair. My pack was never returned to me, and I did not carry a pack for the rest of the war. A person could not afford to sling his rifle over his shoulder and advance with hands in his pockets. Neither did a person feel comfortable or secure with freezing bare hands clutching the rifle stock. After a few days, a new pair of gloves arrived, and I was again able to enjoy hand protection. Little comforts like this were a necessity on the frontlines. I had the opportunity to wear them several times before we were ordered one night to infiltrate an enemy held wooded area.

We proceeded into the woods after dark. There was no moon and it became impossible to keep contact by vision. A person could wave his gloved hands before his eyes and see absolutely nothing. Hence, to continue the advance, we had to hold hands; we were essentially a human chain. The advance was slow but after an hour or more, we were well into the woods. It was spring. Ice and snow were melting. Little brooks were flowing and the weather was cold.

As we slowly proceeded, there were interspersed noises and grunts. As we advanced, the noises became closer with occasional hushed expressions of disgust in some rather foul language. The advance continued and it soon became obvious that the links in our human chain were having to cross a flowing stream. If the maneuver was performed just right in the blackness of the night, a person could successfully jump across. To do this right, the person had to position himself correctly on the near bank so that his jump would carry him over to the far bank. The banks were not visible. The alternatives were to jump too early and land in the middle of the stream, or a person could crowd the near bank too much and fall in before the jump. There were more options to do it wrong than there were to do it right. A good healthy grunt with no subsequent whispered outburst meant that the person made it; he did it right. But the same healthy grunt followed by a splash and whispered expletives not worthy to repeat, meant that the person landed in the stream, got muddy and wet, and then had to crawl out.

This exercise went on for some time and everyone in the approaching line had time to ponder his strategy. Jump across a flowing stream that you cannot see; maintain contact; if you do it right, you win and stay dry; if you do it wrong, you get wet and live with the consequences.

The line was getting shorter and shorter. The shrouded noises became more and more explicit. The human chain was only momentarily broken for the great leap that was necessary. We slowly and cautiously approached the tiny brook; the noises and grunts were now very near. Finally, the man ahead of me reached the brook's edge. He inched forward... and more forward as we held hands. It nearly seemed like he was expecting me to hold him back if he advanced too far. I was inching forward with him but leaning back so that both of us would not fall in at the same time. I could give him just a little more slack if I opened my hand a little. Finally, he made his tremendous leap and made it across the stream while still clutching my glove and pulling it right off my hand. My time had now run out. I quickly inched forward and with a forceful grunt made my leap. Hallelujah! I made it. I quickly reestablished contact and whispered, "Hey, give me my glove! Hey, give me my glove!!" His reply, "What glove!?" Several days later, I put in another requisition for a pair of gloves.

We finally reached our destination and were able to dig in. When morning came, we did not know from where we had come or if we were going to head out again. For the time being, we were quite happy to hold.

This form of advance was typical—move forward in a single column to a designated area, dig in and hold. Manpower for such a mission was usually a platoon. A Lieutenant was usually the highest-ranking officer around. Other platoons in our company probably made similar advances in adjacent areas. If there was no opposition, a second advance was often made before we had our first foxholes dug. After getting to a hold position, we dug in and stood guard for twenty-four hours a day. After several days of such maneuvers, the GIs were dragging, and relief was welcome.

Our withdrawal from the front lines was in a similar single column fashion and was usually at night. In darkness, the terrain was more treacherous, but our position and movement were less obvious to the enemy. Both civilians and German soldiers were less likely to see us. Presumably all of the German military behind our lines had fled or otherwise was captured. We could leave our guard down commensurate with the distance that we had walked to the rear. With time and distance our stress level lowered; we felt more secure and our bodies relaxed. Usually we did not go back far enough to find army trucks. Such vehicles often stayed behind the range of enemy artillery shells.

Our relief was similar to that of the intermission in boxing rounds. We were still in the ring, but for a brief interval, we were not fighting to advance or to defend our position. But we were still on the front with the front lines before us. During its entire period of combat, the Seventy-Sixth Division was never withdrawn from the front lines for a rest period.

One night we made a withdrawal toward the rear. The terrain was forested with rolling hills. We had about three paces between men. There was sufficient moonshine to maintain contact with this spacing. We came upon a cleared lane as the moon was lowering in the west. As I looked ahead, I could see the moon's reflection in a narrow slew of water that we had to cross. A healthy jump was necessary and nearly everyone made it across without getting wet. Yet as I was attracted by the moon's reflection, the GI crossing the slew managed to jump right into it—he hit the moon. Of course he got wet and in my estimation, woke up!! We were all very tired and ready for sleep. I felt sorry for the man. At the time there was nothing funny about the incident. Yet, this was about the closest thing to humor that could be found on the front lines. In looking back, I believe this type of incident could cause most GIs to chuckle when otherwise there was nothing to laugh about. We made it back to our reserve area without further incident.

Guard Duty on the Front Lines

When going into the hold position on the front line, the platoon was usually dispersed into a perimeter appropriate for the terrain—along the edge of a forest, on the rim of a plateau, or along the bank of a stream. We were never told, "We are now going into a hold position." Instead we were told to dig in. If the hold position was temporary, everyone dug his own hole. The first few minutes of digging were always vigorous ones. The hole provided cover for the individual in case of an attack. About as often as not, the individual GI would never get his hole dug before the order came down to move out.

If such an order did not come down, the digging never stopped because the hole was made to be an accommodation—knee room and security were always factors. GIs with ponchos could spread them over their holes to keep the water out and still be able to guard the area. All I ever had was a raincoat.

If the prospect was good that we would spend the night, two GIs were assigned to a foxhole. There was guard duty at night in two-hour shifts. Toward evening, the Sergeant would come by and give us a "password" for that night. There was a different password every night. The GI on guard duty in the foxhole would halt anyone at night who approached the position. The uttering of the password allowed the individual to proceed. The individual was a friend. I never encountered a situation where the individual did not know or have the password. Individuals not knowing the password would be considered enemy. It was not unusual for the Sergeant to check his squad's positions during the night while using the halt password procedure.

For those weary GIs who needed motivation to increase the depth of their shallow foxholes, there was always the rumor that if a

German tank spotted a foxhole, it would charge to it until one tank tread was directly over it. Then the driver would slam on the brakes of the tread over the foxhole and turn the tank around over it. This provided a tremendous motivation to keep on digging. We seldom stayed in one hole long enough to trim it out for body configuration. Also when there were two men in a hole, such finesse was usually not possible. In those cases, one man usually rested while the other stood guard in the same hole.

Those fortunate GIs with ponchos could dig their foxhole and then spread their poncho over the top. As long as there was no action, they had a cozy little security nest even when it rained. A raincoat did not afford such convenient weather protection. We were very fortunate. The spring of 1945 was not such a wet one. Only the melting snow and ice kept the small streams flowing.

I was on guard duty one night at a billet when I halted our Corporal twice as he approached the billet entrance. There was no password response. The subsequent sound was the off-safety click of my M-1 rifle. That sound caused him to skid in his tracks and produce the password. On guard duty, every individual was his own judge as to what the next action must be. Usually the system worked very well.

Our actions were stop and go for several weeks. The enemy was disorganized and we took ground wherever and whenever we could. The resistance was sporadic but we never knew what or how intense the resistance would be. Occasionally shots were fired at us while we were advancing. But these did not seem to come from trained snipers. The shots were not good enough. I would surmise that they were from German outposts. As we kept advancing, the shots would cease. The Kraut at the outpost probably fled or retreated. Also we found telephone lines strung on the ground. We usually cut them to neutralize their potential value. With such advances we often took much ground. Finally, the order would come to dig-in and hold. Individually we never knew just how precarious the situation was.

While holding, the company would send out patrols and these often proved to be quite dangerous and perhaps even deadly. On several occasions, one of our patrols walked into a machine gun outpost and not all of the patrol returned. Also some of those who returned might have become wounded. A medic known as Pat (Patrick) was usually with our platoon to treat, bandage and provide immediate medical needs, but then the wounded had to be transported to the rear by some means.

Also if we were in the holding position for more than a day, a detail of two or three men had to be formed to return to the rear for a mile or more and get rations. On at least one occasion, I was selected for such a detail. Our Sergeant gave us the necessary instructions and then told us in what direction to proceed. We moved out of the woods onto a clearing with a ridge that ran the length of the clearing and perpendicular to our path. This was quite an exposure. From our vantage point there was a barn or similar structure whose roof projected above the ridge on the back side. This structure served as an excellent landmark by which we could keep ourselves oriented. We moved across the opening and over the ridge. There we picked up the necessary rations before returning to our platoon. At least we knew which way was back from the front lines because of this detail.

About a day later, we had a wounded GI who had to be returned to the rear. I do not know how he was wounded nor do I know what the wounds were. But he was a stretcher case and had to be carried to the rear. Again I was picked for this detail. It consisted of seven men. Six men were to carry the wounded man on the stretcher and the seventh man was to carry his own rifle and the six other rifles belonging to the stretcher-bearers. I do not know how the selection was made, but my assignment was to carry the M-1 rifles and stay thirty paces behind the stretcher-bearers and the wounded man. This did not seem to be such a bad detail. Certainly, we needed to get the wounded man to the rear. Before departing, however, I was informed that according to the Geneva Convention and the rules of war, I was a legal target for the enemy, while the stretcher-bearers were unarmed and therefore not legal targets. What a position to be in!! (Say your prayers and get going.) Since I had made this trek the day before to get rations, I felt rather confident that the situation had not changed to become a more dangerous one. We moved along a narrow opening through the woods (it would be called a "sandera" in south Texas).

I kept my distance behind the stretcher-bearers and the wounded man while very cautiously scanning the woods on both sides of me. We delivered our patient and then returned to our platoon without incident.

After being on the front lines for four or five days, we were tired and dragging. There is no real rest on the line. The adrenalin is always flowing or ready to flow. A person stays on guard during the day and at least for half the night doing two-hour shifts in a foxhole. This was dangerous and serious business. On several occasions, I "halted" people who did not take the directive seriously, but kept approaching me. If the hushed halt command did not get the intruder's attention, and no password was given, instructions were to shoot. Usually the off-safety click of the M-1 rifle caused the password to leap forward.

After another day, we were ready to withdraw from our holding position. We were told that we are going to the rear. Our Lieutenant appeared and proceeded to tell his non-coms where to go. This was not in the direction of the old barn whose roof was projecting over the cleared ridge. Evidently the platoon's First Sergeant did not agree with the Lieutenant. The First Sergeant knew that some privates had gone to the rear to pick up rations and again to carry out a wounded GI. The First Sergeant's sense of where the rear was did not agree with that of the Lieutenant. Our Squad Sergeant was then consulted, and he knew which privates had been to the rear. Subsequently the privates were called into the decision-making process.

We told the Lieutenant the direction to the rear, but he disagreed. We told him, "We have gone back to that barn twice in the last two days, and that is where the rear was then." The enlisted men were unanimous in agreeing what direction to take to get to the rear. After a lengthy exchange of convincing stories as to who had been where and for what, the Lieutenant finally conceded with the comment, "Well, men, if all of you agree that this is the direction to the rear, I am going with you." We made the trip back safely for the third time.

The Lieutenant had evidently stayed close to or in his foxhole during our stay in the hold position and had either never oriented himself or he had become disoriented during our stay. I had not seen him before while in the hold position and cannot remember that I saw him thereafter.

The higher command should be commended for not routing troops leaving the front line through troops going to the front line. As tired and bedraggled troops, we were happy to have a road to ourselves where we could move at our own pace. The jaunts toward the rear were often long; the tired men simply became more tired. We finally came to a little dorf when darkness moved in. We were allowed to sleep in an empty barn with a wooden floor. Nobody had to stand guard and we were able to relax. I remember finding myself a spot on that floor where I could lay down. I did this with my shoes and clothes on with my head in my helmet. The webbing in the helmet liner was an excellent pillow. The M-1 rifle did not give much warmth but it was beside me. I fell asleep immediately and slept without making another move. The same can be said for the other troops – a peaceful, carefree night. What a blessing; what a relief; what a great regenerated feeling the next morning. The sun was smiling on us. I thanked God that I was alive and ready to face whatever the new day might bring.

This was the most relaxed environment that I had been in since leaving Luxembourg about two weeks before. After getting caught up on our rest, I Company was marched out to an isolated hillside where we were put at ease and gathered into a group to hear the Captain speak. He read to us the "Articles of War." I probably had heard these read to me in basic training. But after being baptized with time on the front lines, we were once more reminded of the battlefield conduct that was expected of us. In summary, the message was "You stay and hold your ground until you are told to do otherwise." The consequences for doing otherwise without being told were also mentioned. They were equal to that of being shot by the enemy. No one complained. Our resolve was strengthened to complete the task in which we were engaged.

As the days passed, our forced marches continued and engagements with the enemy became less frequent while the hunt for the enemy continued to be intense. The aim was to keep the enemy running with little or no opportunity to reorganize, dig-in and hold. The enemy was on the run and the next great natural protective barrier for them was the Rhine River. Our goal of course was to prevent them from even reaching it.

We never moved to the rear on the same road on which other troops were moving forward. At the private's level, there was no communication between troops moving forward and those moving towards the rear. Quite often in our advances we were told who might be on either side of us. I do not recall that we ever made contact with such groups. However, on one occasion, we were moving forward while one of our Tank Destroyers was going to the rear. This was most disturbing. We wanted to get on that TD and turn it around. There was no communication between us at our level. We never found out why the TD was going to the rear. The TD was not running as if it was being chased. But it certainly was not giving us support. It was simply idling at a healthy pace and going in the wrong direction. The foot soldier on the front welcomes all the help that he can get. Armor going to the rear does not convey the message of optimism—that all is well ahead. As I recall, we did not find anything formidable before us. Yet the retreating TD left that message with us.

To make our pursuit faster and more efficient and effective, army trucks were used to make us more mobile. Sometimes the moves may have been laterally along the line for some ten to fifteen miles before we moved into the front again. Another alternative was that we would simply disembark and hold a little burg perhaps for a night. We never knew what our schedule was because someone else, more informed than we were, was making it for us.

Chicken or No Chicken?

We had become accustomed to the walk-ride mode, when one day the army two-and-a-half-ton trucks picked us up and transported us for several miles before unloading us in a little burg in the country. It was still early in the day. If the area was safe for truck transport, the enemy was at least several miles away. We unloaded and there were several homes that had been vacated for us. We always explored the home and most everyone laid claim to a corner, bed or other place to call his own. The kitchen was always explored rather thoroughly. Things bottled or canned were usually safe to be consumed. Everyone was tired of eating GI rations. If a bottle of champagne was discovered, there was an immediate squad or platoon party. We did not need glasses to share in the bottle's contents.

On this particular occasion, further exploration yielded a frying pan and some lard along with salt, pepper and some other condiments. The facilities at hand, soon brought out the bond, camaraderie, imagination and ingenuity that had developed among the men during the months and perhaps years of training in the States. They knew how to work together as a squad or platoon. Most everybody knew who could do what quite well. Someone had spotted a hen in the compound in which the house was located. The set-up was perfect for some fried chicken. Details were quickly organized. Several men were to go and catch the hen and wring its neck before plucking its feathers and cleaning it. Others started a fire, while still others made sure the skillet was hot and the lard ready to fry chicken. This was going to be the best eating that we had in weeks. The hen was caught, killed, plucked, cleaned and cut-up. The fire was going, and the grease was hot. We were about to smell that delightful, mouth-watering odor of frying chicken.

Just then some trucks rolled up and the order came down to load up and move out. There were no ifs, ands, or buts about it—"We are moving out!" Everybody grabbed his rifle and other gear. We loaded onto the trucks; we were on our way, and we left the chicken behind. We were so close to a good, fresh, tasty meal, but we missed it—so close.

After an hour or so on the moving trucks, we reached our new destination. The trucks stopped and we unloaded. The situation was very similar as in the previous burg. We were put into a home in a somewhat urban environment. It had all the facilities to fry chicken. How stupid can we get? We should have brought the chicken with us! But we did not. But hey! There are chickens in the courtyard. The detail did not have to be reorganized; everyone knew his job for a fried chicken dinner. Another hen was caught, slaughtered, plucked and cleaned in record time. Within minutes, we had it in the kitchen. Before doing a second rehearsal as to how to cut up a chicken, another order came down: "We are moving out!" But there were no trucks. This time we were walking. We had learned our lesson; take the chicken with you. So one GI, most interested in having some fried chicken, took the hen, and stuffed it into the pocket of his field jacket. We started to walk and walked all night, then did the same the next day and into the next night. Our movement was interrupted by brief fifteen or twenty-minute rest periods. This continued into and through the second night. Early in the second day, a person could begin to smell both the GI and the chicken. The fellow with the chicken finally made the decision to discard it along the side of the road because there was no indication whatsoever that we would soon reach a place where we could have fried chicken. You could call this little episode "the chickens that did not get away." Or did they?

Where were we? I did not recognize the names of the little burgs through which we passed. We had no maps, and no one kept a diary. No one seemed to be particularly familiar with Germany as a land or as a country. The smaller roads on which we traveled had few if any road signs. At one time we passed a road sign that showed Koblenz to be about a hundred kilometers away. My thoughts were *I won't have to worry about that place for awhile yet.*

We had moved fast enough to where neither the German military nor the civilians had put up any demoralizing signs. However, before the end of the war, we did get to see a few of them. At that later time we had enough momentum that the signs had no effect on our morale.

A Welcomed Hot Meal

From time to time during our advances, we were surprised with a hot evening meal and a pair of clean dry socks. The kitchen trucks would set up a kilometer or so ahead of us and we would walk in just when they were ready to serve. Or we may have walked all day and were taking a short break when the kitchen trucks rolled in. We did not carry mess kits or cups, so the kitchen had to supply them. Such hot meals were always a real surprise and we loved them. What an uplifting realization. Someone knew where we were. Also, if the kitchen trucks could feed us, we could relax a bit because the area was assumed to be relatively safe. After such a meal, the kitchen crew picked up the cups, mess kits and dirty socks before departing. We would continue our advance.

The terrain in the area did not change much; there continued to be rolling hills that were forested while the valleys and flatlands were generally cleared. There was little agricultural cropland production because this was late February and early March. The potential for a war environment was not conducive for planting crops that would require several months to produce something to harvest.

Our marches, advances and truck movements continued until one day we arrived at Oberwessel on the Rhine River. War histories that have been written indicate that we were rushing toward the Rhine River with the hope of getting there ahead of the retreating German army units. By doing so, we could cut off their retreat across the Rhine and take large numbers of them captive.

15

The Watch on the Rhine:
Die Wacht Am Rhine

The River's Nature and Importance

In the area of Oberwessel, the Rhine River flows from south of southeast to north of northwest. It finally reaches the Netherlands and discharges into the North Sea. The Rhine is the most important river in Europe. Its valleys form part of the highway system from the North Sea to and across the Alps to the Mediterranean Sea, and to the Black Sea by way of the Danube River. The Rhine River has high embankments generally on both sides. In the river's valley, there is generally a highway and a railroad track on each side. Several miles below Oberwessel was the town of St. Goar.

The river in this area is characterized by sharp turns. It forms a Z between Oberwessel and St. Goar. The river flows from the bottom leg of the Z at Oberwessel to the top leg of the Z at St. Goar. The section between the bottom to the top of the Z is quite straight. The Lorelei is located at approximately the top corner of the Z near St. Goar.

Legend has it that a young lady threw herself into the river from the top of this rock (the Lorelei) because of a faithless boyfriend. This action then spooked the area with noises and visions that distracted the crews of ships and often caused them to crash because they failed to negotiate the turn in the river. My Grandfather was familiar with the legend of the Lorelei and related it to me when I was a child. He even taught me a little song about it that I learned to sing with him. Today German visitors to our country are amazed to hear me sing it. None so far have volunteered to sing it with me.

The version of the song as it was taught to me follows:

> *Ich weiss nicht was soll es bedeuten,*
> *Das ich so traurig bin.*
> *Ein marchen aus ur alten zeiten,*
> *Das kommt mir nicht aus dem sinn.*
> *Die luft ist kuhl und es dunkelt*
> *Und ruhig fliesset der Rhein.*
> *Der gipfel des berges funkelt*
> *Im abend sonnen schein.*

A literal translation of the above verse would be somewhat as follows:

> I know not what is the meaning
> That I so sorrowful am.
> A fairytale of ancient times
> It comes not out of my mind.
> The air is cool and it's darkening
> As quietly flows the Rhine.
> The top of the mountain sparkles
> In the sunny evening time.

The poem (song) has six verses. It was written by Heinrich Heine in France in 1823 and was published in 1824. In 1837, Friedrich Silcher set the words to music and it became the Lorelei song. The young lady (Lore Lay) in the song was originated by Clemens Brentano in about 1800 before Heinrich Heine wrote his German folklore. A published version of the Lorelei is in Appendix A along with a translation into English by Mark Twain.

The river was a natural barrier that temporarily separated us from the enemy. It was quite formidable and thereby provided protection for both sides from a sudden attack. There was occasional sniper fire across the river and no one could expose himself. The highway running through Oberwessel had essentially a solid string of houses between it and the river. This provided excellent protection and cover for us. Other than guard duty, we had no reason to be out. The German soldiers across the river could not see us and we could not see them.

Our stay there was one of anticipation and concern. What might be our next assignment?? If we had moved any closer to the river, the order would probably be to cross!! The veterans of Echternach and the Sauer River did not look forward to another river crossing, but no one flinched if that was to be our task. However, for this moment, we were poised to be spectators and did not know it. We were on center stage where we could view a whole panorama of events around and above us without being greatly involved or severely threatened.

Guard Duty on the River

My platoon was billeted in a home from which there was an excellent view down the leg of the river that connected the two horizontal legs of the Z configuration. Our home was just one home further down the street than the last home on the other side between us and the river. We were not only looking down the river, but we were also looking down the highways and the railroad tracks on both sides of the river. There was no traffic on the German side and neither was there any traffic beyond us on our side.

We made ourselves at home. Various types of guard duties were assigned to platoon members. My assignment was to make the highest window in the house facing down and across the Rhine my station from which to view and report any activity on the river or on its sides. I was duly warned to make my observations from well within the room, never get into the window or even get close to it. I heeded the warning and never attracted a shot from across the river. We were on German soil and the enemy was reluctant to damage or destroy German property unless they could claim a prize by the destruction.

From my window, I could see the highways and railroad tracks on both sides of the river and of course the station was a picture window of the Rhine River itself. During the day there was no traffic on the highways, railroads or on the river. The situation was tense enough that any human being, perhaps other than a small child, would attract gunfire. Across the river from us and beyond the river's bend were two small boats anchored on the river's side.

They had the configuration of tugboats and were just anchored on the inside bend of the river en route to St. Goar. They did not look like speedboats or attack ships. Instead they looked like workhorses on the river. There was no visible armament on them. Yet two such boats could give the enemy the potential to do a lot of things. Why were they there? I never observed any activity on them. On about our second day, perhaps an outpost from our group took several shots at them but received no return fire. The next day, the tugboats were so deep in the water that they were about to sink. Only the superstructure of the boats was visible. I doubt that our shots forced them to submerge. They probably submersed themselves to give us less target to shoot at. The boats made no attempt to leave.

Sixty-two years later a lady from Germany (Uschi Mueller) was in the States with her husband who was employed by Siemens. She spent several nights in our home during which we were able to visit. She was born after the war in the area of the Lorelei. In our conversation, I mentioned my service in the army and my guard station on the Rhine River. When I mentioned the two tugboats, she was not surprised but immediately knew what I was talking about. "They are used to guide and assist larger ships and water craft to negotiate the bend in the river." So these boats never left their station as the frontlines approached. I doubt that the pilots for the boats stayed around; yet I would not be surprised if they did.

The railroad tracks on the enemy side of the river could not make the sharp turn that the river and the highway made, so there were two tunnels that entered the river embankment before the bend and then emerged after it. This allowed an increased radius for the turning tracks. About fifty meters after the upstream entry of the tunnels into the embankment there was a short smoke stack projecting out of the rocky rubble. I never saw any smoke come out of it during the day. However, they could have cooked at night. Also soon after the tunnel entrances and at the tunnel level, there was a window opening in the embankment which faced across the river towards Oberwessel. These railroad tunnels were substantial cover for German soldiers. We knew they were there but we did not know how many! Also we did not know how much combat equipment was in them and the type of equipment that it might be.

The Night Watch

Toward evening one of our Tank Destroyers would slowly and quietly come rolling down the street until it reached the last home on the river side of our street. There it aligned itself, half hidden by the house, with its 90mm cannon pointed down the middle of the highway on the enemy side of the river. The first night passed quietly without incident. In the morning the TD withdrew but in the evening before dark it was back in the same position. Then during the night, there was the thunder of the cannon and the distant explosion of the shell. Several shots were fired. When morning came, several destroyed vehicles were sitting on the highway on the enemy side of the river. The TD continued to monitor for night traffic on the highway, river and railroad for the rest of our stay. There was no more traffic or other action. The highway was never cleared for traffic while we were in Oberwessel.

The Flights of Our Bombers

We were now far enough into Germany to where our bombers would fly over us while enroute to their targets. These were interesting sights to watch. As the bombers approached us, they were in close and precise formation. But after they passed over us into enemy territory, they became the targets for anti-aircraft-artillery (AAA) fire. After only a few squadrons had passed, we knew the general locations from which the AAA fire would originate and could anticipate when the shooting would start and the intensity of the fire that a squadron would encounter. But we could not communicate this information to our planes even though we were so anxious to do so. How do we tell our planes, "Hey, you are headed right into the middle of the anti-aircraft-artillery batteries." Our planes would not veer from their charted path, but like a mighty freight train moved steadily forward.

We were spectators and the game was being played out before us. We did not see any of our fighters escorting the bombers and neither did we see any German fighters attack them in our area of vision. We would sweat them through for as far as we could see.

About an hour or more later, the bombers would return from their run. Again there was the need and the desire to communicate, but there was no way. We just had to sweat them through again. By now some formations were not so precise. Occasionally the formation was incomplete. This in itself told a story; the missing plane was struggling far behind or perhaps it had been lost. Sometimes a plane was struggling to keep up with the formation. Maybe it was just a little lower and a little bit behind, just out of the formation but trying to stay with it. In such cases, its pilot could see what was happening ahead and might veer a little to avoid the hot spots. When such a maneuver occurred correctly, we wanted to burst out with a cheer. When it was executed incorrectly, we just had to hold our breath, pray and sweat the plane through. Then there were also lone stragglers who had to make it on their own. They were too far behind to have seen what was ahead. How can we help it; what can we tell it? Nothing! So we just hoped and prayed and held our breaths. What a relief to see such a "wounded duck" come on through and over into friendly skies and then struggle on in for the rest of the flight. Hopefully such heroes were able to sleep in a comfortable bed that night.

During our stay on the Rhine River, we never saw one of our bombers go down. The war was far enough along to where the Allies were conducting daylight raids. We never heard our planes overhead during the night. Did we see any of our fighter planes go down? We will come to that shortly.

Our Watch Station

Oberwessel was in the valley of the Rhine River, perhaps thirty or forty feet above the water level. The embankment of the river rose several hundred feet on both sides of the stream. We could not see the upland but we were left with the sensation that it was flat. It was somewhat crucial for us to know what was happening or if something was happening on the upland across the river from us. The embankment behind us started up nearly immediately after the home in which we were billeted. There were no trees on the steep slope, only pathways. The entire slope was covered with grass. About two-thirds of the way up, there was an anomaly of some sort. Perhaps a rest station or if someone was working on the slope of the embankment, it would serve as a center for break time. I had no occasion to go up there but one of our platoon members was assigned to be an observer from that point. It provided enough shelter for the individual to hide. We may even have had a telephone line run to his post. His assignment was no secret. I will call him "Joe" because I do not remember his name. Joe had to get up every morning and climb the embankment to the shelter before daylight. In the evening after dark he could return for the night to the billet in which we were staying. I never saw him exposed up there and he was faithful in getting there before daylight and for not leaving until after dark. Civilians in the area could have seen him come and go.

Well, Joe was hidden but had little or no substantial protection at his post. On about the third day of observation, there was the thunder of a cannon across the river, the whine of a shell over us and then the explosion as the shell hit perhaps a hundred meters from Joe's post. After a few minutes, there was the second thunder, whine and explosion of the shell only about twenty-five meters from where Joe was. The second shot left no doubt as to what the target was and Joe came out of his hiding place. He headed down the slope in double time. He made it safely into town. No further use was made of the observation post.

Each day we were watching the Rhine and contemplating what our next action might be. Was this developing into a site at which to cross the river? The embankment on the other side had two railroad tunnel entrances and a window out of the embankment facing Oberwessel. The rising embankment itself was bare with no obvious pillboxes in it. Mortar rounds could be dropped into the river valley but the exposure of the valley for enemy artillery seemed to be somewhat restricted. The other side of the river appeared to be much less threatening than was the Siegfried Line across the river at Echternach. There did not seem to be a build-up of men, equipment or materials in our area. What were the plans for us at this place? Would we get another night of rest or might we be ordered to attack before morning?

The Crash of Our Fighter Plane

Another night passed as we kept close watch for activities across the river. The day was relatively quiet when we suddenly heard the sound of a plane at low altitude heading in our direction from the other side of the Rhine River. As it came into sight, we recognized it to be one of our P-47 fighter planes. It was losing altitude quite fast, but was not tumbling or turning. It nearly looked like it was at the bottom of a dive and was unable to pull out. The pilot ejected himself and floated to the ground while the plane crashed in a huge ball of fire just a few hundred yards further but before reaching the embankment of the river. Both the crashed plane and the pilot's landing were in enemy territory. The river's embankment on the other side hid the pilot's landing and the crashed plane from us. We did see the pilot parachute to the ground and the ball of fire from the crash of the plane. Some days later after we had left the Rhine River, we were informed that others (US soldiers) saw the Germans take the pilot captive soon after he had safely landed with his parachute. A vehicle was driven to the site and picked him up. After another few days, we received word that our forces had recovered the pilot and that he was unharmed.

I do not know anything about the plane's mission. We saw no planes in the sky before the crash. There were no unusual noises that alerted us to think that the plane may have tried to strafe a German gun position. It seemed to be by itself. If the plane could have stayed aloft another half mile, it could have crashed on our occupied side of the river. If the pilot had parachuted into the river, he would have been the victim of German gunfire. The crashing of the plane was unfortunate, but considering the subsequent events, maybe it was fortunate that it crashed where it did.

A quiet day on the front lines literally means that you are shooting at no one and no one is shooting at you. It does not mean that there is no rumble of the cannons and the subsequent explosion of the shells. Quite often such rumbles became exchanges between the two sides. Even if the shells are screaming or woofing over head, the front still can be relatively quiet right on the line. Both sides watch, wait and try to enjoy the quietness until something happens somewhere. This watchful quietness prevailed on the Rhine River but every day there was an episode or two that would shatter the quietness and put everyone on the alert.

Ammunition Truck Explores Enemy Territory

We were enjoying such a relaxed quietness one day when one of our two-and-a-half-ton army trucks came down the street at perhaps thirty-five to forty miles per hour. The driver was a colored GI and seemed completely confident and happy as if he were delivering some goods to Battalion Headquarters. He had his eyes on the road and felt assured that both sides of the street were secure. He was right. He seemingly knew where he was going. There were no roadblocks or checkpoints nearby. Well the street was ours to our billet but it was no man's land immediately thereafter. The enemy was on the other side of the river and could watch our traffic just as we were looking for theirs.

The truck and driver whizzed happily past us and soon turned right from the bottom leg of the Z configuration of the river. It then proceeded down the Rhine on the middle leg of the Z towards St. Goar. After only a short distance, we began to see successive splashes of water cross the river in the direction of the truck. Also, there was the sound of machine gun fire. This happened several times before the truck made a left turn at the top of the Z and disappeared in the direction of St. Goar. We all wondered where the truck was going. But before our wondering ended, the truck reappeared from the top of the Z. It was not going anywhere; it was coming! This was not at a leisurely pace. If it had wings, it would have flown. As it was, the driver must have had a heavy foot that was trying to push the gas pedal through the floor. Again there were the little splashes of water crossing the Rhine in the direction of the truck and the subsequent sound of machine gun fire. The little splashes never quite caught up with the truck to make a fatal hit. The driver came to the bottom corner of the Z and made the left-hand turn toward us while also crossing some railroad tracks never letting up on the gas pedal. While going out to make the delivery, the driver passed our billet rather leisurely, but while coming back he left the impression of still being in enemy territory. The gas pedal was still on the floor, but he made it back safely. Wonder how far he was behind the front line before he realized that he was in friendly territory again? The next morning, some civilians came by with one of our bazooka rounds and informed us that it was lost off the truck on its way back as it crossed the railroad tracks the day before. That was just another little episode during a quiet day on the front lines.

GIs on the Other Side

While we were on the Rhine, the weather was generally fair, cool and pleasant. Our guards were on the river's edge during the night and during the day we watched the river and beyond from our various observation posts. On this particular morning, we observed someone move to our right a short distance up the river. Then another person appeared, and soon we could see four or five of them slowly moving parallel with and down the river on its embankment. No shots were fired. Everyone breathed a great sigh of relief and wanted to yell for joy when we recognized them to be GIs. They were coming down the river from the area of Dörscheid. I do not know from what outfit they were or where they had crossed the river. What a relief. Someone was across the river, and we were not the ones who would have to cross it here. For the moment, we were poised to give supporting fire if they were fired upon. Their movement was slow and deliberate. Once more we were the audience, and they were the performers. Slowly and cautiously they approached the railroad tunnel entrances. There was no gunfire. After reaching the first tunnel, two GIs cautiously stuck their heads around the entrance to take a peek inside and then listened for a few moments. There was no sudden withdrawal to indicate that a sound was heard. After a brief wait, they scouted the second tunnel in a similar manner with the same results. They then continued in a dispersed line along the embankment toward the bottom corner of the Z leg in the river. The window, in the embankment, that opened toward Oberwessel was approached with great caution. It was peaked into and then checked for sound. Seemingly nothing was seen or heard. A little further up the embankment and further into the tunnel was the little short smoke stack that projected above the ground. After it was spotted, it was keenly observed before an approach was made. The stack was checked for sound. If there was no noise, the GI still questioned it. After a further inspection of the stack, the GI removed a hand grenade from his belt, pulled the pin and dropped it down the stack. As expected a portion of the explosion blew out of the stack. After a few moments, the GI approached the stack once more and checked it for sound. Apparently there was none and the dispersed line of GIs moved on. After a while they approached the corner of the embankment, where the river turned, and disappeared around it. The other side of the river across from us was now ours. What a relief. While we were still watching, a white flag suddenly was projected from one of the tunnel entrances. It was waved up and down for awhile before a German soldier stepped out into the open. Soon a second German soldier appeared. The two slowly made their way down to the river's edge. All we had to do was find some means to get them. But that was not our charge. Instead the order came down to "move out." The task of taking the Germans captive was left to someone else. We moved out of Oberwessel on the same street as we had entered but soon diverted our march away from the river. No one told us, but all of this happened on a Sunday.

The End of Our Watch

What can be said about our stay on the Rhine? In time of peace, it would have been an outing and a place that a person would love to travel to and enjoy. How did we feel? We were not in direct combat. We were, however, on the front line for every minute of every day. Most anything could come at us from across the river. Also, we were subject to an "attack" command at any and every moment. A person was a potential target at any window and every time he exposed himself on the outside. We were always subject to German artillery shells, sniper fire and even civilian snares. We could never afford to be at the wrong place at the right time and no one could tell us where that wrong place was and what the time might be. We were at ease but we were never able to let our guard down; we were always ready to jump at any moment. The beauty of the Rhine River and its valley was largely suppressed by the dangers that were hidden therein.

16

The Rhine River at St. Goar

After leaving Oberwessel, we took some back roads away from the Rhine. Neither I nor my squad mates knew where we were going but after several hours we came to another town on the Rhine. It was St. Goar, just a few miles down the river from Oberwessel. There we moved into a billet from which we could plainly see the river. We were not deployed to repulse an attack. Instead we were appropriately grouped to make an attack. Upstream, about two hundred yards on our side, there were two pontoons in the water at the river's edge. There was every indication that this was the beginning of a pontoon bridge. The enemy was well aware of this and was shelling the area with 88mm artillery. I saw no further action on our side of the river to put additional pontoons into the water. From my point of view, the effort had been momentarily stalled by German 88mm artillery fire. Otherwise it seemed that the bridge was being built for us and we had arrived ahead of schedule or the construction was delayed. We were able to observe the area for an hour or more before darkness set in. Soon after dark the command came down to "move out." We moved out but not in the direction of the partially constructed pontoon bridge.

We Ripened Fast – Hutnik (1946), reports that Boppard and St. Goar were selected for crossing sights (P. 147). The Third Battalion of the 417th Infantry Regiment (this included I Company), the Second Battalion of the 385th Infantry Regiment and the 901st Field Artillery

Battalion joined in with the Eighty-Ninth Division to deliver combined fire across the river at St. Goar, a maneuver which successfully befuddled the Krauts. This was obviously the big picture of what was going on.

I must say it also befuddled the GIs of I Company of the Third Battalion of the 417th Infantry Regiment who had walked there but did not cross the river. The Second Platoon of I Company of the Third Battalion of the 417th Infantry Regiment did not engage in any combat while waiting at St. Goar to cross the Rhine River. The GIs whom we saw across the Rhine before we moved out of Oberwessel probably engaged some resistance soon after passing Oberwessel. They should now have been very close to St. Goar also, if they were able to continue their advance.

17

The Battle for Germany

Beginning of the Big Push

We moved out of St. Goar on foot and walked throughout the night and during the next day (Monday). This march was somewhat away from the front lines because on Tuesday we were picked up by troop transport trucks (two-and-a-half-ton) and became more mobile. The mobility was faster but our movement was not necessarily forward. We were not taking ground while on the trucks but we were traveling on ground that had already been taken. According to *We Ripened Fast* – Hutnik (1946), the Eighty-Seventh Division crossed the Rhine River during the night of March 24, 1945, at Boppard. It may be that we crossed the Rhine River there before being located back on the front line. The GIs whom we saw on the other side came from up the river somewhere.

The troop carrier trucks may or may not have had a tarpaulin cover. Along each side of the bed was a bench that could be folded up against the sideboard. For troop transport, the bench was down. There may have been a short bench across the front of the bed. The back of the truck bed was open and may not even have had a tailgate. When the trucks were being loaded, the most aggressive GIs took the first choice of seats. The last GIs usually had to settle for whatever space the seated GIs would make for them. The GIs sat on the benches in full garb. The cartridge belt, bandoliers of ammunition, hand grenades, canteen, shovel, bayonet and folded raincoat were worn continuously. The M-1 rifle was generally held between the legs in a vertical position with the barrel pointing up. When the GI stood up from his sitting position, he was ready to move. He had everything with him.

As the enemy retreated, it put into place as many roadblocks and other obstacles as possible. They used explosives to fell trees across the roads, blew up small bridges and used every other means to delay and detain the Allied soldiers. These obstacles were cleared before we arrived to pass through. Often small bridges were temporarily repaired. We saw many tree trunks with small blocks of explosives strapped around them and appropriately wired to explode and fell the trees. But the enemy did not get to use them.

We were again trying to push the enemy back faster than what they could retreat. This seemed to be a favorite tactic of General George S. Patton. Make the enemy run, then keep them running and, if possible, push ahead faster than the enemy can retreat. This tactic is good, it sounds great, but someone has to execute it. How? Push hard and long to make it happen. The Rhine River was the last stopping place at which to catch a breath. We were now in a position where we could push and we pushed hard.

The roads on which our trucks traveled were often only tenuous one-way passages. Slowly but surely we continued the truck ride through the night and into the next day, (Wednesday). If anyone wanted to get some sleep, he did so in the sitting position. Any given GI was rubbing shoulders with the GIs on either side of him. Somewhat like sleeping in the chair of a plane or passenger train. The trucks moved without lights and occasionally there were momentary stops. We did not know why they stopped or how long the stop would be, but we used such stops to accommodate our personal needs. Soon we would be underway again. There was very little conversation among the troops. Everyone sat silently and was contemplating what our next action would be. At sometime during the night we must have crossed the Rhine River.

When on trucks, we were usually several miles behind the front lines. Our guard was somewhat relaxed because we were in someone

119

else's hands. This trust was never severely shaken, because we were always delivered to our destination.

After the Ride, We Walked and Walked

We were on the trucks for about twenty-four hours before we disembarked and began to walk again (Wednesday noon). We walked till evening when we were pleasantly surprised by our kitchen trucks. They knew where we were and had come out to serve us a hot meal. The meal was served before dark. We also restocked our rations. By nightfall, the kitchen trucks were gone and we continued our march. These marches were usually in train fashion one man following the other. We were not taking ground but instead we were crossing ground that someone else had taken ahead of us. I wonder who that was? In a sense we were reserves trying to keep up with the front lines.

Some outfit was ahead of us moving as fast or faster than what we could walk. From what was visible on the road, the enemy was offering little opposition. Yet there were occasionally strong indicators that the front lines were very near. On one occasion, there were perhaps three or four dead human bodies lying out in an open meadow, maybe 200 to 250 yards on the left side of the road. The loss of these lives was so recent that no one had yet come to pick up the corpses. It was not yet safe to do so. The clothes indicated that these could have been civilians, but why should civilians be out here? Maybe they were camouflaged German soldiers. I could not tell. The bodies never moved. Why were they shot? How were they shot? Were they running away from the road when they were shot? Could they have been enemy observers trying to get back to their post to report that our armor was advancing through the area? Could our armor afford to let running people run away? Should the victims have raised their hands while near the road and just watched our armor go by? Both the attackers and the enemy have to make decisions and in both cases their respective lives may be at stake. A wrong decision can well be the last one that the individual on either side will make. But a decision has to be made and the consequences must be lived with.

My guess is that our armor came over the crest of a hill in the road. These individuals were in the valley and saw it; they (soldiers or civilians) attempted to run away but never made it. Somewhat further down the road, there was a battery of German 88mm artillery perhaps a hundred yards off the road to our right. These artillery pieces all seemed to have barrels that were exploded. They were probably German anti-aircraft artillery that was defending Frankfurt. I would guess that the Germans themselves destroyed the weapons in place before they retreated from them.

We walked on through the night and into the next day (Thursday). We were exhausted but after several hours of walking, we were usually given a short break to sit and relax against a tree, an earth bank or a fence post just to take the load off our feet. Then the word would come down the line: "We are moving out," and the march would continue. As we neared the front lines, the roar of the cannons and the explosion of the shells were common noises. What was now important? How close are they? Are we getting closer? Are they directly before us or to either side? We saw some road signs which showed "Frankfurt: 25 kilometers." Then later we saw signs that showed "Frankfurt: 14 kilometers." For a while it seemed as if we were headed toward Frankfurt. But we never approached it. Personally, I preferred combat in the woods, rather than in a town or city. Really, I felt pretty good in a foxhole.

Towards evening we arrived at a little burg and the order was passed back "Kunze up front!" I moved forward and once again was given the privilege to oust an older man with a middle aged woman and then perhaps a granddaughter (about sixteen years of age) from their home. "We are staying in your home tonight. You are out!!" This was a sudden and tremendous shock to them. But they were well disciplined and did not even ask to get back into their home. However, the young granddaughter was very upset and pleaded, "Can we please stay in our barn?" The Lieutenant saw and heard the plea and when I poised the question to him; he briefly thought and granted the request. As I remember, they turned and headed for the barn being thankful that they could stay in it. I was pleased that we could accommodate them in this way.

The home was not necessarily on a street. It was at the end of a little road which led directly to the home, barn and courtyard. We were too tired to explore anything. I can still see a flash vision of the home but remember nothing on the inside. We were very, very tired. The non-coms usually took the beds and the rest of us each found some corner in a room not in the line of traffic that looked like a peaceful place. Indeed it was. I presume that someone stood guard during the night as most of us had a welcomed night of rest.

The next morning (Friday), we fell out as usual. Our squad received a short briefing by our Corporal. His message was "We are going to attack!! There is a little town ahead of us. As our armor approached it yesterday, there were white flags out; the town was ready to surrender. Our armor rolled in and when in the middle of town, all hell broke loose. There were German soldiers everywhere. After a furious battle, the result was that the Germans knocked out three of our tank destroyers and captured twelve of our jeeps. (Other sources report different figures.) Today it is our assignment to take the town." Its name was Schmitten, located in the Taunus Mountains about twenty-five kilometers north of northwest from Frankfurt. Thereafter we moved out. It did not sound like an easy assignment. Any engagement would probably be on the opposite end of the spectrum from a friendly one.

Over the years, additional information has surfaced that begins to show the order of battle, but some details and times are still shrouded and unclear. The battle for Schmitten lasted for two days and involved units from the Tenth Armored Division as well as Infantry units from the Third Battalion of the 417th Infantry Regiment.

Units of the Tenth Armored Division were the first to attack the town. Their first wave moved into the Village with the full assurance that the "white flag" message was genuine. When fully in town, they were ambushed by German SS Troopers in the homes and business buildings on both sides of the street. The enemy was everywhere. The result was the destruction of three of our tank destroyers (TDs) and the capture of a dozen or more of our jeeps. Another GI author

(Knight, Appendix B) also mentions that half-tracks were knocked out. The remainder of our armor was beaten back and driven out of town. I am still searching for an account of the battle by the Tenth Armored Division but have found none. The consequence of the disaster was that the Third Infantry Battalion of the 417th Infantry Regiment was now ordered to "Take the town!!"

I believe that all of I Company stayed in the little dorf with us. My platoon was not necessarily leading the charge. I had no information about any other outfits that were with us. As we trekked along the country road through the hills, the sound of rifle and machine gun fire became louder and more distinct. We were headed towards it!!

The name Taunus Mountains is really misleading because there were no mountains. In Texas we would have called them hills. These covered the terrain and the road wound around and through them. The area was covered with nice straight forest trees with occasional underbrush. There were no fields. Between the hills there were little cleared valleys that seemed to be meadows. The town of Schmitten was located in one of these larger valleys. There were essentially no trees in Schmitten. On the outskirts of town, homes extended on up into the forested area of the hills. On our side, the town's edge had been cleared of trees to where the valley was an open meadow. Roads were not in the bottom of the valleys but were hewn out of the hillsides. On the hillside of the road, there was just enough of a bar ditch to drain the water from a rain. The ditch was not deep enough to provide cover for an advancing soldier.

We followed such a road until about 11:00 a.m. As we approached Schmitten, our road followed a hill which had a J configuration. We came down the long leg of the J toward the bend. We were on the inside of the bow. The road continued around the bow to the tip and then followed the outside of the bow for a short distance before it veered away from the hill and into the town of Schmitten. After reaching the inside of the bow, we paused there and remained uncommitted for several hours.

The Battle for Schmitten

The battle for and in Schmitten was going on just over and behind the hill from us. Machine gun and rifle fire were sporadic but persistent and continuous. We knew the battle was being waged but had no idea if any progress was being made. If there had been any progress on our side, I am certain that we would have advanced to secure the taken ground. We made no such advance. The platoon in which I served was dispersed in place along the road. The ridge of the hill gave us excellent protection. We could have been subject to mortar fire but there was none. Our attacking troops received the full attention of the enemy.

Who were the attacking troops ahead of us? The Third Battalion of the 417th Infantry Regiment was assigned the task of taking Schmitten and Dorfweil. All companies in the battalion were probably not committed into the battle. Some were surely kept in reserve. I do not know which ones were engaged, but those who were committed lost a lot of men. The terrain favored the enemy and not the attacking troops. Units from the Tenth Armored Division were the first to be repulsed. This was followed by units of L Company being unsuccessful in a "marching fire" attack. Then the Second Platoon of I Company was unsuccessful in its first attack. I will report the activities of the Second Platoon of I Company because I served in it. The actions of L Company will then be related to the actions of my platoon.

The battle for Schmitten raged on through noon while we sat and contemplated what our specific mission might be. In the early afternoon, there was suddenly the rumbling of our cannons and the wafting noise of our shells as they passed overhead. This was followed by the immediate thunderous explosions in the targeted areas of town, behind the hill only a quarter or a third of a mile away. I looked up the hillside and thought to myself: "*I hope there is someone up there directing the fire.*" I do not know if these were 90mm shells from our TDs (Tank Destroyers) or perhaps 105mm shells from our artillery. What was the objective of the artillery? The battle had been raging all morning—rifle fire and machine gun bursts. If our GIs would have had any success, we would have moved forward to occupy the ground. We did not move forward; no ground had been taken; there was no progress. Instead there was a continuous rifle and machine gun battle that produced casualties but no gain. Our advance had been stopped. How and why?

Our advanced troops had been engaged long enough to know exactly where the enemy was and where artillery support was needed. We, the GIs behind the hill, knew that there had been no progress. The machine guns were a logical target for our artillery. How close to the nest did our artillery shells have to hit to deactivate the guns? What was the deactivation range of our shell bursts? How effective was the artillery? Could the shell bursts get down to the street level? After several volleys (three or four shells per volley), the shelling stopped. We were hoping for many more. Our forward troops must have been able to make their move. The machine gun nest had been silenced. I momentarily thought, *"We are doing nothing while the big guns are at work. They can shove another shell into the magazine and hurl the projectile into town without having to see the consequences of their work. For me, a rifleman, that compares to encountering a machine gun in the woods. I open fire against it, and it opens fire against me and others around me. With every shot, I hope to hit the target while not seeing the target itself. I can fire one clip (eight shells) of bullets after another without having to see the life or lives that my bullets may take. How different is it going to be when I go around the hook of this hill and begin to fire into Schmitten. I will be shooting at a specific live enemy. I hope and pray that I will be able to shoot and hit him before he will be able to shoot and hit me. I will be exposed. The enemy will be at least partially hidden in a house, behind a wall or in a hole."* I guess at that time I was preparing for the worst and hoping for the best. There was the little prayer which I had inscribed into my soul while we were in Luxembourg: "Who knows how near my end may be..." My thought was *"God be with me and let things happen according to Your will."*

We, as attacking infantrymen, were hoping for many more volleys to soften up the town. Why did they quit? Why no more shelling? The battle is still going on! Well there seemed to be a standard answer to this question. The answer was "the Colonel wants to use this place as regimental headquarters and does not want it to get all shot up. Let the infantry take it; they do less damage."

Recent publications have verified this rumor. The *417ᵗʰ Infantry Regiment: WW-II Historical Events:* Veterans—Post WW I & II (page XI) states that "On April 1, 1945, Colonel Bruner moved his command post to Schmitten." In the same manuscript, the chronology of the 417ᵗʰ Infantry Regiment reports that "the Regimental Command Post was moved to Schmitten, Germany, for which we had sweat the Third Battalion's blood." (page 32). Also, in the same manuscript, a tape transcription (Appendix C), by Sergeant Carl J. Kittleson of I Company, 417th Infantry Regiment, reports (page 217) "Our Colonel didn't want the town messed up too much, because he wanted it to become his Regimental Headquarters." The real answer was: "No further shelling was necessary; our attacking GIs could now cross the incoming road that the machine gun had defended." The dead GIs at this crossing will be discussed later.

The Second Platoon Enters the Battle

At about 3:00 p.m., the word came down the line "We are moving in!!!" As soon as we passed the tip of the hook in the hill, we would be in view of the enemy and hence be targets. Just after a few moments, we passed that tip. There was Schmitten in the near distant foreground while the evidence of battle was immediately before us. We approached two foxholes, one on each side of the road. There was a dead German soldier in each one. There was no sign of retreat in these warriors. They had held their ground to the very end. The foxholes were not very deep. The hole and the mound hardly gave enough protection to hide a body. The dead bodies were not down in the holes, but the upper part of the body lay exposed behind the mound. Our attack was in single file like cars in a train. We were well dispersed with ten to fifteen yards between us. We followed each other's path as closely as possible because the area could have had anti-personnel mines.

We carried our guns in the rifle ready position while keeping our eyes on the town before us. As we passed the foxholes, I could not resist taking a fast glimpse at the closest dead German still in his hole only about two strides away. His helmet was still on his head with the chinstrap in place. The helmet had a bullet hole through it right in the temple area. If I had a German helmet for a target that is exactly where I would aim for and hope to make the hit.

The dead soldier's gun was there and to my amazement, there was still a cigarette clutched between the index and middle fingers of his left hand. The cigarette had continued to burn until it also died leaving about three-fourth-inch of ashes still attached to the cigarette. Did he light up a cigarette as he engaged in battle or did someone give him the cigarette after he had been hit and was dying? Was it a normal cigarette or did it serve a particular purpose? I do not know. It just turned out to be a glimpse of a pale face and hands that I can never forget. His only option was to die there and he did.

We turned off the road to our right and advanced along the tree line on our side of the valley. Schmitten was seemingly northeast of us and we were proceeding in an east of southeasterly direction. Our armor may have used the road to attack the town. We saw no burned or destroyed vehicles or tanks. The foot soldiers before us seemingly had used the same road without much success. We were now using another avenue to attack the town. Instead of using the road, we were now in the process of making an attack through the woods. The lead men of our column soon received gunfire. These GIs were not within my view but the gunfire was close and came from the other side of the valley. The head of the column was at about the end of the cleared valley and the distance across the valley at my position was only about fifty yards. Much happened within my platoon but I will first tell that which I saw. My field of vision was probably only two or three men before me and the same for the men behind me. I will recapitulate these moments again a little later.

Our advance was sporadic and slow but persistent. There was no protection or shelter other than to hide as much as possible. We were on a wooded hillside. As more GIs became engaged, the German outposts were soon overwhelmed. We experienced casualties and so did the enemy. Soon there were cries of anguish and desperation on the enemy side. The indication was that one of their men had been mortally hit and was immobilized. There was the cry *"Last mich nicht hier"* (Don't leave me here) along with that of pain and anguish. But the tone of desperation in the victim's voice left the impression that his comrades were pulling out and leaving him behind. Perhaps they could not retreat fast enough if he had to be carried or helped in some way. The anguished cries were repeated several times and soon there was silence, as the gunfire continued.

The lead GIs of our platoon had advanced far enough down the valley to engage the entire platoon in the advancing line. We were now ordered to form a front by turning ninety degrees to cross the valley. With this formation we would comb the woods on the other side of the valley and attack Schmitten not along a road but through the woods.

We crossed the valley without further contact but knew the enemy was in retreat just ahead of us. As we proceeded I came upon the German soldier who had been screaming. He was now dead and beside him laid his German Luger pistol, which was an item that was on my "take-home" list. I glimpsed at the dead trooper (He could have been an officer) and his Luger pistol but never broke stride in moving forward. Did the trooper finally shoot himself in preference to being captured? Did his comrades shoot him? Or did he finally die from combat wounds? I do not know. I do know that it took only one moment for me to reach the decision to leave the wanted pistol behind.

I am sure that some cadaver clean-up crew came along behind us and must have celebrated the find and wondered how the advancing troops could have left such a gem of a souvenir behind? I could have told them why. My immediate thought was that I would be dead if by some means or for some reason I should be caught or captured with it. Of course there was no assurance that I would get to live even if I was captured without it. If I should get killed with the pistol in my possession, I doubt that it would have been shipped home as part of my belongings. The decision to leave it was made without any hesitation in our advance.

The armor attack of the previous day must have been conducted on a road that led into town. Our armor was dealt a punishing blow while being partially destroyed, captured and otherwise repulsed. The infantry ahead of us then attacked Schmitten along a road on the left side of the valley from which we had approached it. There was no direct frontal attack from the valley, but the day's battle had been largely fought from the bar ditch between the road and the hill as the road meandered into town. Knight (Appendix B) in L Company reports that a frontal attack (marching fire) was tried early in the morning. It was repulsed before the troops were able to get out of the woods into the open valley.

Now we were attacking below the town from the right side of the valley as we left town. The manpower that the enemy still had now needed to defend the town on two fronts. The town was small and the battle for it was well into its second day. How much enemy manpower was left in the town? Were any reinforcements coming in? How much ammunition did the enemy have? The enemy did not seem to have artillery because it did not respond to our artillery attack. There was never any air support but we did not have air support either. We encountered no mortar fire and neither did we drop mortar shells into the town. From our point of view, the enemy had a lot of rifle and machine gun ammunition because they were using it on us.

Our wave of men, one man deep, moved forward toward Schmitten. The area was wooded with young trees about one foot in diameter. No sky was visible ahead because the tree population was too dense. Occasionally there could have been some visible blue sky directly above us. Our immediate battle area had little underbrush. In general, we directed our fire in the direction from which the enemy fire came. We had crossed the valley and were moving up a gentle incline towards the top of a hill whose ridge ran parallel to the valley on the right side of Schmitten. We did not see the enemy and the enemy did not see us, but both of us were exchanging shots at each other. After advancing perhaps a 125 yards from the valley's bottom, we began to encounter short bursts of machine gun fire. These bullets did not seem to hit anyone and neither did we see dirt being kicked up where the bullets could have hit the ground. Our advance continued and we soon discovered that there were two machine guns immediately ahead of us. Both were just beyond the crest line of the hill. The crest of the hill was protecting us from their fire but it also made our fire ineffective towards them. From my position in the wave of advancing men, the first machine gun was slightly to my right before me. The second was twenty-five or thirty yards further back towards Schmitten. It was nearly straight ahead of me. Both were ten to fifteen yards behind the crest of the hill. Our advance was now fifty to sixty yards from the crest. As we approached, the machine gun fire became more intense. But interspersed with the machine gun fire were occasional single rifle shots. We had more than just two machine guns ahead of us.

The GI on my left was a rifleman. He was much older than most of us. He could have been in his thirties and I had learned to know and to respect him. He was a fatherlike figure for me and served as a role model. He was mature, deliberate, considerate, friendly and patient—a fine gentleman. His morals and character were very much compatible with mine. As a rifleman, he also carried two rounds of rifle grenades along with the grenade launcher and the blank bullets with which to launch the grenades. The GI on my right was a rifleman just as I was. There was no BAR (Browning Automatic Rifle) man close to me but there was one about three men from me on my left. All I can remember is the rapidity of the German machine gun shots compared to the slow motion fire of our Browning Automatic Rifle. The comparison between our BAR and the enemy machine guns did not inspire a feeling of superiority. The enemy's rapid-fire weapons (burp guns and machine guns) probably fired nearly two shots whenever ours fired one. In the article *World War II – A Personal History*, Bye (2005), he reported that the enemy machine guns fired 1,200 rounds per minute.

As we neared the machine gun nests, we could no longer stand up but made our advance in the crouched and crawling positions. We soon reached the point where the machine gun bullets were just above us. The crest of the hill was still beyond our capability to successfully lob a hand grenade. We would have been the victims instead of the enemy. So for some period, we exchanged our rifle fire for the enemy's machine gun fire and their occasional single rifle shots. We were pinned down and would have been the enemy mortar man's dream target, but it seemed that the enemy had no mortars. We had no protection other than the small tree trunks to hide behind. The tree trunks were not big enough to stop a rifle bullet. From time to time someone would raise up to get a glimpse of the machine gun nest, but no one was able to take the needed shot to silence the nest. I made such an effort and was somewhat startled to see a German helmet with a swastika on its side. When I saw the enemy helmet, my helmet was also in their view and promptly drew a barrage of machine gun bullets. Every GI was thinking and wondering, how do we proceed?

The GI on my right, perhaps twenty feet away, pulled his knees up under himself and proceeded to raise his head to take a quick look. Even before his body straightened up, there was the single crack of a rifle from the enemy side. His body was jolted and shocked as every muscle momentarily contracted before slumping down and becoming limp and motionless. He was shot in the head. There were no cries of pain or anguish, but within the blink of an eye, life had turned into death. So far the machine gunners had stopped us but a single rifle shot had inflicted the first casualty near me. The machine gun bursts continued and so did the occasional rifle shots. I do not know that each single shot had a specific target. The single shots came from several different locations. We knew where the machine guns were, but had no idea from where the single shots were coming.

Somewhere there were snipers who were in a better position to see us than we were to see them. The crest of the hill protected us from the machine gun barrages but it did not protect us from the sniper shots. The exchange of our rifle fire with the machine gun nests continued, but our concern shifted from the machine gun barrages to the individual rifle blasts. We were depending on sight and sound to find the hidden snipers. The nearest sniper seemed to be up in the trees just beyond the nearest machine gun but ahead of the second one. I thought his gun blast would cause some tree branches to sway and he would be in the area behind them. I was then ready to blast that area with at least a clip (eight shots) of bullets. But I could see nothing move in the area from which the shots seemingly came.

My early farm life taught me that the squirrel is where you see the branches moving in the trees.

After a few more minutes passed, the GI on my left (my role model) raised his head to take a peak. He was behind a tree that was about fifteen feet away. As he slowly raised his head, there was the single blast of a rifle again, his muscles contracted as his body seemed jolted and shocked before slumping limp and relaxed to the ground without any cry of anguish or pain. The single shots were deadly.

I prayed for keener sight and hearing but had only what God in his providence had given me. I was ready to meet my Maker because I could not see the deadly snipers but they seemed to see us. Any time now the next shot should be directed at the little tree behind which I was seeking shelter. I was never closer to God and during these moments God must have focused on me. The little prayer "Who knows how near my end may be..." was in my mind and heart. My thought was "Lord when that bullet strikes me, give me one last sane moment in which to raise my hand to grasp yours." It seemed that the time could very well be this moment, now, or now, or now—but now never came. In retrospect, I wonder whether I was scared of the enemy or was it that God was so close whispering to me "Otto, as long as you use the good senses and judgments that I have given you, nothing bad shall happen. I have plans for you to give many more years of service to my people on earth."

I had the feeling that I was in view of the sniper with dead GIs on both sides of me. If I want to live, I cannot afford to raise my head or even move. The machine gun cannot harm me. My focus has to be on the snipers. I laid as low as I could behind my tree and kept straining my ears and eyes to locate the snipers before us. I never did find their positions to get off the needed shots.

The exchange of machine gun fire began to slow when the more distant machine gun opened with a long burst. This was followed by a long burst from the closer machine gun. I heard the sound of running feet come to the nearest machine gun nest. In my mind an ammunition carrier brought several more canisters of ammunition to the machine gun before us. The enemy now probably had enough ammunition to continue the battle well into the evening.

It was now early evening when suddenly my squad Sergeant was hunched over the GI on my right. He turned the dead man's head to see his face and then quickly scooted on his hands and feet to the dead man on my left and did the same thing before scooting back toward the rear. This was an act of compassion, duty and loyalty as well as of bravery. He risked his own life to confirm the physical status of his men. If there had been a moment of hesitation, the sniper probably would have had another victim. There was no call for a medic. The dead men could not make the call and the squad Sergeant confirmed that such a call was not necessary. The men in the squad did not know that our first Sergeant was dead, and our Lieutenant was wounded and out of action. I doubt that the squad Sergeants knew who was in charge.

What could we have done or what should we have done? Among other potential approaches, we were too far back to lob a hand grenade. If the GI on my left had stayed alive, we could have tried to use rifle grenades in several ways. There was the possibility of shooting a grenade just over the crest of the hill to hit the machine gun nest. A second possibility was to hit the biggest tree in the forest with a grenade. This tree was only fifteen to twenty feet to the right of the machine gun. We probably could have stunned the gunner long enough to deactivate him and the gun. Maybe two rifle grenades would have worked; the first to hit the tree and the second to hit the machine gun nest. Additionally, such a strategy could possibly have blasted a sniper out of that tree. But this never happened because the enemy destroyed our potential for destruction before we were able to deactivate their potential for destruction. The final result was that we kept the enemy engaged until darkness set in. Thereafter we withdrew to our original point of attack and all indications are that the enemy also withdrew back into Schmitten.

Our Second Attack on Schmitten

The battle for Schmitten was not over and neither was our combat for that day of Friday. After reassembling in the moonlight near the tip of the *J* configured hill, we proceeded down the bar ditch along the road where the battle had been raging all day. The battle along this road had continued when we were first committed to comb the woods on the right-hand side of Schmitten. The difference was that the time was now night, the moon was out and we were able to move forward without immediate opposition. Those who had gained this ground had now left and we were moving in to repossess it. We used the bar ditch until we arrived at the left side of town. Our previous attack through the woods was toward the right side of town. There was still some gunfire but it was not directed at us. We came to a road which led into the heart of town while our road was a crossroad going up the valley. Our bar ditch had a culvert over which the incoming road passed before going into town directly towards a church. The culvert was about twelve to fourteen inches in diameter. No one could crawl through it!! Immediately before the incoming road and culvert, there were three or four dead GIs on each side of the bar ditch. Their bodies had been moved aside to clear a path to the mouth of the culvert. There had been one or more machine guns in town at the head of this road near the church. These controlled the road as well as our crossing road. Any GI that tried to cross the incoming road was machine gunned down. Those who were hit immediately were pulled back into our approach side. These dead have been mentioned before. There must have also been wounded GIs, but these had been moved out before us. We did not know if the machine guns were still in position or not. But our men were able to move across the road without drawing machine gun fire. Obviously, the top of the incoming road was not a safe place to be. Everyone dashed across the road at top speed and leaped into the bar ditch on the other side. There the dead GIs had not been removed either. They had simply been pulled off the incoming road and into the bar ditch. So after I dashed across the incoming road, there was just a pile of dead bodies to leap onto at the far side of the culvert. Again, there were no wounded left, but there could have been between eight to ten or more dead bodies. No one hesitated to make the leap; no one stopped to view the dead; we did not have time to feel sorry for them or for ourselves; our goal was not to become one of them. War is more than cruel and inconsiderate. The individual's senses are hardened to where sympathy and respect become very much a secondary priority to life itself. The soldiers who initially took this ground could have been from I Company. Sergeant Kittleson (2005) describes a battle that could have produced many wounded and dead. See Appendix C for his version of the battle.

Soon after the road crossing, there were buildings on the town-side of the street. A little further along, there were apartment buildings on our side. The advance was slow and unopposed. We continued until we were near the backside of town. No other GIs were in the area, but they had been there. So we knew that we would soon make contact with the enemy. It would have been considered a beautiful moonlit night in time of peace. We finally came to an apartment-like building on our side of the road and each man dashed into it as he left the bar ditch. Rifles were in the "ready" position. Immediately before the stoop of the doorway lay a dead GI. We jumped over the body and ran into the building which was lit only by the moonlight through the windows.

The Enemy's Final Roundup

It appears that our soldiers, who had taken the area, had withdrawn, and we hastened to reoccupy the ground. We came in from the town-side of the building, and everyone positioned himself near a window looking out towards the country. We were looking for enemy troop movements. Just a little farther down the street from our apartment house there was a road leaving town.

The apartment building seemed to be unoccupied. There was no furniture in it. It did not appear to be new but it was empty. There were no beds, no curtains, no floor covers. Other writers report that Schmitten was the home of an Officers Candidate School (OCS). These could have been their quarters. Otherwise the structures could have housed families who had been bombed out in the larger cities like Frankfurt.

After we had watched out of the windows for a few moments, our squad Corporal saw enemy soldiers on the road leaving town. He brought his rifle up and took several potshots at them without targeting any particular individual. This attracted their attention quite fast. Our building was sprayed and raked several times with bursts from their burp guns. That got our attention equally as fast and no one was very eager thereafter to stick his head out of a window to see where the enemy soldiers were. We knew the enemy was leaving town and were glad to see them go.

We no longer saw any enemy soldiers and also received no further gunfire from them. The time was past midnight and the gunfights had ended. We had been on the road and in battle since early morning and everyone was ready for a break. We were no longer advancing and the Germans were not attacking. Everyone was content to relax a little. Keeping our guard up but not having a target to shoot at was a welcomed relief. The tense situation gradually subsided and became quiet.

At about 2:00 a.m., there was the sound of a jeep coming down the street with the bar ditch that we had used to get into the building. It puttered right by at idle speed and kept on going. I thought the situation had really improved; the Captain has come in. The jeep moved toward the street where the enemy soldiers had left town. Now things really became quiet. All gunfire ceased. Everyone relaxed a little.

Before long the order came down: "We are moving out." We withdrew along the bar ditch of the street by which we had come. After a few blocks we headed back out into the woods where we kept on moving until the next morning (Saturday). We were told that the jeep which we had heard going by our building was not our Captain at all. It was the German's picking up their last outposts in the town of Schmitten. The jeep was one that was captured when our armor first attacked the town.

After our infantry battled for nearly twenty-four hours, the town of Schmitten finally was ours. What a battle. The defenders had been in battle for at least forty-eight hours. The enemy soldiers were real tough warriors. We obviously had more resources and more reserves to keep the pressure on. That finally won the battle for us.

Other Units in the Battle

What you have read is my perspective of what happened at the town of Schmitten. The battle is also recorded in the book *We Ripened Fast* – Hutnik (1946). I will briefly paraphrase his comments while also recommending that the reader review the Lieutenant's perspective of the battle from a broader and higher level of command.

After the Seventy-Sixth Infantry Division crossed the Rhine River, it was opposed by the Sixth SS "Nord" Mountain Division, which had been brought back from Norway. Additionally, there were the 276th Volks Grenadier Division and the 159th Infantry Division. The Third Battalion of the 417th Infantry Regiment was assigned to take the towns of Schmitten and Dorfweil. Before the Third Battalion received this assignment, three of our tanks were knocked out in Dorfweil and a fourth was captured. In Schmitten, troops of the Third Battalion moved in and fought house to house. The enemy launched a counterattack and successfully (but only temporarily) captured a platoon of Yanks. The enemy was finally driven out of Schmitten in the early morning hours of March 31 (Saturday), 1945.

The following two paragraphs are directly from the book *We Ripened Fast* – Hutnik (1946), page 155. I was in I Company of the Third Battalion of the 417th Infantry Regiment. The incident reported here occurred when my platoon was first committed into the battle. The Sergeant was my Platoon Sergeant, and the Lieutenant was my platoon commander. I was not directly in this action but was only a squad or so behind where the action occurred. Our medic was known to us as "Pat."

> "Pfc Patrick J. Finn was his name, a medic with I Company, 417th Infantry. When it happened the company was clearing the woods near Schmitten. Finn was behind the line of fire but was watching the men approach the woods where the Nazis were. Two soldiers were out in front and were rushing across the field. They were almost to the woods when out of the trees came the sputter of a

German machine gun. One soldier spun around and then crumpled. The other dropped for a moment and then was up and running forward. He got it, too. Finn could see them."

The bright red crosses on Finn's helmet were prominent and maybe the Krauts knew the Geneva rules about medics and maybe they didn't, like the ones who fired at him earlier in the day. He looked at the wounded men and that was enough. He worked his way out of his spot of safety, moved across a small stream and then across the open field to the wounded men. One, a Sergeant, was dead. The other, an officer, was seriously wounded. Finn administered first aid, heedless of the machine gunner and snipers in the woods only a few yards away. He managed to get the officer back in time for medical treatment."

Pat became well known and was highly respected within our platoon. The foregoing quoted engagement goes back to when our battle started on Friday afternoon. I joined I Company on February 20, and this battle started on March 30. Within thirty-eight days, my platoon lost three Lieutenants, and we were now in need of a fourth one. I never learned to know any of them. They were known to me only through my translation duties where it was necessary to communicate with some German people. Otherwise I probably saw them at platoon formations from time to time. I do not recall that we ever had a company formation while I was on the front lines.

The Sergeant was better known to me because of his platoon activities. I recall the name as Sgt. Stett but cannot find him in the Seventy-Sixth Division roster. Maybe he was a replacement as I was. My name is not in the Seventy-Sixth Division roster. Sgt. Stett was a mature soldier who stood solidly on his feet. His demeanor was such that he was respected by his men. I liked him and thought he was a great leader. He was mild mannered and not overbearing; the kind of individual that a person would want for a friend and leader. With days and time, we could have become close personal friends. Well, the report was that he was gunned down by a machine gun and received five or six wounds as the machine gun bullets raked across his body. This machine gun nest was taken and the resultant cry of an enemy soldier of *"Last mich nich hier!"* (Don't leave me here!) is what I wrote about earlier in this chapter.

Aside from *We Ripened Fast* – Hutnik (1946), several participants in the battle for Schmitten have written their account of the actions. Kittleson (2005) reports in the *417ᵗʰ Infantry Regiment: WWII Historical Events*, that I Company (First Platoon) encountered a small village (Schmitten) which contained an Officer Training School. There were a few diehards left with a mortar and machine gun to guard the only road going into town. Kittleson and his platoon moved forward one by one and an awful lot of guys were hit. By the time he ran into town, he was running over dead and wounded bodies. A machine gun bullet hit his M-1 rifle and splintered the wood to produce a wound in his finger (see Kittleson, Appendix C).

James Richard Knight of L Company gives another account of the battle (Appendix B). Knight describes the battle for Schmitten as it was experienced by his platoon in L Company of the 417ᵗʰ Infantry Regiment. Knight saw some of the blown up jeeps and half-tracks that had been lost by the Tenth Armored Division the day before. Early in the morning (Friday) L Company was ordered to use marching fire to attack the town across the open valley. They quickly found that Schmitten was occupied by a sizeable and stubborn battalion of SS Troopers. The marching fire attack failed. Then the Second Platoon (Knight's platoon) was ordered to circle around Schmitten and take the town of Dorfweil on the same road behind Schmitten. Two tank destroyers were assigned to the platoon to assist in the assignment. A frontal attack on Schmitten (my platoon at night) now pushed the enemy back toward Dorfweil.

The task force of L Company successfully took Dorfweil and managed to dig in before the enemy began to retreat out of Schmitten. (My platoon saw them withdraw.) When the enemy retreat started, the Second Platoon from L Company was quickly overrun. The final group of GIs was trapped in a house and was taken captive. One of the TDs became the victim of a *panzerfaust* (bazooka round). The other was captured intact and its personnel were taken prisoners.

The enemy moved these GI prisoners back with them in their retreat. While the TDs and the Second Platoon of L Company were fighting for their lives and were being taken prisoners, the Second Platoon of I Company (my company) was pushing hard to drive the enemy out of Schmitten back into Dorfweil. For more details about the activities of L Company, see Knight (Appendix B).

We moved out of Schmitten several hours after midnight (Saturday morning), but the day of the week was of no particular consequence. Being able to see another day was more important to us. We lumbered along slowly through the remaining hours of the night and shortly after sunrise we arrived in another little town (Dorfweil). There we moved into an empty home at the edge of town and kept watch through the windows. The town was small. There seemed to be primarily one street with a row of homes on each side of it. The town could have been five hundred yards long.

About thirty or forty yards down the street was one of our tank destroyers just sitting in the middle of the street facing into town away from us. GI helmets and other battle gear were scattered in the street. Right now the time was more peaceful than what it had been sometime before. Was it safe? Or how safe was it? As the time passed, a well-dressed US soldier wearing a jacket, pistol and helmet ventured out into the street just beyond the TD and began to pick up the scattered battlefield gear. We watched when our Corporal suddenly exclaimed, "Hey, that is Major Moe, our Battalion Commander!!!" After just a moment, his comment was "Let's go and help him." And we did. The area was obviously relatively safe, but we did not know how safe it was. I walked up to our TD, that was knocked out. In the armor, right in front of the driver, was about a one-inch hole burned through about four inches of metal armor; the result of a German bazooka (*panzerfaust*) shot. No one mounted the tank. The hatches still all seemed to be closed. Otherwise the TD seemed to be intact. We all saw the results of the instant impact and power of a bazooka round. Just from observation, I guessed that everybody inside was killed and the dead bodies were still inside. We cleaned up and checked the street a little more before the order came to move out once more.

We were battle weary and unnerved but we kept on. No one was falling out. From time to time we would take a ten- or fifteen-minute break (not necessarily predictable). I am sure someone knew where we were going, but the privates in the ranks did not. Our move was in single file on dirt roads through some small hills and along some valleys. While proceeding along a cleared valley, we had nearby woods on our left and then about fifty yards of clear valley on our right before the woods started in again. Something seemingly happened in the nearby woods on the left and in front of us that startled a GI. His response was to run toward the clear valley on his right. His fellow GIs responded in the same manner, and the run extended both up and down the line. I just saw the wave coming toward me, and I ran with them. There was no gunfire, and the pace of the run slowed only as we reached the woods on the other side of the narrow valley. There still was no gunfire. The run finally stopped in the woods. At that time we looked at each other and began to ask, "Where is the enemy?" Well there was none. We were just a bunch of shell-shocked troops. After regaining our composure, we cautiously walked back out to the road and continued with our march.

A day or so later, we were reprimanded by our non-com and squad Sergeant for this spontaneous action. We were told, "We do not run unless there is a very definite reason for doing so (being shot at could qualify)." Our scrambling was not an acceptable battlefield maneuver. Obviously, the non-commissioned officers had momentarily lost control of their men. They were running with them. The reprimand was appropriate and we were fortunate that the enemy was nowhere around.

Since there was no opposition, our march was obviously toward the rear (away from the frontlines even though the frontline was not well defined). We walked until evening at which time we arrived at a village that was essentially deserted. We were assigned to some empty homes for the night and slept very well.

A Church Service? What a Surprise!!

Morning came and after we started moving around, the word was passed to us: "There is going to be a Protestant church service. If you are interested in attending, fall out at 10:00 a.m." That was welcome news. We had not had the opportunity to go to church in a long time. This was probably my first opportunity to attend church in Europe. Well it could be Sunday, but no one had kept track of the days or months.

At the specified time, a number of us gathered in the street. We marched off in full battlefield regalia. After several blocks, we arrived at a church. We entered and sat down in chairs. The setting was a familiar one. I felt at home in the church. The furniture and ornaments were what I expected. The difference was that the fronts of the entire balcony were covered with framed certificates honoring those of the congregation who had lost their lives in the war. Counts in the teens or twenties were common and normal in churches which we saw. What a tragedy.

Every church in Germany had the same story to tell. Many of their young and middle aged men had lost their lives in the war. I finally had to ask, *"How does this compare to my church back home?"*

My church also wanted to honor its young men in the service. It developed an Honor Roll (Fig. 9), with names of all enlisted men. As additional members volunteered or were inducted, their names were added. The Honor Roll was hung on the right-hand side of the church front wall and stayed there for many years. Names of men who gave their lives were enclosed within two cross symbols.

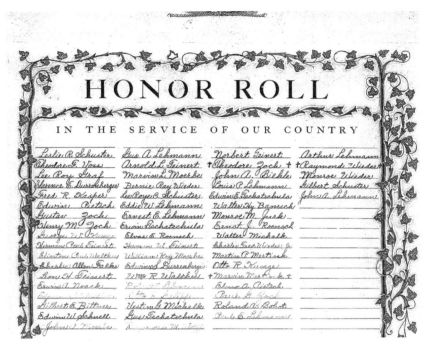

Fig. 9. The "Honor Roll" of Holy Cross Lutheran Church in Warda, Texas, which lists the members who served in the Armed Forces during World War II. Three of the fifty-eight men lost their lives. Their names are enclosed with the sign of the cross.

The Honor Roll is still on exhibition in the church display cases. Three of fifty-eight men lost their lives. I expect that the ratio in Germany was nearly the opposite. Few of their service men survived. Before the war ended, most German soldiers had to take an oath to fight to their death. This made their capture extremely dangerous. They were eligible to be shot by us or by their own men. I know of none that were shot by us but saw at least one who had been shot in the back because he tried to surrender to us.

The exhibition of the death certificates was an extra meant for us to see. We were there to enlarge that list while their goal was to increase ours. Our previous days of battle left absolutely no doubt in our minds about their intentions. We were happy and thankful to have the opportunity to be in the church alive.

The church service was started with a song or two. The Chaplain then entered the pulpit to give the sermon. He told us it was Easter!! Who had given any thought to Easter? Who among us even knew what day it was? What a change of spirits!!! Well, if this was Easter Sunday, we were in Dorfweil on Saturday morning.

The day before that was Good Friday. That is the memorable day when we battled in Schmitten. The Bible tells us the story of Good Friday. I also have my remembrance of my Friday in Schmitten. For more than seventy years now, I have been able to celebrate the biblical Holy Week, but along with that I remember the events of those days on the front lines in 1945. I am thankful that I am here and often ask myself the question "Why was I selected to still be here?" I have tried to answer that question with my work and service, hoping that the Good Lord will continue to smile on me with the whisper "Otto, keep it up; you are doing fine."

You, the reader, can reconstruct our activities during Holy Week 1945. On the afternoon of Palm Sunday, we pulled out of Oberwessel on our way to St. Goar.

We Ripened Fast – Hutnik (1946) reports that "Easter was not forgotten by the men of the Seventy-Sixth… GIs crowded into ancient pews with their rifles and steel helmets." A picture on page 156 shows a service in progress. I attended a service in that church on that day but the service which I attended did not have that many GIs in attendance. I sat in about the fourth or fifth row from the front on the right side of the aisle. There were only a few GIs in the side pews on the right and the same is true for the regular pews on the left side of the aisle. I cannot find myself in the picture on page 156. Yet there was at least one picture taken in the service which I attended. While the service was in progress, there was a flash in the church without the usual bang or boom that we were accustomed to. We nearly came out of our seats but managed to hold on to them while hearing the good news that was coming from the pulpit: "Christ is risen, He is risen indeed." We are alive to celebrate his rising.

After the war, I studied to be an agricultural engineer at Texas A&M University. I received the BS degree in 1950 then earned the Master of Science degree at Iowa State College in 1951 and subsequently a PhD degree from Michigan State University in 1964. My PhD research was with the rice grain. This work had some merit and garnered attention around the world. Eleven years later (1975), I was invited to the Indian Institute of Technology (IIT) at Kharagpur, West Bengal, India. While en route, I stopped for one day in Frankfurt, Germany, and secured a taxi and driver to take me to Schmitten. My taxi driver was in the war; was captured and became an interpreter and translator for the Eighth Army. He could speak better English than I could speak German. We drove to Schmitten and tried to find someone who was there during the war. More specifically we were looking for someone who was there during the days of our encounters (the Battle of Schmitten). We had some difficulty in finding such a person. We finally drove out of town where there was an open valley on our right. The road was carved out of the hillside as needed on the left and there were houses on the right side. On this road we met a couple taking their afternoon stroll. My driver asked them if they had any knowledge of Schmitten during the war. The lady replied, "Oh yes, I lived here". She had been bombed out of Frankfurt and had moved to Schmitten. She was there during the battle. The *J* hill was just behind the houses and across the valley from where we stopped to talk. The road which we had used to attack Schmitten was now closed and a better one had been built. She knew the exact houses in which the Germans had machine guns in the basements that faced across the valley to the road on which we were trying to come in. She also knew of other machine gun locations in the town like the one in front of the church that caused us so many casualties. She related that a Schutz Staffel (SS) Captain was in charge of the enemy troops. After the enemy lost the battle and Schmitten was ours, the Captain's clothes were found lying on a bed in a home and the Captain himself had changed into civilian clothes before he disappeared into the local civilian population.

Every GI had a wonderful and meaningful Easter. It was a meaningful and comforting day. My death might be near, but Jesus died and then rose for me over 1900 years ago. I was glad to be alive but also felt reassured of my life with God if death was to come.

In our society, death is normally viewed as something sad and undesirable. We struggle for life up to our final breath. But that is the only way that God has chosen to call us to himself. Imagine God in heaven looking down on his beloved one in battle and saying "Otto you do not have to put up with that heathen rage any longer. Just come on home." A single bang would have done it. But I have to tell myself, that is not what God wanted. Rather His message was "Otto, hang in there. You have a lot of work to do before you can rest in your Savior's arms." That period of grace is now more than seventy years.

As I remember, we lost no time in the village where we celebrated Easter. During the day we were called to "fall out" and were briefed and lectured as to how we would approach and take any future machine gun nests. The bottom line was "marching fire". We would not let ourselves get pinned down again. Marching fire would still result in some casualties but the hope was for fewer ones along with a greater degree of success. Why did we not use marching fire on Good Friday? Well, we had lost our Lieutenant and First Sergeant. I am not sure that the squad Sergeants knew who was in charge. Were any of them ready to take command?

We Ripened Fast – Hutnik (1946) states that the powerful and aggressive German Sixth SS Nord Mountain Division now could be written off the books. The Seventy-Sixth Division had reached its assigned east boundary on Easter Sunday. Officers wrote on their staff reports concerning their men "Morale – Superior."

The sentiment among the riflemen was probably more accurately "Let's get on with the task. We are looking forward to more pleasant, interesting and desired goals in life."

More of the Same:
Clear the Towns and Comb the Woods

We moved on, and so did the war. Our transportation continued to be by foot along country roads. From time to time, we would comb some woods to assure that they were clear and secure. More and more often as we approached small villages, there were foxholes dug on the hillsides in strategic positions to defend the road on which we were approaching the town. Such foxholes were probably not dug by German soldiers but rather by prisoners of war or by displaced persons. We were happy to find them unmanned and unfortified.

After a day or more of marching, we were combing some woods when we encountered machine gun fire before us and to our left. The combing ceased momentarily as the squad Sergeants aligned their men for the attack. We were formed into two parallel lines with alternate men forming the second line about ten yards behind the first. During the attack, if someone in the front line was to get hit, one of the alternates was to move forward to fill the slot. Both lines were to direct fire at the machine gun's location with the second line being very mindful of the men in the first line. We would not converge on the machine gun location but would continue our advance forward with our fire directed toward the machine gun location. After the machine gun was silenced, it would no longer be a target. We would then continue to look for targets before us. I do not know how long the double line was, but our attack most likely consisted of all the men in I Company.

After getting appropriately positioned and organized, the attack began. The machine gun responded. With every burst from the machine gun, we were able to more accurately zero in our fire towards its location. The battle was short and the machine gun position was taken. Our immediate squad and platoon suffered no casualties. We never saw the machine gun nest or the gunner. For a single machine gun, the marching fire approach was quite effective. Just imagine a company of men firing at an unseen target whose position was determined by the sound of the machine gun. Thereafter, we continued on the country roads and combed specific woods without much opposition. Our advances were slow but certain.

One day we moved into a town without encountering any opposition. This was not a combing operation but rather one in which the GIs followed one another. In such an attack, the lead men become the first target. Ground was being taken but the advance was sporadic. This produced an accordion effect in the line of troops which followed. We would advance and then hold, then advance and hold again. As long as there was no gunfire ahead, our adrenalin was not flowing. Yet other interesting things did happen.

The town which we were taking was a typical German village with a solid row of buildings on each side of the street. Usually the buildings were quiet and seemed unoccupied. The streets were bare and our hunt was on. During one of our advance and hold movements, I stopped at a door that could have led into a dwelling. The inside was not quiet. There was a woman's voice breaking through the silence. "*Die verdampten Americanische schweine sind hier...*" (The damned American pigs are here...). She really scolded, berated and degraded us without a whole lot of profanity. She was not immediately behind the door that led to the street but was perhaps in a hallway, or at least a room away from the entrance. She was expressing her feelings about us coming into town. Her words were not threatening us in any way. There were no indications that she might have a gun. She could have been performing for her neighbors through the walls, but there was never a response or comment by anyone else. I do not know when this monologue began but it showed no sign of ending when we made our next short advance. As it was, she was releasing her pent up emotions and as long as she was not threatening us, we did not bother her.

After several more accordion cycles, there was a little boy out in the street watching with interest and amazement. Our particular advance stopped as I was in the vicinity of the boy (about five or six years old). He stared at each one of us. I wonder what his thoughts were? He seemed curious and harmless. When I reached him, I probably said something like "*Gutten tag, wie geht es mit dier?*" (Good day, how are you?) He was startled and amazed but understood; he seemed unafraid and did not turn or move to run. It took just one moment to get a conversation underway. I became my own S-2 unit. "When were the last German soldiers here? How many hours ago? Were they walking or were they riding? What were they riding in or on? Were they living here in town or were they just passing through? How many men were there? Were they just carrying rifles?" And so on. I was getting myself the latest intelligence and felt quite comfortable in doing so. Yet my squad members before and after me saw this.

My conversation with the little boy was reported on up the line and within a day or so my Sergeant came to update me on the "non-fraternization" rule that was in effect. I was expected to abide by that rule. Failure to do so could result in some rather severe consequences. Any conversation with persons on the enemy side had to be done in the presence of and by the request of our Lieutenant. I accepted the censure and toed the line thereafter. Otherwise my visit with the little boy had no adverse affects on anyone.

Liberation of Our US Factory

We took one town after another. Sometimes we just walked through if there was no resistance. On other occasions, we were more cautious, and still other times, we actually were looking for something.

One day we just stopped in a little burg and were seemingly waiting. Soon the command came down: "Kunze up front!" I proceeded forward and found the platoon Lieutenant and the First Sergeant. The Lieutenant had been asked to investigate a particular building. We proceeded down the street and found the structure. It was the biggest building in town; perhaps fifty or sixty meters square and three or four stories tall. We needed to get into that building.

There were some German civilians around, and we found a man who had keys. This was some type of factory that produced electrical or electronic equipment. The Lieutenant gave me questions to ask the German civilian. Soon there were some German women that joined our group. They tried to help the civilian man answer our questions. "Whose factory was it? What did they build?" The operation was shut down but things were clean and in order. The man and women answered our questions but the answers made no sense to me. I was not familiar with their terminology. We continued to ask questions as we slowly toured the plant. Electrical items were being fabricated which were in the area of electronics. They described what was being built as *"torpedieren kopffe."* The terminology was not known to me but the inquiry continued. "What did they do with *torpedieren kopffe?"* Their answer was "They were used to make *torpedierens.*" "What is a *torpedieren?*" I asked. "Well, it is used to sink ships." I finally came to realize that the conversation was about torpedoes. This factory was putting together the electronics for torpedo heads. And who was building them? This again took several questions before I could make sense out of the answers. But to ease things a little, they told me who built the plant. The original builder and owner was the *"Allgemeine Electrische Geseltshaft."* The more I talked, the less I knew. I was really getting lost. The Germans were amazed at my lack of comprehension. One of the older women finally spoke up and said, *"Ihr habt die geseltschaft in die Vereinichten Staten."* (You have the company in the United States.) This was the clue that I needed. The *"Allgemeine Electrische Geseltschaft"* turned out to be "General Electric" or GE. The factory was initially built by GE possibly for the fabrication of electric motors. But as Hitler came into power and began to wage war, the factory was nationalized and its production was changed from its original purpose to the production of torpedo heads. The factory was not operating now and we did nothing to destroy it. I do not know when GE first lost control or if GE was able to reclaim it after the war. With this information, we finally felt that our task was done. I was sent back to my squad and we soon continued our advance.

Mail Call on the Front Lines

We had been on the front lines for over forty days now. Perhaps at some time or other there was a mail call but no one could really handle a package. If there were any mail calls, they were meager ones (very few letters). As I remember, I was really looking forward to a letter from home, a friend or even a girl friend. But for a long time, there seemed to be nothing. I envied the few who did get a letter. Someone remembered them. They could have been the veterans in the division whose address had always been the 417th Infantry Regiment of the Seventy-Sixth Division. Someone was probably still following the paper trail to see where I was so that my mail could be sent to me. I had hopes that there was mail on the way but it had not yet found me.

How lost was I? My last address was probably Camp Maxey, Texas. I had no address at Fort Meade, Maryland, because I did not stay there long enough. I was in no particular company or outfit. We were all individuals grouped together on a sheet of paper for the purpose of troop movement. I doubt that we were all infantrymen. Platoons were organized primarily for shipment. This procedural organization was probably good for our trip to Boston, on board ship, our trip from Glasgow, Scotland, to Weymouth, England, then across the English Channel and on to Metz, France. At Metz, the individual soldiers probably reassumed their identity and became that for which they had trained. The subsequent truck rides were specifically for selected groups. The two or three truckloads of men in my group went to Luxembourg. Some of these men were known to me. We had no address because we were troops on the move. Perhaps two squads of men left Luxembourg with me and I am not sure that I knew any of them. When reaching the front lines, I was plugged into a hole, but I had finally reached a destination. During all of this time, I probably had an APO address in New York. Did they know where I was going? They probably knew that I was going to Europe!

When the Seventy-Sixth Division retraced its path across Germany in 2001, the Division's Mess Sergeant was among the group. When I identified myself to him, he seemed to know exactly who I was. He said, "Oh, you are one of those SOB's who caused us to water down our meals for a week or more. You were suddenly on the front lines when we did not know you had arrived." We did not get watered down meals on the front lines; we probably would have enjoyed them. But we may have caused some rear echelon groups to not receive their rations and they then had to eat watered down meals to allow everyone to have some food.

On the front lines, ammunition to engage the enemy was probably the first priority. Food (C rations) and water probably ranked second, health needs and dry socks may have ranked third, and then somewhere down the line was mail from home. Pay probably did not even make the list because there was nothing to buy.

While low on the "priority list," letters from home and friends were high on the soldier's "wish list." But in reality, the environment

151

was such that such letters would not find me very soon. Such letters were probably being sent but we never were at a place long enough for them to reach me. I would guess that the postal clerks were continuously frustrated. Other priorities preempted these communication amenities.

While living along with my Grandparents during my childhood, I probably spent as much or more time with them as I did with my parents and siblings. Even though Grandpa did farm chores, Grandma was always at home or in the garden. Nearly daily, I would dash into her kitchen yelling, *"Kaffee, zucker, milch!"* (Coffee, sugar, milk!). She knew exactly what I wanted and poured me a cup of left-over coffee with milk from the farm and sugar from the store. I enjoyed that. During such visits she took the opportunity to acquaint me with the Bible. She found John 3:16, and before I left, she made sure that I could recite it from memory and also knew where it was in the Bible.

Her Bible was in a living-bedroom combination. Aside from the kitchen, that was the only other room that was heated in her living quarters. The living component of the room contained a table against the east wall. Grandpa had a chair at the south end, and Grandma sat in an easy chair on the north end. Above the table was a mantle with a clock that had to be wound every twenty-four hours. Above the clock on the wall were three large frames for pictures. The one on Grandma's end was a word picture of cloth. It contained the words *"Glaube, Hoffnung, Liebe; Aber die Liebe ist die groszte unter ihnen."* (Faith, Hope, Love; But the greatest of these is Love.)

This is a Bible verse that I had not forgotten. It gave me support and served me well. It admonished me to keep the faith; wherever there was life there was hope; and although ours was not a "lovely" task, love and compassion were in my heart. On the front lines, the word picture probably would have read "Life, Faith, Hope and Love." Without the first, the other three were unnecessary. On the front lines, I was exceedingly thankful to start each day with "life, faith, hope and love." When everything else failed, these attributes always proved to be fundamental and sound.

So in the face of these odds, what were the options of the soldier on the front lines? What were my options? I could pray and pray and pray. God was the meeting ground between me and my family and friends. I was confident that such ardent prayers were placed before the throne of God by all of my family and friends. I also sent my prayers to Him who was my refuge and strength. Although we were thousands of miles apart, our petitions and requests were all received by God himself. This gave me the courage and strength to proceed from day to day.

The last payday was probably on January 31, back in the States. No one was worried about getting paid. There was nothing to buy! But the entrepreneurs who would rather search through drawers and cabinets in homes in which we spent a night soon came up with merchandise to sell. My old high school wristwatch cost six dollars through a Sears mail order catalog. It still ran but no longer kept time. I made a major purchase when I bought myself a stainless steel wristwatch made in Switzerland from one of these vendors. It cost about thirty-five dollars. It kept good time for many years. Other items remaining on my wish list were a German Luger pistol and a good German camera (Leica). I continued to watch for them.

Ride on Tank Destroyers (TDs)

Then one morning as we were getting started, some of our Tank Destroyers (TDs) rolled up, and we were ordered to board and ride on top of them. I do not know how many men a TD could carry, but each TD was loaded to capacity. I would guess that each TD carried about two squads and every two TDs carried a platoon.

The ride was most welcome, but from my standpoint we had suddenly become a dream target for the enemy. I enjoyed the ride but being such a lucrative target was another concern. Hopefully all the German artillery had been destroyed or captured and was behind us. What about the German bazooka? Well, we were on the TD to protect it from such an attack.

The routine quickly developed, we ride the tank destroyers as long as there is no opposition. When there is potential opposition or whenever the opposition has revealed itself, we disembark and attack while the TDs take their positions behind us and give support as needed. Whenever we reached a village or town, we disembarked into a battle line. We then advanced on the town. We could not trust the "white flag" message because the battle of Schmitten had taught our armor that such flags could be an invitation for disaster. Whenever we were through the town, the armor (TDs) would come on through, and we would resume our ride.

In some towns, we captured some German soldiers without opposition. Somehow they came out of the houses without a fight. Maybe only one surrendered initially but he knew where some others were. If the surrender was successful, the others were no problem. In other towns there were none. Sometimes we interrogated the Bürgermeister to determine the status of the town.

When was there a battle and when was there not one? This decision often depended on the German officer in command. A staunch and loyal SS trooper would sooner shoot his own man in the back than have him surrender to us. We never knew how many men were in a town or what type of command they were under. Just routinely, captured German soldiers were asked to roll up their sleeves and we would look for tattoo marks under their biceps. SS troopers had tattoo marks which indicated the blood type of the man. The tattoo mark gave us an indication of the quality of the soldier that we had captured.

Enemy Reconnaissance by Air

Our daily routine soon became one of "ride and walk." Depending on the terrain, territory and circumstance, we perhaps walked all day. One day we were advancing in a sparsely forested area along a small winding road on top of a plateau. Suddenly the sound of a plane began to break the silence and the sound level quickly increased. The plane was coming towards us. Our eyes began to sweep the sky in the direction from which the sound came. We did not know of any air support and therefore assumed it to be an enemy plane; a single engine Messerschmitt fighter plane. It was three to four thousand feet high but low enough to observe what was on the ground. It was tipping its wings from side to side to observe our location. Even after we fired on it the pilot and plane never made any effort to strafe us. We had no luck with our shots and the plane quickly disappeared. I assume that the plane was on a reconnaissance run; just where was the front line? What did we accomplish? Nothing! But with our gunfire we did let the enemy in the air and on the ground know exactly where we were.

Our little road was on a plateau that led us to a ridge from which the land sloped down into a valley in which there was a little village. Between the village and the rising wooded landscape was a meadow of perhaps a hundred yards or less. We were accompanied by a jeep that was armed with a light thirty-caliber machine gun along with a gunner and a driver. As we neared the village, we saw some German soldiers trying to escape by running across the meadow into the adjoining woods. One enemy soldier had run across the meadow and was charging up the rising wooded landscape approximately ninety degrees from our line of advance. The machine gunner in the jeep opened up on him. We joined the gunner with rifle shots. The fleeing Kraut demonstrated to us the art of "hit the dirt." Machine gun tracer bullets were all around the fleeing German, but from my observation, he was not hit.

A moment later another Kraut was running across the meadow between the village and the woods in which the first Kraut hit the dirt. Among numerous shots, a well-aimed shot was fired by one of our older men in the squad. This GI was a middle-aged, mature man who could have had a family back in the States. He was no longer an eager, adventurous young man; rather, he was one who did not fire at random, but when he did fire, he had a target. His shot hit the Kraut and brought him down. Since the Kraut was no longer mobile, we ceased to fire at him, and continued our advance on the village. There was no opposition. Soon we were upon the wounded Kraut in the meadow. Patrick Finn (Pat), our medic, was called forward and he proceeded to dress and bandage the wound. The bullet had gone through the calf of the German's leg.

The soldier was in a tremendous state of shock; his color was deathly pale; he was in agonizing pain and was gasping heavy breaths. To me it was a demonstration of what a bullet from a high-powered rifle does to an individual when it hits but does not kill. The bullet itself is small, but its speed produces the shock effect. Common sights in a battle area are trees that were grazed by bullets. When the projectile hits an inch or so in from the edge of the trunk, the wood fibers on the outer edge from the bullet's passage are splintered and broken open like two broom bottoms that were pushed together and then pulled apart on one side. The wood fibers fail in tension because the bullet's velocity accelerates them outward away from the tree trunk. In this manner, a machine gun can cut down a tree. When such a high velocity projectile passes through human muscle (flesh), it can also make a tunnel several times the size of its own diameter. The result is a shock effect.

We took a moment to watch Pat practice his profession in a very confident and professional way. He had a wound to bandage and the agony of the individual did not distract him. Pat had what he needed to handle the job. Even though Pat was shot at by Germans several days before, he was now binding up the wounds of one. He showed kindness, compassion, mercy and concern to one who just minutes before had been our enemy.

We all took a look at the wounded soldier and realized that the pain which we could inflict on them was exactly the same pain that they were trying to inflict on us. We stored the mental image in our minds. It remains unforgotten by those who were there.

After a few more moments, a Kraut came walking out of the near woods and across the meadow with his hands over his head. This was the German soldier whom we had pinned down earlier in the woods. After seeing the compassion that we had shown to his wounded comrade, he took the opportunity to surrender himself. The prisoner and the wounded prisoner were moved to the rear. We raised our vision to the near distant perimeter which was still in the hands of the enemy. Our day of work continued as we took the land one step at a time and as we took prisoners dead, wounded or alive. We had the firm hope and conviction that someday soon the sun would rise and there would be peace on the horizon.

The days of ride and walk became routine. The backbone of the enemy's resistance was behind us. But a single shot from one enemy soldier, or from a dozen enemy soldiers, was still deadly. Our goal was to move forward fast enough to prevent the remaining enemy to organize and dig-in. The prospect that the Allied soldier could someday be inside of Germany had been anticipated. Defensive positions had been prepared on many roads, hills and forests. Trees were girdled with blocks of TNT so they could be blasted and felled when desirable. When passing among such trees, the thought was always "I hope that this is not the moment." Had the detonation wires been cut? Where are those wires? Step lively this is not a very safe place. No one broke rank to check anything. The whole place could be booby-trapped. The fellows ahead made it through here - so will I, and the advance continued.

Within Germany there were many displaced persons from neighboring countries that had been conquered. These people were often used as "forced labor." Often defensive foxholes had been dug on the German side of any straight stretch of road; such foxholes were on hillsides and many were probably hidden and could not be seen. The enemy expected us to come down such a road and we were to be the target for the German machine guns in the prepared foxholes. At this point in time, there were few defenders in the foxholes. We did not even know if we were the first Allied soldiers to come down that road or if some had already been there. Whenever we made contact with the enemy, we knew that we were the first ones there.

The German nation had not yet surrendered and there were many small and large enemy pockets of resistance. Some of these were sprinkled with SS troopers who would not let their men surrender. These situations were always dangerous and unpredictable. Each of us had only one life to give but many lives to protect within our platoon, team or squad.

Even though we had moved beyond most of the German artillery, there were German antiaircraft batteries throughout the country. Some of these were probably mobile while others may have been in emplacements. Such units could be used to repel us. We did not know where to expect them. To my knowledge, we were never assigned to take such a gun position. If the area around the gun was taken, the gun itself soon became ineffective.

German 88mm Cannon Fires on Our Column

One day we were taking ground in a single column formation. We were in rolling terrain with clear and wooded areas. We reached a long cleared hillside area and proceeded to cross it parallel to the ridge but well below it. In such an advance, the distance between successive men could have been thirty or forty meters. Everything was quiet. Our advance was slow but sure. I do not recall how many hours we had walked. The troops were tired. Suddenly there was the rumble of a cannon, the short eerie swish and the explosion of a shell, probably a German 88. The original rumble of the cannon was perpendicular to our advancing column. The shot fell short and was perhaps three hundred meters before me. As the next GI approached the vicinity of the shot, there was another rumble, swish and boom. This one was nearer to our advancing column but still short. When the next man approached the line of fire there again was the rumble, swish and boom. Now this one was too long. By now we had identified the line of fire quite well, and individuals were double timing across the area. The observation for the artillery unit may have been good, but the communication from the observation post to the artillery battery must have required some time. The enemy had a difficult time synchronizing the shot as the individual crossed the line of fire. After five or six shots, we still had no casualties. Our column never hesitated or broke stride. Like a juggernaut our advance parallel but below the ridge of the hill continued. The enemy finally decided that their success rate was not great enough to justify artillery shells to pick off individual GIs. Our column proceeded without any further shelling by the enemy.

Dismounted but Combined Attacks

Then there were days when we did not ride the TDs, but rather, they moved along with us along the road. These advances were no faster than we could walk and were indicative of imminent danger. There must have been a reason for this mode of advance but we were not informed of it. Perhaps the potential for an artillery attack was high or maybe German armor had been reported in the area. Seemingly the TDs needed to maintain their maximum mobility. The terrain was flat and the area was not forested.

In such an attack mode, where did I want to position myself, where is the safest place from which to engage the enemy? I could walk beside the TD and be exposed to only one side. Yet if the TD was a target, I might be a bonus for any shell that might hit it. If I advanced slightly behind the TD, it could give me frontal protection from a surprise attack. To advance slightly ahead of the TD was also a possibility. If the TD were attacked from any angle, the TD would be the target and not the GI. This looked like it might be the preferable position.

We proceeded along the road together, the armor and the advancing GIs. Soon we came upon a GI in full battle gear lying on the side of the road. We saw no blood and there were no visible wounds. His field jacket was draped over the top of his body and head. The body was completely motionless. No one was giving him any attention. The fact that his field jacket was draped over him indicated that someone had already attended to him. Our advance never stopped. We passed up the lying body and wondered what had happened. When we finally reached a holding position, the information spread that the GI was slightly ahead of a TD when it fired its 90mm gun. The muzzle blast was close enough to take him out! How? The concussion was too great. Was he unconscious or dead? No one said that he was dead, but his motionless body made it look that way. So ahead of the TD was not the safest place to be. Where did I want to be? It depended on the situation and the moment. This incident reminded me of my first day on the front on the outskirts of Trier when we walked into the German armored vehicle with its 88mm cannon. If I had been just a few steps closer and a few steps further to my left, I would have definitely faded out. A few additional steps would have probably ended the war for me on the first day of combat.

On another morning, we boarded the TDs and were on our way through the woods and rolling hills. After a while we came to an open expanse that seemed to be a flood plain of a river bottom. In the immediate clear area there were several well- constructed metal buildings. There was some free space around each structure and then there was a sturdy eight-foot hurricane fence to form an enclosure. They seemed to be unoccupied. There was nothing in the yards to indicate how the buildings were used. Their location and appearance indicated that they may have housed displaced persons who could have been used as forced labor.

In the distance before us, the flood plain led to the stream or river. Immediately thereafter, the terrain rose to a higher level. Directly before us (perhaps six hundred meters) was a village on the other side of the stream. The buildings extended up on the rising slope. The village was not fully in our view because there were nice trees on our side that hid part of it. This wooded area could have been a convenient park for the villagers. The village was on the backside of a bend in the stream and on our side the trees were in the bend.

As we emerged from our wooded area toward the fenced in buildings, we received gunfire from the town. Our advance was halted, and we deployed into a single attack line with ten or twelve meters between men. The TDs positioned themselves closely behind us. After the lines had been established, the order came to attack. As we advanced beyond the buildings before us, the enemy's fire intensified. The TD closest to me and only a few yards behind me was faced directly into the hurricane fence. The gunner simply raised the gun barrel and the TD moved into and right over what I thought was a good looking fence. The TD was behind us, so we used the space between the fences of the respective buildings to advance.

After passing the buildings, the enemy fire began to intensify. We had no place to hide. Then enemy soldiers came running out of the village to a bridge across the stream that was on the left side of the wooded area. After crossing the bridge, the Krauts headed into the woods and took up prime positions behind the trees.

Their fire forced us into the prone position. Each of us became a smaller target for them. As the Krauts came across the bridge individually, we visually followed them into the woods to their selected trees. As each one took his position behind a tree, each one of us fired perhaps four or five rounds at the base of that tree. This kind of exchange went on for several minutes. Since each Kraut came out individually, each one had our attention when he selected his tree. Our bullets were headed his way, before he could raise his head. There were probably a dozen or more of us firing at the same target whenever the Kraut tried to position himself. The return fire from them was minimal. After most of the enemy soldiers had reached the woods, our TDs began to provide tree bursts with their 90mm cannons.

Eventually a final Kraut came out of the village, crossed the bridge, scurried into the woods, dashed around the trees momentarily and quickly decided that was not a place to stay. He did an about face, headed back towards the bridge in a mad dash and, while crossing the bridge, threw his weapon into the stream. Thereafter, he disappeared into the town.

The battle continued until there was no more gunfire from the woods. We then advanced and took the town. We walked close to the woods but no one checked them. No more enemy fire came out of them. All of us walked across the little bridge. The TDs did not follow us. (The bridge was not big and strong enough.) They did an about face and went elsewhere. We continued our attack on foot.

Several days later our Sergeant commended us for our marksmanship. When the battlefield cleanup crew came along, they found seventeen dead Krauts at the bases of the trees where they had tried to defend the town.

How could this battle have been different? How was it similar to the Battle of Schmitten? Our individual battle capabilities had not changed. Perhaps they were even less, because our ranks were not full. Collectively, we had our artillery with us, the tank destroyers. How was the enemy's capability different? They were not SS troopers! The quality of the enemy's soldiers was much different. They were not deployed to defend the town. The local residents may have even told them to get out; "We do not want our homes to be shot up and destroyed." The terrain was less protective for them. They were not a dug-in, well-organized, battle group with machine guns in place. Seemingly we surprised them and they were not prepared. If there had been several well-hidden snipers (like in Schmitten) deep inside the homes in the village, we would have been ideal stationary targets with no protection. They could have picked a dozen of us off before we could have spotted any of their positions. In such a case, we probably never would have gone into the prone position. Instead we would have had to storm the town. This could have been costly in terms of wounded and lives lost. As it was the command decisions were excellent and timely. We greatly appreciated how the battle was conducted to take the town and to achieve the victory.

We were experiencing a kind of warfare for which we had not been trained. I had received twelve weeks of signal corps basic training at Camp Crowder, Missouri, and never saw a tank. This experience was followed by six weeks of basic infantry training during which we saw no tanks or TDs. I wonder if the tanker crews ever practiced hauling infantrymen during their maneuvers? What could or should a TD crew do when their tank was attacked while it was loaded with infantrymen? What should the infantrymen do when riding a tank if there was an attack? The tank had not been built to haul people. Some of us were barely hanging on. How severe is the jolt, blast, concussion, pressure wave for men riding on a TD when the 90mm gun is fired? Thank God we never had to experience the answers to these questions.

There was no communication between us and the TD crew. Just about as much conversation as there was between us and a two-and-a-half-ton truck driver when we were being hauled, or as much as there was between us and the Germans when we passed through a town. Did the TD crews like us on board? Did their commanders suddenly restrict their effort to that of a two-and-a-half-ton truck driver? Did we like them? I would say "yes" for the ride but "no" for the lucrative target that we made. The TD crew stayed buttoned up while we were on board. We seldom saw any of them. How much did we restrict their procedures for which they had been trained? Could the turret be turned without knocking some of us off the TD? If a crew member opened his hatch, it was for just a moment, and then he buttoned up again. Seemingly the armor and the infantry had a non-fraternization rule that had never been announced. One time the TD driver opened his hatch and someone asked him "Where are you from?" His reply was "New York," and he buttoned up again. The information promptly spread all over "The TD driver is from New York, the TD driver is from New York." That was the most news that we had on top of that TD all day.

As we continued our advance into Germany, it seems that the armor began to shed us and instead moved out on its own (the American version of blitzkrieg). Small pockets of resistance were by-passed. They were looking for bigger and better targets. The pockets of resistance were mostly riflemen on foot without mortars or artillery. The armor could create more havoc, confusion and loss of morale by being miles ahead of us. We were left behind to clean up pockets of German soldiers wherever they exposed themselves.

Within a few days, we were riding two-and-a-half-ton trucks moving forward. The front line was beyond us. En route we cleared towns and known pockets of resistance.

The Battle for Zeitz

Then one evening we entered Zeitz on foot. It was one of the last enemy military centers in our path that the Germans could not afford to lose. We were billeted in a home. There was no opposition for us, but there was a battle in progress within the city. We could have been in reserve. The noise of battle was common on the front lines. The foot soldier was seldom so far behind that he could not hear the noise of battle or feel the tremors of the earth from the battlefield explosions. The nearness of the thunderous barrages, the rumbles of the artillery and the machine gun and rifle fire were the factors that determined the rate of adrenaline flow.

During the evening hours, an enemy fighter plane flew overhead, but it did no strafing. The pilot could not see us. We were inside and could not see the plane. I suspect that it was a reconnaissance flight to determine the status of the city. For details on the battle for Zeitz, the reader is referred to *We Ripened Fast* – Hutnik (1946) for their contributions to the war effort. The battle for Zeitz is eloquently described in several of its pages.

Leapfrog Operations

We now began a leapfrog operation. We rode forward on trucks as far as safely possible. The trucks took us to the front and we then advanced the front line until we reached a hold position. Then other outfits advanced beyond us. We were moving from central to southeast Germany.

On one occasion we liberated a porcelain (china) factory. It was not operating. The workers had left, but the factory was intact. An elderly man (German) had elected to risk staying with the factory as the front lines approached, reached and passed it. We saw some of the manufactured wares but what could we do with a porcelain dish? The old gentleman was proud of the products but we were hardly the consumers that he wanted. At that time I was not familiar with brand names but soon learned that Meiszen porcelain was considered to be nearly "white gold." Our platoon Lieutenant did some wheeling and dealing and bought a set of dishes packed in a wooden crate. The old gentleman was told to send them to the Lieutenant's home address in the States when such activity became possible.

We were about a hundred kilometers west of southwest from Meiszen, a city that is world-famous for its porcelain wares. I was not hooked on porcelain then, but sensed that it was something extra ordinary.

Area of My Grandfather's Birth

My Grandfather was born in the Kingdom of Saxony (*Königreich Sachsen*) in eastern Germany at Lauske (baptized in Hochkirch) in 1857. He migrated with his parents to the United States and Texas in 1869. So far there was no town that we had taken whose name I recognized from my previous conversations with him. I grew up in a home with him and my Grandmother. My parents had a kitchen, dining room, porch and pantry on the west side of a two-story home while my Grandfather and Grandmother had a kitchen, dining room and porch on the east side of the living complex. The Kingdom of Saxony was an area that he often spoke about. We were now beginning to hear that term being used in our area of conquest. This made me a little more interested in the area and I began to look at road signs a little more. The first city that I recognized from my Grandfather's conversations was Leipzig. It was still some sixty kilometers away.

My German accent was soon to match that of the area from which my Grandfather originated. My use of the language continued to be with captured German soldiers and with the Bürgermeister in the villages. All of my communications were under the supervision of our platoon Lieutenant.

How Do We Meet the Russians?

How Do We Identify Ourselves?

After a few more days, we had advanced eastward far enough that contact with the Russians was possible but not yet probable. We received daily briefings on how that contact may occur. At night, rifle flares were to be used to identify ourselves to them. We would use several flares of one color and the Russians would respond with several flares of another color. After surviving the battlefields across Germany, we did not now want to lose lives in combat with an Ally.

Our moves from Zeitz carried us southeast to Zwickau, where we took up a holding position. The information was that we had advanced beyond a line determined by Higher Command to be the boundary for United States occupation. We were billeted in a railroad switching station which had numerous sets of rails in its yard. Seemingly we were on the east side of the city. The railroad tracks went west into Zwickau and east out into agricultural lands.

We set up guard outposts in two-man foxholes. These were manned twenty-four hours per day. We took German soldiers prisoners wherever they appeared. These were no longer in organized groups. Remaining organized groups were in holding positions. The prisoners which we took had defected from their units or perhaps their units had been taken captive but they had managed to escape. Generally, they were still in uniform but were no longer armed. It was general practice to frisk every prisoner that was brought in. If one still had a pocketknife, we liberated the knife. The end of the war was near, but we did not know how near.

Since we were no longer advancing, the members of my platoon became a little more adventurous and began to explore nearby buildings and homes. What else was there to do when a GI was not on guard duty? Alcoholic beverages of various kinds and strengths were common in German homes. These reached the troops one way or another. Whoever could liberate such a bottle did so. Everyone had his own way of consuming such a find. This type of liberation was in no way recommended. Rather it was prohibited because there may have been no truth in the labeling. Yet, depending on how the bottle was picked up, most GIs were willing to take the risk. They probably could not even read the label.

On perhaps two occasions during our battles across Germany, someone found a bottle of champagne in a home. Such a find was consumed on the spot by those who were present. On one occasion our Lieutenant had the honor to "pop the cork" and then consume the first drink. For the rest of us, the bottle became a common cup. The bottle did not last through the first round.

Checking the Guards

Since I could talk German, I was kept in reserve at platoon headquarters. My assignment was to routinely check the guard outposts on foot. Each post was manned by two GIs. After a day or so, we had telephone lines to each outpost. I was also used to interrogate prisoners that were brought in.

On one occasion, I came upon a post where two guards had carried a bottle of liquor to their foxhole. They had consumed enough to be far beyond their capacity to be sober. One was so intoxicated that he did not recognize me to be a GI. As I approached the post, he realized that someone was coming. He grabbed his rifle and pointed it toward me, while calling "Come here, you damn Kraut." He clicked his rifle off safety and had his finger on the trigger. I did not know what to do but felt that a sudden move in any direction was not advisable. I stayed my course with the hope that his first shot might miss and I could then take evasive action. I knew the man and he knew me. He was perhaps in another squad.

Several times while I was in the army, I experienced that the man who really befriended me while sober, was at the opposite end of the spectrum when he was intoxicated. While under the influence of liquor, he would challenge me in most any way. I never learned how to solve that problem. The simple answer might have been "stay away from him when he has been drinking." But what do you do when he comes in drunk at night and looks you up and you find that absolutely nothing that you say is agreeable with him?

The other guard at the post was not that far gone. He was simply a spectator or an innocent bystander. He did nothing and said nothing. Both men were at their post, and the enemy was not threatening. After completing my tour, I reported back to the Sergeant of the Guard, "All posts were secure and manned with the guards on duty." Nobody got into trouble, and my subsequent relationship with the intoxicated guards was cordial and friendly.

In addition to checking the guards at their outposts, I was given the duty to observe the crest of a ridge during the hours of daylight. The ridge was perhaps 1,000 to 1,200 yards away. The crest was bare with the exception of a large wooden barn located right on the crest. I observed no activity, but the building was suspect. After several days of observation, guards at an outpost fired several rounds of tracer bullets into the structure. It caught on fire and burned to the ground. We saw no one exit the structure as the blaze spread. Thereafter, there was only the bare ridge to observe. I never saw any activity. The Russians did not come over that ridge to make contact with us.

On another occasion, I was at platoon headquarters when a call came in from a guard post. Something with a gray-red color was moving just beyond the crest of a hill which they were facing. It would appear for a few moments and then disappear. Shortly it would reappear. The Sergeant of the Guard was told that it looked like a big backpack. The Sergeant told the guards to halt the individual. They shouted "Halt!" but the backpack kept on moving. The distance was probably 150 yards. The conversation continued back and forth, but there was never a response from the backpack. It sounded like someone with all of his goods was trying to sneak through our lines. The Sergeant finally told the guards to fire a shot into the backpack. This they did, and the backpack dropped out of sight. The Sergeant then told the guards to go and investigate. Did the backpack really disappear? After an on-foot investigation, the guards called back. They had shot a deer!

In retrospect, I would guess that the guards knew exactly what they were seeing. But they could not afford to fire a shot which would have been heard far and wide. Also I suspect that the shouts of "Halt!" were at best soft whispers. As it was, they made the shot legal without arousing anyone. I do not know if someone was able to consume the venison, but it made a lonely, boring stand of guard duty into an interesting and lively one.

The War Is Over!!!

Then one day, we were called into platoon formation by our Sergeant. Our Lieutenant had an announcement to make. The word finally reached us: "The war is over!!!" Germany has surrendered! Yet we were cautioned that there were still pockets of enemy soldiers who had not yet received the news or their commanders were afraid to break the news to them. These pockets were still dangerous and they were holding their positions.

We all took a deep breath and then breathed a sigh of relief. What a load had been lifted off our shoulders. The mission was accomplished, it is over. However, for most everyone, the end of the mission would only be reached when we arrived back home with our loved ones. What a task! The first step had been taken. We were one step closer. Our final goal was still thousands of miles away. We now needed to be extra careful and vigilant that no more lives would be lost before our ultimate goal was reached. We all rejoiced very silently. The serious faces broke out into smiles. There was now a greater hope. Many silent prayers of thanks were sent heavenward. The sun in all its glory was beginning to rise once more in our lives.

We had experienced no combat in our holding position and we knew that the war was over. Our vigilance was much relaxed and we began to roam and survey our area with a little more ease. The Russians had not yet reached us.

Inspection of the Railroad-Switching Yard

I remember walking through the railroad-switching yard looking at the railcars and wondering what was in them. Some were empty, some were locked, some were open and some were flat. I climbed up one with an open top to see what was inside. To my surprise, some railcars contained the structural bodies of fighter planes. They had no wings or tail assemblies, but the structural cockpit and the windows were in. I marveled at the thickness of the windshields. Were they trying to build one that was bullet proof? The craftsmanship of the structure was impressive. The trip through the rail yard was most interesting. The next day I went to explore some more. Sure enough, some GIs had put the plane's windshield to the test. Someone had hit, banged and beat on the windshield. It was badly cracked but still intact and in position.

An Enemy Soldier to an Ally Prisoner

German soldiers were now becoming refugees. They could appear most anywhere at any time. Often they were in groups of two or three. They may or may not have been in uniform. Our GIs brought in anybody that appeared to be of military service age. The captured Germans were generally unarmed. Many were wanting to surrender to us rather than to the Russians. I believe that some walked into our lines to surrender to us.

The transition from being an enemy soldier to becoming an Allied prisoner was a sensitive and dangerous one. How did a German soldier find the GIs on the front line? Could the German soldier get shot before he surrendered? How is the trip made across no-man's land? How many rifles are pointing at the German soldier? I know of no German soldiers that were shot while surrendering to us. But they were looking down a lot of gun barrels in the process. I did see the evidence where a German soldier was shot in the back while he tried to cross into our lines. This will be discussed later.

Captured Germans were brought into platoon headquarters. Usually they had their hands on their heads while we proceeded to frisk them. Every prisoner was checked for knives and small weapons. Additionally, each one was checked for a tattoo under his biceps. Our Lieutenant would have me question them individually and collectively.

On one occasion our lieutenant thought that we had a group of tough prisoners. He proceeded to pull out his switchblade pocketknife, opened it up and proceeded to rub his thumb over the cutting edge of the blade. Evidently he wanted the captured Germans to think that we were tough warriors, especially when we had them out numbered with both men and weapons. Who was the Lieutenant trying to impress—his own men or the German captives? I thought the exhibition was juvenile and felt a little embarrassed myself. After being frisked and briefly interrogated, the prisoners were whisked away. We went about our business of looking for more of them.

Repositioned at Zeulenroda

As mentioned earlier, we had penetrated deeper into Germany than allowed by the higher command. We were beyond our designated boundary. Consequently, we were loaded on trucks and repositioned in Zeulenroda a town west of southwest from Zwickau.

The war was over, but our rules of engagement had not changed. We were still forbidden to fraternize. Our platoon was billeted in a two-story home on the outskirts of town (Zeulenroda). The German people stayed in their homes pretty well. I do not know if this was by choice or by directive. Perhaps it was their most secure place. Yet they seemed to be more curious to see us than we were to see them. I do not know what the German propaganda had told them about us. I am sure that it was nothing good. Now they were probably looking for the horns on our heads (devils) but were pleasantly surprised that there were none. We were just as ordinary as they were.

During the day, people (mostly females) would sit by or in open windows and look out as far as they could. This was never the case during the war. Quite often there were two people in a window and they would be conversing with each other. Also, the second-story people would converse with those on the first floor. This behavior was perhaps popular with them because we were living next door. In Zeulenroda there was some space between the houses. The neighbors were very interested in observing us. I do not know how long the town had been captured. Also the people who lived in and owned our billet could have just moved in with the neighbors next door.

Their curiosity was very interesting. I could understand their comments but they never suspected it. They talked about what they could see. After we were there for awhile, they would talk and politely ignore us and we would politely ignore them.

We were still in combat attire. We slept in the home and in our clothes. But during the day, we were on the outside by choice. Our demeanor was switching gears. The stress of battle was wearing off and our energy levels were building up. Nobody was standing guard at our billet, but there were guard posts just outside of town. Our days were relatively free but we stayed mobile and ready to move. We were allowed to canvas and roam the neighborhood.

I do not remember what the plumbing was in the home (our billet), but it probably did not have the capacity to serve a platoon of GIs. Perhaps the plumbing was adequate for the platoon Lieutenant and the non-coms (non-commissioned officers). Soon after we arrived at the billet, somebody was assigned the detail to dig a slit trench in the rear of the back yard. A slit trench on the front lines serves the function of a commode in a home. It was dug long enough to accommodate three or four people at once. That trench became our bathroom. This was an accommodation that we had not had in Europe before. We had used such means of sanitary disposal on maneuvers in the States. The slit trench was in view of everyone and it immediately became a functioning bathroom. All the troops used it.

My Picture Taken

However, one morning while I was straddling the trench and relieving myself, our platoon Lieutenant stepped out of the back door of our billet and walked to about fifty feet of me. He took a picture, did an about face and walked back into the billet. He did not say a word and what I said was well under my breath. Needless to say, he did not get a salute because he did not deserve one. Was he worthy of a salute? I am probably a famous GI in his World War II photo album in Oklahoma somewhere. The experience made me wonder if all individuals who carry bars on their shoulders are worthy of the respect that a salute signifies.

In front of our billet was a street and then there was clear and rising meadowland. On the crest of this land was a cemetery. With nothing on the agenda, I decided to visit the cemetery one day just to see the names of people who were buried there. I was not allowed to talk to the people in the town but in this way I could relate to the town. The names were interesting but I found none that were particularly familiar. After a while I did find a gravestone for Otto Albert Kunze. He was born in 1924 and died as a young man. My name is Otto Robert Kunze, and I was born in 1925. The first and last names were exactly like mine. The middle name was different. It would have been interesting to pursue the "Kunze" name in Zeulenroda, but communication was forbidden.

The Lord's Prayer in German

A lesson learned in combat was to always scan and canvas the immediate area around you. When night comes, where can you shoot and where should you not have to shoot? What do you do if something happens? While doing so one day in Zeulenroda, I just sat down on the rising land across the street from the billet. I immediately became the subject for conversation by the women peering out of the windows. They had become brave enough to exchange comments at the normal level of communication. After listening for a while, I startled them by injecting a bit of German into their conversation. They were surprised and astounded. Rather than get into a real and unallowed visit with them, I asked if they could recite the Lord's Prayer for me? They were stunned and silent. So I said, "Let me recite it for you!" This I did. They were surprised and overwhelmed. *"Der kann das Vater Unser gebet in Deutsch!!"* (He can recite the Lord's Prayer in German!!) In that area, my German should have been nearly without accent.

Soon after we withdrew from Zwickau, many Germans living in the relinquished area decided to also withdraw into US occupied territory. This migration was forbidden. We were ordered to post guards along all roads coming out of the area. We stopped the migrants but they did not want to return to their homes and face Russian occupation. The result was a population buildup on the border. They just parked their carts and baggage along the roadside with the hopes that the border would soon open up. Well it never opened while we were there. This was probably the East Germans' first experience with what was later to become the Iron Curtain. We initially closed the border to them. In the years to come the East German Army would permanently do so.

Returning Displaced Persons

During our wait and hold operation, I had another interesting experience. There were many "displaced persons" (DPs) who wanted to return home. They had probably served as laborers, but now suddenly, they were free and without a job. We were not involved in identifying these people, nor was it our job to bring them together. But one day, we were asked to supply escorts for German civilian truck drivers who were to transport these people back to Chemnitz. This was probably the first leg of their journey back toward home. Each truck had two drivers and there were perhaps three or four trucks. It was not a convoy. Very little had yet been organized. I do not know if this continued for days but our trip was the first one for the German drivers.

I was simply picked up one morning and was told that I would escort a truck with DPs to Chemnitz. After being delivered to the staging area, there were the drivers, truck and DPs loaded and ready to go. The drivers and I climbed into the truck which had a bench seat. I had a driver on each side of me while I sat in the middle with my M-1 rifle between my legs. This was not a military truck but rather a civilian one. I was surprised that such operating vehicles could still be found in the civilian population.

There was no discussion between me and the drivers, but I was a good silent listener. I never did let them know that I could understand their conversation and concerns. The truck was fueled by wood chips. These were converted into a low-grade of gas vapor as they were burned with a limited supply of oxygen (air). The Germans had developed this technology to such a degree that it provided reliable fuel for transportation. By watching their gauges, the drivers could tell when it was time to stop and refuel the system with wood chips. They knew what they needed to do and I did not. I never left the bench seat in the truck. The trip was between fifty and sixty miles. We probably started with the system generating at full fuel capacity. We then stopped once to recharge the system before we reached Chemnitz, and then we recharged once more before reaching Zeulenroda on our return trip.

The low-grade gas vapor generator consisted of a large cylindrical container like a water heater. It was located between the truck cab and bed. At that time, the vapor generation process was of no interest to me. The drivers operated it with some concern but did an excellent job. I just listened. The technology was not familiar to me, and I did not recognize it to be new and in the experimental stage. Yet I have found it quite interesting that forty years after the war, historians were still searching to find this technology documented somewhere. How could it have become so completely lost when it had been developed so well. No one has been able to find a good and workable design for such a unit.

We traveled on the autobahn (super highway) that led to Chemnitz, but not necessarily at a super speed. The concern was that we could not afford to use the gas vapor faster than what the generator could produce it. Also it appeared that there was essentially no storage capability. The speed of the truck was dictated by the rate of gas production. The truck engine labored, but I was never concerned that the engine would stall. If we had stalled, we would have had to wait awhile to raise the rate of fuel generation so that we could proceed again.

We drove into the outskirts of Chemnitz. The drivers knew where to go. The street on which we traveled had been cleared but the city was in rubble. We never reached its center. The place was deserted. What a disaster! We delivered our human cargo and then promptly started on our return trip. We drove just as fast as the generator could produce the gas. I really did nothing during the trip, but my presence was needed to make the trip official. The truck could have been challenged somewhere at which time my presence would have been crucial.

Pecking Order Among the Troops

As the days passed, a pecking order began to emerge among the troops (privates). For the original troops in the platoon, this order was probably already established in the States during training exercises. But for the new additions to the platoon, this order had not yet been determined. The privates began to challenge each other in various ways. There was pent-up energy among the men. Who did I challenge or who challenged me? Of all people, it was the medic, Pat. It seemed that we could not pass each other without seeing who could push the other out of the way. A test of strength!! There was no animosity between us because we were good friends. Pat was a wonderful guy, everybody's friend. He pushed me out of the way numerous times but I never refused the challenge when it presented itself. The pecking order was really never decided between us. At least I never did admit it.

An Enemy Nest Remains

The war was officially over, but there were still surrounded nests of enemy troops that either had not heard the news or they did not believe it. Late in the war every German soldier had to take an oath to fight to his death in the defense of Germany. Nests of such soldiers had a difficult time surrendering alive. One day the information reached our platoon that a nest of enemy soldiers wanted to surrender. But they could not afford to do so without faking a battle with us. This information came from higher headquarters. We were the ones who were to stage the sham battle; the German soldiers were to surrender themselves and the nest would be cleared. We were informed and instructed about the location and the terrain of the battleground. Such briefing and planning never occurred during the war. During combat, our morning briefing usually was "Today we are going to attack!"

The enemy soldiers were in a forest. On one side of this forest was a railroad track built on a landfill dam that led across a valley or flood plain of several hundred yards in width. There was forest on one side and field or meadow on the other. We were to deploy behind this dam on the field side. When the command was given, we were to fire our rifles into the air to simulate a battle. We had only live ammunition. After some time, the German soldiers would come out of the woods from behind the railroad tracks and surrender themselves. It sounded like a great plan. It nearly sounded like a battle that we could have staged in the States while out on bivouac. However, in the States we always had blank ammunition.

Trucks (two-and-a-half-ton) picked us up at our billet, and we were off to the mock battle. We arrived at the battleground, deployed behind the dam and were ready for the simulated battle. We would not have to advance or charge. The designated time came, but the order to commence the battle never came. We waited and waited some more. Shots that we heard were not fired by us. After some time, we left our deployed position and randomly moved further out along the dam with the railroad tracks.

We soon came to a trestle where the railroad passed over a country dirt road which came out from the forest. I suspect that this was where the German soldiers were going to file through in their surrender to us. Well, one enemy soldier had made this attempt and was shot in the back, dead, while trying to do so. His body lay in the road under the trestle. No one could afford to view the forest through

176

the trestle. No one crossed the road. We did not look forward to charge the forest. We had heard that the war was over, but perhaps not over for us. Germany had lost it but some enemy soldiers were still fighting. The Higher Command that had sent us to do a sham battle now had to decide if a real battle was necessary. I do not know what the means of communication were. Obviously they were slow and possibly not direct.

We took guarded peeks at the dead German soldier. No more enemy soldiers attempted to surrender. We never staged the mock battle and neither did we storm the forest. Time was on our side. The area around the forest was occupied by US troops. We let the situation take care of itself, and to the best of my knowledge, it did.

If the enemy could get no food, ammunition or reinforcements, there was only one destiny for the nest; it had to degenerate and capitulate. The Krauts had to come out for supplies, but there were no supply sources. Instead of getting supplies, such troops were probably informed by the civilian population that the war was over—Germany had capitulated. Such troopers probably did not return to the nest with the bad news and no supplies were obtained. Instead they probably deserted the nest and preferred to be captured by US troops.

We returned to our trucks without any casualties and without any prisoners. It was a "dry" run. The command above us made some good decisions which all the troops appreciated. After completing our assignment, we returned to our billet in Zeulenroda.

Visit a Concentration Camp

A few days passed before we again were loaded on trucks for a journey. There was little, if any, briefing, but we were probably told to carry our rifles and a day's ration. If someone would have told us where we were going, the information would have been meaningless. After awhile we reached the autobahn and really moved. We probably traveled seventy to eighty kilometers before we left the autobahn. We then traveled on smaller roads and passed through some town. Then we proceeded to get into a forested area that seemed to be on a mountain-like hill. The terrain was not rough, but it was rising. The

177

forest was quite dense. After a while, we arrived at our destination. We were told that we would be there for perhaps three hours before we would assemble again and reload for our return trip.

We had arrived at the infamous concentration Camp of Buchenwald. Most of us had heard and read about concentration camps but had never seen one. The camp was intact but deserted. The prisoners had fled, been removed or otherwise been released. There were still a few men around who seemingly had been prisoners. We did not converse with them. They did not seem to be Germans. Their faces, demeanor and body language spoke volumes. They were stressed out, undernourished, poorly clothed, elderly and had no sparkle in their eyes; but they seemed calm, relieved, relaxed and showed no fear. We did not excite them because they had already seen GIs for a week or two.

Schutz Staffel (SS) officers and troops who manned the camp had lived in beautiful homes in the forest adjacent to the camp. Then there were some administrative buildings immediately outside the prison compound. Also there was a complex where prisoners could or perhaps were forced to work.

The camp is located on the northwestern slope behind the crest of this small mountain (Ettersberg Hill), *Buchenwald Memorial* (2000). The country terrain to the northwest can be viewed for miles. Over the crest and about three miles to the southeast is the city of Weimar. The camp itself is isolated and deep in the forest.

The prison compound was enclosed by multiple strands of electrically charged high voltage wires. During the night this barrier fence was well illuminated with lights. Elevated guardhouses were located all along the fence line. The entry gate was of malleable steel. Across this gate were written, in flat steel, the words *"Ein jeder das seine."* This roughly translates into "To each his own." We were there just a few weeks after the war. The camp was open but not clean. It looked like the administrators and those in charge (officers and guards) had vacated the area. The terrible stench of death and burning flesh was present in every breath that we inhaled. There was no fresh air. Fly ash from burned bodies saturated the area. The scene left most of us speechless and gave us a new appreciation for why we fought the war.

One building housed a crematory that consisted of two fur-
naces with three ovens per furnace. Dead human bodies were burned
in these. The building also contained a corpse cellar into which dead
bodies were dropped through a chute. The cellar also served as a place
to strangle and hang people. The victims were any people (German
or foreign) who resisted or did not support Hitler's dictatorship.
Many were brought in by the Gestapo to be murdered.

Another building was used for medical purposes. Human organs
were preserved in jars filled with formaldehyde. These were displayed
and stored on hallway shelves. I was particularly interested in the
hearts, but I am sure there were other organs like livers, lungs and
kidneys. There were no guides to take us on tour. We just wandered
through the camp as we pleased. When we saw preserved hearts, kidneys and other human organs, we had to draw our own conclusions
as to why they were there. How were the organs obtained and what
functions did they serve?

We looked into the barracks where the prisoners slept but no
one ventured into them. The barracks were not a place where I would
want to sleep. I would have preferred a private foxhole. Our hearts
went out to the prisoners who were so helplessly and so hopelessly
incarcerated there. We thank God for our country where people are
free and we want to keep it that way. After our tour of several hours,
we re-boarded the trucks and were on our way back to Zeulenroda.

Volumes have been written about the Buchenwald Concentration
Camp; who were the people that were imprisoned there; who were
the people that died there? What purpose did it serve and how well
did it serve its purpose? The reader is advised to read other volumes
to get more particulars about the camp and its activities. Also I would
suggest that people who travel to Germany take the time to travel to
Buchenwald and see the history that is recorded there.

According to the book *We Ripened Fast* – Hutnik (1946) our
combat path was along a line north of Gotha, Erfurt, Weimar and
Jena. Prisoners in the camp liberated themselves when their SS guards
and administrators fled before the advance of General Patton's Third
Army.

In the year 2001, some members of the Seventy-Sixth Division (I was one of them) retraced the path along which they fought their way across Germany. Buchenwald was one of our stops.

Today only selected buildings remain. Only the foundations of the prisoner barracks are still there. The entrance, compound fence, crematory and a few other structures are still intact. If you are in Germany and happen to travel near Weimar, take the opportunity to visit Buchenwald. It is a testimonial to the depth that mankind can stoop if the citizenship of a country does not have the authority to run its own government.

Today the camp is a pleasant place to see many horrible and unpleasant things. It is a memorial to those who died there. Relatives and friends bring flowers and wreaths to the crematory in memory of their loved ones who died and were cremated there. Schools take their children to Buchenwald to show them a piece of German history of which no one can be proud. The entire camp is self-informational. Plaques on building walls indicate what happened there. Pertinent historical information is written on them in at least four different languages. In the administrative buildings near the parking lot is a scaled down model of the entire camp when it was fully functional.

We veterans were happy to revisit Buchenwald. We had no guided tour, but the pictures, plaques and monuments provided us with much interesting information.

While we were there in 2001, busloads of primary school children were visiting the camp. These were chaperoned by their teachers. As usual, some of the children moved through the buildings faster than others. I was outside one of the buildings when three young girls came through and began to chat on the outside as they waited for their remaining group. I approached them and said, "*Ich war hier sechs und fünfzig Jahre zurück.*" (I was here fifty-six years ago). They were surprised, and one of them exclaimed, "*In diesen lager!!!*" (In this camp!!!). I explained that I was not a surviving prisoner but rather a soldier who had the opportunity to visit the camp soon after the war. They suddenly became really interested. Instead of visiting the camp as we veterans did, perhaps I should have taken the opportunity to bring more life and reality into what the school children were seeing while visiting Buchenwald.

The visit to Buchenwald in 1945 lasted for only a day; the war in Germany was over and the troops were anticipating what our next assignment might be!! The war with Japan was still raging. There were strong rumors that we would go to the Pacific.

Since we were no longer chasing the enemy, our company kitchen began to serve us a hot meal about once a week. Now we were able to really enjoy it. After eating C rations for months, everything that came out of the company kitchen was delectable. Additional months of practice had made the foods prepared by the mess Sergeant and his crew much better than what it was in the States while we were out on bivouac. Simultaneously with the hot meal, we received a clean pair of dry socks.

Some historians write about newsletters that were published and distributed among the troops. I remember none except an occasional copy of "Stars and Stripes" that we received only after the war. Events like President Roosevelt's death, the end of the war in Germany, the atomic bombs and the end of the war in Japan were verbally announced to us. While on the front lines, we were on the move. Everyone was looking for mail; we regularly received rations, but did not expect to get paid and we did not know that newsletters existed.

A Little Shooting Practice

With the war in the Pacific still going strong, GIs could not afford to lose their marksmanship. Perhaps their shooting expertise even needed to be improved. So one day we were loaded on trucks and after a short ride we arrived at a rifle range. It was not a German army training facility. There was nothing military around it. The range was a makeshift setup near a road in a wooded area. The firing line was closest to the road and the targets were on the other side of a valley vegetated with brush. Down the middle of this valley ran an electrical high voltage transmission line. The target observers on the other side of the valley were in communication with the firing line by telephones. I do not know who manned the stations. To my knowledge, our platoon just went in and had their target practice. I did no more than just shoot my clip of rounds. The M-1 that I carried into and during battle was not new, but it functioned properly, was generally reliable and was preferred for battle.

The rifle range practice was a routine matter. Generally, the GIs were happy with their M-1 rifles. No one became a hero and neither did anyone lose his pride on the rifle range. I had never shot my rifle for target practice and really feel that I did not shoot too well. For now, the war was behind us and no one was particularly concerned about his marksmanship. After shooting our rounds, we re-boarded our trucks and returned to Zeulenroda.

Another day or two passed, and we received the word that two GIs died out on the rifle range. During target practice, someone hit a transmission line wire and caused it to break. The high voltage line fell across a telephone wire, and the GIs on each end were electrocuted. That is the last that we heard of rifle range practice. A few days later we passed the rifle range while riding in a truck. It seemed unmanned and appeared to be abandoned.

What!!! A Bath??

Winter and spring were now essentially behind us. One day we were ordered to board some trucks. We needed no rifles or battle gear. The day was nice and the sun was shining. After a short ride, the trucks unloaded us and we were led to a fifty-five-gallon drum with a valve and sprinkler head on its bottom. The drum bottom and sprinkler were mounted about eight-feet high on planks held up by some posts. We were going to get a bath!!! Everybody disrobed and turned in their underwear and socks. The valve to the sprinkler head was opened, and every GI was allowed one minute for his bath. The water was cold, but no one refused the opportunity to take the shower. After the shower, each GI received a towel with which to dry and some clean underwear along with a pair of clean used socks. My last bath before this one was in the salty Atlantic Ocean water used on the USS *West Point* on which I crossed the Atlantic Ocean.

Entrepreneurs at Work

We were now operating in a relaxed environment. The dangers of war were behind us. Everyone suddenly had some free time and there were those who found ways to use it. Some GI entrepreneurs surfaced who had things to sell. Most of the items were small and portable. No questions were asked from where the goods came and the items were not new. I was looking for a good camera but was willing to buy a cheap one just to get some pictures. I would have paid a good price for a Leica but none could be found. One of the entrepreneurs sold me a collapsing bellows camera. Film could be ordered through our PX (post exchange) service. So with a little effort, I became the proud owner of a camera with some film. I was ready to take pictures whenever there was an opportunity.

The devastation of a war is hard to imagine. In general, we now had money, but there was little or nothing to buy. We ate army rations and were supplied with water. There was nothing to buy with our money. Much of the German population was on the road somewhere going or coming. Those who remained in our area had nothing to sell.

Our platoon was still responsible for posting one or more guards on roads just outside of town. I was not involved with these and do not believe that there was much traffic. Maybe we were more interested to know what the traffic was?

One day I took my position once more on the rising landscape just across the street from our billet. By now the word had spread that I could speak and understand German. Two middle-aged women soon came to the window of the two story home and sat in it. As usual, they were conversing, and it soon became obvious that they wanted to tell me something. *"Wie sagen wir es zu ihm?"* (How do we tell him?) There was some excitement in their voices. They got my attention and proceeded to tell me about one of their immediate lady friends. The fact that I did not know her made no difference. Their friend had wandered out to the guard post: *"Und er hat ihr geimft!"* (And he vaccinated her!) They burst out in laughter, and I was speechless. It was time for us to move, and we did.

Music from the Heavens

We had accomplished our assignments at Zeulenroda. Hence, we were loaded on trucks and moved about forty kilometers south to a billet on the outskirts of Plauen, in the State of Bayern (Bavaria). Our stay was brief—just a few nights. Our billet was located at the bottom of a gorge that was between two hundred to three hundred feet deep. I do not recall that we had any assignments there. However, we did have some memorable moments. Every evening at about an hour before sunset, a German musician who lived nearby took his violin and bow and started on a winding steep trail that led to the cliffs at the top of the gorge. After reaching his destination, he would prop one foot on a huge stone and then fine-tune his violin. In just a few moments, his music was flooding the residents below. It was music from heaven. The music was wonderful. The valley was quiet, and for thirty minutes or more we could relax and enjoy the lovely sounds, while being able to see the silhouette of the virtuoso between us and the evening sky. It was beautiful, relaxing, peaceful and fulfilling. We were in a natural theater. Just before sunset, our violinist started his slow trek down. He had to be careful, because the path was narrow and steep. He reached the bottom just as dusk set in. Among the many experiences that I would like to forget about the war, this is one that I am happy to remember. It was a little bit of heaven after all the hell that we had gone through. We were on the heavenly end of life's spectrum for just a few moments each evening. I do not know if he played for us, for the German people or for both of us. Music is a universal language that is appreciated and understood by the people of all tribes and nations. It was a common ground for both the Germans and the GIs.

Somewhere at about this time our duffel bags caught up with us. Here came my bag with my name and serial number on it (Kunze, 38701724). It was pad locked just as I had left it in Metz, France. Back there the word was "You will not need this for a while." To receive it back, meant that the "while" had passed; we were over the hump. Instead of looking forward to the darkness and dangers of the battlefield, I could now look up to the heavens with hope, peace, light and life. The sun of my life was beginning to rise once more. What a difference and what a relief. Praise God from whom all blessings flow.

After VE Day we did not envision any more battles in Europe. But the prospect of going to the Pacific war arena was very real. But soon after VE Day, the US Air Force dropped the atomic bombs on Nagasaki and Hiroshima and the Pacific war came to an end. Now everyone began to think about going home. The prospect for this opportunity was based on a point system. The initial requirement was eighty-five points. Then it dropped to seventy-five. As the months passed, the points needed decreased still more, but I could not muster more than about thirty points for (1) time in the service, (2) time overseas and (3) combat battle stars. My prospect to go home was at least a year away.

The Seventy-Sixth Division was activated in 1942 and trained in the United States for over two years before being deployed to Europe. I trained for less than five months. The division earned three battle stars during the war, I earned two. Original members of the division had between fifty-five and sixty points by the end of the war and could qualify to go home in a few more months. I remained eligible to stay for many more months on other assignments.

The Seventy-Sixth Division was demobilized in June 1945. This caused all the GIs to be reclassified. Some were going home very soon, some not so soon and some were going to stay for awhile. As a consequence our combat squad and platoon reached the end of its service life. Its men were redeployed. Some went home, some prepared to go home and others with few points were redeployed to stay awhile. I can tell you where I went. Comradeship, bonds and buddies that were born out of battle were broken and dissolved.

I entered the service by leaving La Grange, Texas, with other inductees. Perhaps there were one or two others whom I distantly knew; perhaps we both knew another individual. I shipped out of Fort Sam Houston in San Antonio with no one that I knew. I had no known friends at Camp Crowder, Missouri, with whom I trained. We were shipped to Camp Maxey, Texas, as individuals and not as a unit. I knew no one at Camp Maxey. We were shipped out of Camp

Maxey as individuals and not as a unit. I knew essentially no one at Fort Meade, Maryland. The mix continued on my way overseas on the USS *West Point*. After landing at Le Havre, France, we were formed into squads and platoons for the purpose of troop movements. In Luxembourg, I was called out of our compound with GIs unknown to me to march to the front lines. Near Trier, I was plugged into a hole in a squad whose men I did not know. The hole that I filled was open because the buddy who had been there had either been wounded or killed. No great effort was made to develop a close relationship with a new replacement who could also get killed. I do not know that the holes which developed in our squad at Schmitten were ever filled. As I remember, we just closed ranks and proceeded. Now as we shipped out from Plauen, the bonds which had been born through battle were broken once more. The veterans who trained in the Seventy-Sixth Division in the States were soon ready to go home. The replacements who joined the Division in battle had many more months of service before them. I shipped out of the Seventy-Sixth Division, not with buddies or friends, but rather with other GIs, whom I did not know, who had the same low number of "go home" points as I had.

18

Germany to Le Mans, France: A New Assignment

My next truck ride, along with selected other GIs, was a long one. By now I had acquired the small pocket atlas that I found in a German home (Figs. 7 and 8). In it I marked the path according to the road signs that we had seen from Luxembourg to Chemnitz. Also I could now trace my journey as we were leaving Germany. We traveled into the area of Hof, which earlier had been the headquarters for the Seventy-Sixth Division. With the division demobilized, there was no reason to stop. We then continued by truck on a path toward Bamberg, Würzburg, Aschaffenburg, Offenbach, Mainz, Kaiserslautern, Saarbrücken and back through Metz, France.

Our nights were spent in military barracks or centers that were a permanent part of the city in which we stayed. Some of these had been shelled or bombed (Fig. 10), but a few remained undamaged. These were put to use. My Father served in World War I. He was stationed in France. While en route to the front lines, he was stricken with pneumonia. As we were sheltered in some of these old structures, I wondered if I was perhaps billeted in some of the same housing in which he stayed some twenty-seven years before. I could not describe the places precisely enough, and my Father could not remember them well enough. I was never able to describe a particular compound which he remembered. By just passing through, I was never able to develop a good description and geographic location myself.

Fig. 10. While en route to Le Mans, France, we spent the night in a military barrack that had not been shelled or bombed. The picture shows one of several barracks that had been hit.

19

Duties at the Disciplinary Training Center

After several days of travel and shuffling of GIs, we arrived at a disciplinary training center (DTC) near Le Mans, France. Le Mans is about 110 miles southwest of Paris and about 100 miles directly south of Le Havre. There we lived in tents which had been there for a while. The weather was mild. The tent complex (Fig. 11) was located on a hill slope that had good drainage. The mess hall was a more permanent prefabricated building (Fig. 12) which, along with the supply tent, were near the crest of the hill. The residence tents then extended down the hill.

Fig. 11. Company street in our tent camp at Le Mans, France. On the back of the picture I wrote "Company K, 156th Infantry."

Fig. 12. The K Company mess hall where we ate while
living in tents on the outskirts of Le Mans, France.
Private First Class Otto R. Kunze is in the foreground.

The move into this environment was nearly like moving into
the front lines. We were just plugging holes where individuals had
left. The consequence was that I moved into a completely new mix
of GIs (Figs. 13 and 14).

Fig. 13. Several of my tentmates are shown. On the back
of the original picture, the GIs are identified as: top row,
left to right—Smith, Illinois; Still, Iowa; Schlotfield, Nebraska;
Sgt. Karstens, Michigan. Bottom row, left to right—Thompson,
West Virginia; Keleher, New York; and Kunze, Texas.

Fig. 14. Tentmates in fatigues are shown. The following information is on the back of the original picture: Smith, Illinois; Schlotfield, Nebraska; and Kunze, Texas.

Our task was to supply guards or to guard the DTC twenty-four hours a day every day. We were not involved with the inmates or with the management and administration of the center. We manned guard towers and guarded the entrance gate. The inmates were not German prisoners of war. Instead, they were GIs who had not served honorably and consequently were in big trouble. They were essentially mentally sick and their goals were not to be good soldiers. We in no way associated with them, but the gravity of the situation was conveyed to us by a gallow that was positioned near the center's entrance. There were reports by guards that they witnessed an occasional execution by hanging.

The DTC perimeter did not look much different from that which we saw at Buchenwald. At night the perimeter was well lighted. Guards at the entrance gate checked all incoming and outgoing traffic. Garbage trucks were probed with metal rods before they left the gate. This sounds unbelievable but sure enough they found some inmates hidden in the garbage one day.

The guard duties were a routine before I arrived, and the newly arrived GIs fell into the routine very rapidly. When not on duty, the GIs were free and on their own. Individuals could get passes into Le Mans, and the trucks made runs into the city every day.

Somehow, I was not selected for the guard duty routine. Instead, I was put in charge of the supply tent. The supplies seemed to consist of things that had just accumulated over a period of time. Some of the primary items were rifles and ammunition, bayonets, shovels, a shop vice, hacksaw, soldering iron and solder, files, padlocks with keys, padlocks without keys, keys without padlocks and a variety of other things. One of my responsibilities was to keep an inventory of the significant items. I do not remember that the supplies included any blankets or clothing items.

I had my duty hours every day. No one else shared that duty with me. Occasionally my Sergeant would come by and check on me. Also, the supply Sergeant would drop in. On one occasion, even a Captain came by for an inspection. I did so well that I soon was given the title of "armorer" and was promoted to be a Technical Corporal (T/5).

What did a T/5 Corporal do in a supply tent when there was no business? I inspected the weapons and kept them clean and oiled. I did not get to shoot them. After a few days, I had time on my hands. Could I match the keyless padlocks with some of the keys for which we had no padlocks? How many keyless padlocks were there into which I could insert keys? I did not find a single match that would make a padlock work. Nearly all the padlocks were made of brass. How did they work?

A close inspection showed that each padlock had a small oblong plate insert on one end of the two flat sides. If I could file off the bottom end of the narrow padlock side and the rounded end of the insert plate, the remainder of the insert plate would slide out. When this plate was removed, a series of holes were exposed. In each of these holes was a little compression spring and two little steel cylinders (tumblers) about the diameter of a matchstick or smaller. The end of the tumbler that contacted the key was rounded. The other end was flat and the second tumbler was flat on both ends. When all the little compression springs and tumblers were removed, the cylinder into which the key was inserted would fall out of the padlock.

After seeing the inside components of the padlock, I was able to determine how to match a key to a padlock. The key was inserted into the cylinder. Then tumblers, with rounded ends contacting the key, were inserted into the key cylinder. Initially all tumblers had to be flush with or they had to extend above the key cylinder. Tumblers extending above the key cylinder were then filed flush with the outside of the cylinder. The key cylinder with the key could now be inserted into the padlock. With the key cylinder in place another tumbler with both ends flat was inserted into a padlock hole. After all the second tumblers were in place, I could set a small compression spring into the first tumbler hole at the bottom of the padlock. With this spring compressed, I could slide the cover plate over the first hole and repeat the operation with the second hole. The process was then repeated again and again until the last hole was closed, and the cover plate was also in the closed position. The key could now be turned to unlock the padlock. When the key was returned to its original position, the tumblers were perfectly aligned. When pulling the key out of the lock, the tumblers would move up and down until the key was removed. The small compression springs seated the tumblers in the key cylinder. The second tumbler in each hole locked the key cylinder onto the padlock. The filed-off corner of the padlock body was then filled with solder and filed down into the shape of the original padlock. The rebuilt padlocks were as good as new. A few were used as needed and I was allowed to take a few with me. I took them home to Texas where they gave good service for many years.

What did I do before the supply tent became a padlock rebuilding shop? I had time on my hands, and I was curious. I put the bullet of a loaded rifle shell into the vice in the supply tent and then removed the shell from the bullet. As expected, the shell was filled with powder and the bullet was a solid piece of metal. I did not learn a lot. But the supply tent also had loaded tracer shells. I picked up a loaded tracer shell and put the bullet into the vice and removed the powder from the loaded shell. The powder load was about the same. The tracer bullet however was more interesting. It contained a core of the tracer material which ignited when the shell was fired. So to learn more about tracer bullets, I decided to cut the bullet in two with a hacksaw. About halfway through the bullet, the light in my brain came on—"Say this thing could ignite. Maybe this is not such a good idea." During the war I saw tracer bullets ignite and burn down a barn. I could burn down the supply tent. I did not necessarily need this information. I hung the hacksaw back into place and threw both the bullet and the empty shell away. A few days later, I was in the padlock rebuilding business.

The GIs were accumulating points, and we cheered those who reached the magic number to go home. The veterans had trained for many months in the United States and now had also served in Europe for a year or more. We had a Master Sergeant from Louisiana in our tent who had reached the magic number. Before departing, he carefully laid out his goods and decided what to take and what to leave. During his career in coming through the ranks, he had learned to hand-stitch his stripes onto his shirt. Of course he had to first remove the stripes which he already had. For this, he had procured a good little scissor. This was not a cheap "kindergarten" tool but rather one with sharp points. I do not know how or where he acquired it. He gave me that pair of scissors as a departing remembrance. To this day, I am carrying it in my travel pouch. It is still as bright, shiny and sharp as it was the day he gave it to me. Since then, the scissors have been back to Europe numerous times. They have also been to India twice, the Philippines three times, Taiwan three times, Puerto Rico, China, Japan and Thailand. Additionally, they accompanied me behind the Iron Curtain to Hungary, Czechoslovakia and East Germany. "Thank you, Sarge!!"

The primary duty of our unit was to stand guard. All of us did not stand guard all the time. We had some spare time. The opportunity developed for me to attend an algebra class. The class was taught just a short truck ride from our camp. I had taken algebra in high school but felt that a refresher course would not hurt me. Something at a higher level could follow. Well the course material had not changed and the exercise was interesting and refreshing. I really needed the next level of mathematics to prepare me for the college years to come. But such an opportunity never came.

Our commanders were aware that we had leisure time and went to great lengths to help us use it wisely. One day we were loaded on trucks and after a short trip found ourselves on a softball diamond.

The sides were probably picked from platoons. The GIs and non-coms mixed well. But somehow our Company Captain elected himself to play catcher on our opponent's team.

I had played softball in high school and also on Sunday afternoons during the summers of my high school years. My preferred position was that of "roving fielder." This player could rove around in the area between the infield and outfield; he could position himself wherever the batter was likely to hit the ball. After the batter took a swing or two, the roving fielder could usually tell the area to which the ball might be hit. When someone really wanted to knock the "cover off the ball," the roving fielder could become a fourth out-fielder. The field had no home-run fences.

Well, as a fielder in a ball game, the short fast dash is exactly what is needed to catch fly balls. I was allowed to shed my army shoes and play like a kid with bare feet. For me this was exciting.

No one had practiced for our game and only a few players had gloves. The pop fly was a common hit resulting from a tremendous swing. I gathered in a bunch of fly balls and was recognized to be a speedy runner. Well really not a speedy runner, but rather a quick starter.

The game wore on, and we came up to bat. After due time, it was my turn. With a great deal of luck, I was able to get a hit and then managed to get to second base. In softball (fast pitch), the runner cannot leave the base until the pitcher releases the ball. Their pitcher was pitching and our Captain was their catcher. I successively took sprints off second base as the pitcher released the ball. This immediately attracted the Captain's attention. Then on another pitch, I took a longer than usual sprint off second; the Captain caught the ball, and I stutter stepped to stop and run back; the Captain fired the ball to second base. However, after my stutter step, I continued on to third and safely reached the base. Well, we both had fun, while the spectators had mixed emotions; not knowing whether to cheer or remain silent. I tried that maneuver only once and was happy to spend the rest of my service time at the DTC camp as a T/5 Corporal.

In subsequent days, another GI came by my tent and we walked a quarter of a mile to a track. En route we had to cross a stream by means of a suspension bridge (Fig. 15). We ran sprints of fifty and one hundred yards. Neither one of us was a distance runner. In our practice, I was out front for twenty-five yards and behind the remainder of the dash. Then one day the GIs in the area had a track meet. I was heralded as a "bullet." But at the meet there were no short dashes. I just saw runners' heels for the last seventy-five yards of a one-hundred-yard dash (Fig. 16).

Fig. 15. A suspension footbridge that allowed us to get to a field track near our tent living complex at Le Mans, France.

Fig. 16. A soccer field and a field track at an athletic
field near our camp at Le Mans, France.

Mail was now beginning to catch up with us. Old letters came
through that had been written months before. I enjoyed every one
of them. Many GIs took passes and learned to know the city of Le
Mans quite well. Trucks regularly made the run to the city and back.
A big cathedral (Fig. 17) seemed to have survived the war without
much damage. The Sarthe River flowed through the city. The entire
area beyond the stream was off limits to us. But the GIs soon found
what they wanted on the other side and routinely ventured across the
bridge. I did not have the adventurous spirit and seldom asked for a
pass. There was nothing in the city that I needed. The buildings and
the people were the most interesting. I do not know what kind of
restroom facilities the ladies had. Men simply had a rectangular stall
parallel to the sidewalk (Fig. 18). There were panels (on posts) that
started about sixteen inches above ground and then extended up to
about fifty-four inches. A man and woman could come down the
sidewalk chatting with each other. The man would step off into the
stall and urinate while looking over the wall and never break the conversation. This seemed to be normal for the area. The women were a
little more modest. Their facilities were not that obvious, and I could
not read French. But GIs who stood guard around the DTC had

some interesting stories to relate about females who opted to relieve themselves just a short distance from their guard post.

Fig. 17. A cathedral located in Le Mans, France.
It survived the war without being severely damaged.

Fig. 18. The men's restroom (center-left) located on a street and sidewalk in LeMans, France. The bottom was open (about 16 inches). The top was only about shoulder high.

One day one of my tent buddies talked me into going with him on a pass into the city. We took the truck in and then began to walk. He knew where to go, I did not. We arrived at a bridge that plainly displayed the "Off Limits" sign. That did not bother my friend. He said, "It's okay." We finally ended up in a French pub and each ordered a beer. Soon a young lady, probably in her twenties, came out from across the street and ventured into the pub. She greeted my buddy as if she knew him quite well. She hovered and pranced around us for a bit and then began to focus on me. Soon she grabbed my cap and waved it around. When I started to retrieve it, she tucked it into her undergarments. I started to pursue her and she ran out the front door and to her quarters across the street. I did not pursue her, but instead joined my buddy to continue our drink. After a while, she returned and began to tease me once more. She waved and gently slapped me with my cap. Well I finally caught hold of my cap and after a tug-of-war, the cap was mine. I left the remainder of my beer along with my buddy and the "hooker" as I scurried back across the bridge into legal territory. I took a truck back to camp and decided that Le Man's was really not my kind of "town." I believe the area across the bridge could have possibly been another city.

On the outskirts of Le Mans there was an isolated one-story building with parking space that housed a "USO" (United Service Organization). I saw it several times during my visits to the city. Usually there were some jeeps parked on the outside, but the visitors were always on the inside. I do not know how many other US military units were stationed in and around the city. I never heard my more adventurous tent buddies talk about spending time at the USO. One day I ventured out to the place and found the building locked. Some jeeps were there along with some people inside. I knocked on the door and after awhile a WAC (Women's Auxiliary Corp) came to the door. We visited a little. She stayed inside while I remained outside. She informed me that the facility was not open but there would be a party tomorrow evening. If I did come, I needed to bring a bottle of liquor. After getting all the instructions, I left with the intent to make the party. I grabbed my bottle of liquor and arrived at the designated time. When I reached the door, the place was locked, but the party was in full swing. The party noise was so much louder than my knocking that no one ever noticed it. After listening to the tone of the party for a while, I decided that I was more comfortable on the outside than what I would be on the inside. My knocking attracted no attention. The door was never opened. A table full of GIs from my Tent City could have possibly crashed the party. Those inside sounded like they had partied together before. I returned to camp with my bottle and really never did celebrate with it.

Our Tent City environment became more relaxed, and the GIs soon found that they could spend a night out without being missed. Such nights could be spent at a recently acquired girlfriend's quarters. The terminology soon developed that he "shacked up" with his girlfriend last night. "Shacking up" was certainly more preferable than meeting her out in the woods somewhere. There was a wooded area between our Tent City and the DTC. Some romances were started in this area. So it was not unusual for a GI to return to camp and tell how he "shacked up" last night with his girlfriend. The environment was ripe for such visits. The war had removed much of the native male population while the female population was greater in number and looking for male companionship. With this combination, sexual activity was available for most anyone who wanted to indulge.

Tent City was on the south slope of our hill. Entrance to our area was from the east; to the north, there were other military facilities. To the west there were woods and the DTC. To the south at the bottom of our hill there were also woods. There was some GI traffic in and out of these woods. One day I ventured in that direction. Soon after passing the wood line, there was a GI taking sexually explicit pictures of his girlfriend lying on the ground. I seemingly did not bother him, but when she sensed my arrival, she reared up to reposition her skirt to the normal position. This fouled up the picture taking. I had intruded on a private activity. Another GI and his girl friend were nearby enjoying each other's company. If a GI entered those woods, he needed to have a girlfriend with him or she needed to be waiting for him. Entry by a single male was completely out of place. I did an about face and headed back to Tent City.

During my time on the front lines, sex was never an issue. Our energy level was always so low, and the stress level was so high that sexual emotions never surfaced. This is most unusual for a young man who has just become eligible for military service. A person who was not there may not want to believe it. Life itself was much more important than sex. But as the stress of war and battle faded, a number of GIs became sexually active and found themselves partners somewhere. Such relationships developed fast. The sexual drought was equally present among the German and French women. It was not unusual for a young attractive Mother to push her baby in a carriage from one town to another in pursuit of a GI partner who had shipped out of her town.

Promiscuity and lack of morals were driven by the time and situation in which the troops found themselves. A person needed strong morals to stay on the side of chastity. My Father's parting words were inscribed on my heart: "Otto, it is a whole lot easier to get into trouble than it is to get out of it."

Furloughs to Switzerland became a common excursion for those who could get one. I must have been way down on the list because I never made the "go" list. Even though I had sent most of my money home during the months of combat, I now had accumulated enough pay to take on such an opportunity. Many GIs opted to indulge in games of chance with their money, but I tuned such opportunities out of my mind. Instead, I was still hoping to acquire at least a part of my wish list, i.e., a good Swiss watch and a 35mm camera. Both of these could have been available in Switzerland. My hopes for a German Luger had faded out of my mind. I never saw such a prized possession for sale. I never made the furlough list while I was in France.

With the war over and troops shipping home, our GI population was decreasing. The DTC inhabitants were also being tried and otherwise processed. That population was also decreasing. The result was that our services were no longer needed in France.

20

Military Police Assignment

The next assignment, for those GIs who still needed points, was to a military police battalion in Belgium. I believe that this unit was put together on paper because it was never brought into formation for a Major to address or review. The information was that there were three companies. The men from the Battalion would patrol the three cities of Liège, Charleroi and Namur. My company was going to Namur, Belgium.

Our bonds, friendships and relationships were again disrupted. As we left camp at the DTC, some GIs were going home, others were staying at the camp and others, including myself, were shipping out. As I remember, the DTC was still operational, but the intensity of its operation had decreased by several levels.

Our first move was by truck to Paris, France. One night was spent in the city of Paris. There were no passes. For us, it was just an overnight stop. We stayed in a large single-story building. It could have been a factory at one time but now was used to house troops on the move.

Troops were coming and going. I do not even remember that there was a kitchen. The facilities were just the minimum necessary, bunks and latrines. We were warned to guard our possessions because thieves and pickpockets were around. The lights were dim but never out even at night. There were always folks who looked like GIs in the aisles. I did not get very much sleep that night. All of our group were probably equally concerned. No one was robbed or lost any possessions. Perhaps I even gained some. A week or two later, I had to go to a first aid station because I had body lice. I believe I picked them up in Paris. The attendants at the station dusted me and my clothes with some medicated powder, and I had no further problems.

We left Paris on "forty or eight" railway cars en route to Namur, Belgium. This was a relaxed ride. There were no accommodations in the boxcars. Most of the time the train traveled very slowly, but we were moving. The spirit of the men on board was very different from that of the men who rode from Le Havre to Metz, France, on the same type of transportation en route to the battlefront.

In Europe, as in the States, the railroad often runs parallel with a highway. In the States, the railroad tracks are more distant from the road. In Europe, the distance may be only enough for a drainage ditch between the two. We were traveling parallel to such a highway.

After traveling for some time, a beer wagon on the highway approached us from the rear. It was drawn by a pair of trotting horses traveling faster than our train. The wagon could have carried sixteen kegs with eight cradled on each side. The horses were moving at a comfortable and graceful pace. The wagon passed our train car and was moving merrily forward beyond us. When it was about three train cars ahead, a GI from two cars ahead of us jumped off his "forty or eight" boxcar and ran across the drainage ditch to the highway. He ran up behind the beer wagon, snatched the last keg off it, rolled it off the road, picked it up and carried it across the drainage ditch to his boxcar that was approaching him. The keg then disappeared into the boxcar.

The GIs who saw this activity all cheered while the driver of the beer wagon thought we were applauding him. The driver matched our applause and cheers by vigorously waving his arm and hand. He never saw what happened behind him. He was just short one keg of beer whenever he reached his destination. I am not sure that the keg was full. No beer ever reached our "forty or eight" railroad car. Also we never heard or saw a celebration in the second car ahead of us.

After several additional hours of travel, we arrived at the train station (Fig. 19) in Namur, Belgium. We were picked up by two-and-a-half-ton army trucks and soon arrived at our new destination that we called home.

Fig. 19. The railroad station located in Namur, Belgium. We arrived there in "forty or eight" railway cars after shipping out of Paris, France.

We were quartered in a quadrangle of permanent military buildings with an open courtyard in the center. This complex was on top of a knob-hill in the city. The structures could have accommodated several companies of men. I doubt that our strength was that of two full platoons. A small winding street led up the hill to the barracks. At the entrance at the bottom of the hill (in the city) was a guard station that was sometimes manned. There seemed to be no urgency for it to be manned continuously. Across the street from the entry were an army vehicle service and repair shop as well as a small motor pool.

On top of the hill, there were barracks on three sides of the courtyard. The fourth side contained the entry street, a ten- or twelve-stall latrine and urinal, and then there was a confinement center or jail with six cells and a guard station. We were billeted in the barrack immediately to the left of the entrance street. Our Captain parked his jeep beside the jail with the vehicle facing our barrack. The remaining barracks were empty but seemed to be habitable if needed. Across the courtyard from our quarters and in the basement of that barrack were our eating quarters. The empty rooms in the barracks around us offered opportunities for activities other than those expected from a Military Police (MP) Company.

Operating with our company was an agent of the CIA (Civilian Investigation Authority). He wore a GI uniform and was always around but was really not a part of us. The MPs worked only with our military people and with German prisoners of war (PWs). The CIA agent worked with both our military people and with the civilian Belgian population. The scope of his work was much less restricted. He pursued "black market operations" between our GIs and the Belgian civilians. He used our military police to accomplish his raids. For example, one day, half a dozen of us were loaded on a truck. After a short ride, we disembarked while still in the city. We surrounded what seemed to be a shop and dwelling. Orders were not to let anyone leave or enter the building. Then the agent and an MP entered the building. After awhile they came out with a mix of materials, i.e., GI clothing, gloves, overcoats, cigarettes, etc. They confiscated these materials. We caught no GIs in the act of selling the goods. But we were looking for both the buyer and the seller.

One night when I was selected for a specific guard duty I left my overcoat in the guardhouse while doing duty at my post. When I returned, my overcoat was gone. I presume that it was used for black market contraband.

Our MPs could not directly pursue GIs who were absent without leave (AWOL) and in civilian clothes. We did not have the prerogative to stop just any civilian. In such cases, the CIA agent could pursue such leads. During my stay at Namur, at least one AWOL GI was picked up wearing civilian clothes. He had moved in with a Belgian lady. After the GI was coerced to make the jail his home, the female friend routinely came to make the jail cell her second home. I was happy and relieved to see the deserter get moved out. I do not know if the lady continued to pursue him.

Our platoon was housed in a large room with double bunks on the second floor of a barrack which flanked the jail or holding cells. It was on the left side of the road entry to the complex. The platoon was a new mix of men. I had no friends or acquaintances who had been in combat with me. Neither were there any GIs who had been in my tent at the DTC at Le Mans, France.

In 2001, as the Seventy-Sixth Division retraced its path across Germany, I met Robert Sherman who had served in B Company of the 417th Infantry Regiment. Robert followed the same route to Le Mans, France, to guard the DTC, and then was shipped to Belgium. There Robert served with an MP Company in Liege. Therefore, he was in the same MP Battalion with me but served in another town and in another Company.

Within a few days, everyone was assigned to his specific duties in the area to be patrolled. I was probably the smallest man in the company, so I was not put out on patrol. My assignments were to (l) stand guard at the entry gate, (2) receive the prisoners that were brought in and put them into detention cells, (3) take the prisoners to three meals per day and (4) guard the jail. With these duties, I had a full day, but I was never pressed to be at two stations at once. A duty roster on the bulletin board told me exactly what to do. The entry gate was not always guarded, but I did spend time there on duty. Prisoners were brought in at certain times of day. Before I received them, they had been questioned and processed through our guardhouse in the city. All of the detention cells were closed with a sliding bolt. The cells could have been padlocked shut, but I was never asked to lock them.

I developed my routine. At the entry gate, I simply observed the vehicles that entered and left. Also I could observe the vehicle and foot traffic on the public street. After a few days, a person knew what to expect. There was an open electric light bulb at the entry gate that sometimes functioned. Upon checking, the bulb was securely screwed in. I soon spotted a faulty connection in a service wire. I secured some electrical tape and crawled on top of the guard hut to make the repairs. I was sufficiently insulated from the ground so that the hot wire would only bite (shock) me real good if I contacted it. The job was completed and the light worked very well thereafter.

Guard duty at the jail turned out to be a lonely vigil. I found myself a paperback English dictionary and started to study the definition of words, hoping to increase my vocabulary. I started with *A* on page one but never was able to get past the letter *E*.

The meal routine was to get the prisoners out of their cells, take them to the mess hall to eat, run them through the latrine and then put them back into their cells. The cell doors opened into a hallway that led to a single jail exit door. Each cell was about six feet wide and had a one-man bunk across its back end. The length of the cell was about twelve feet. A few cells may have had an additional canvas cot. High in the back wall was a ventilation opening too small for someone to crawl through. It had an iron grill across it. Next to the cell door and about a foot above the floor was another ventilation opening about twelve inches square with an iron grille across it. The cells had little natural light and perhaps no more than a fifteen- or twenty-five-watt bulb for illumination. The structure was constructed out of brick covered with plaster. This detention center was primarily a holding station for inmates to be sent to other stations for processing.

The most common detainees were German PWs. I would have them for a few days before they would get shipped on to a PW camp. Once again my German language was an asset. I could act dumb and listen or I could converse with them. Usually I just listened.

Most often these PWs were quite hungry when they were brought in. The Belgian people speak French, so a German has a difficult time communicating with them. Most of the PWs had never been exposed to American food. They were often a little hesitant to eat what they did not recognize. In other cases, they did not eat what they did recognize. The food in question was "corn." Generally, Americans love it; it is one of our staple foods. Well, the PWs had to serve themselves. When there was a tub of corn in the chow line, the German PWs would walk past it. I finally asked a prisoner, "Why do you not take corn?" His reply was, "*Das ist für die schweine!!*" (That is for the pigs!!) To my surprise, I found that many Europeans did not eat corn at that time. I think that corn has become more edible for them in recent years.

At Namur, we had a regular kitchen crew cooking for us. But in addition, there were about five Belgian ladies who assisted in the preparation and serving of lunch and the evening meal. Breakfast was usually served by our GI personnel. Between lunch and the evening meal, these females would often use a bombed out building, where only the walls remained standing, to relax and get a little suntan (Fig. 20). To my knowledge, they worked in the kitchen as they were supposed to and were not involved in other extracurricular activities. Their ages could have spanned between twenty and thirty-five.

Fig. 20. Two of the Belgian ladies from Namur who assisted our GI kitchen crew to prepare and serve the noon and evening meals. During the interim, they spread a blanket on the ground in a bombed out adjacent building and enjoyed a little sunshine.

The Belgian female helpers spoke French and some English. My German did not work! Our military police also had such a Belgian lady who assisted them whenever language became a problem. All the foreign females were professional in their work. They attended to business and mixed little with the GIs.

However, with time, one of my new friends was able to break the barrier and began to develop a relationship with one of the female workers. They were beginning to date, and their affection for each other was rapidly growing. But then the inevitable happened. Her male friend acquired enough points to go home, and he did. He had mixed emotions when he left, but she was heartbroken. She did not hear from him and kept asking me if I had. After about a month, I received a letter from him. He asked me to convey the message to his girlfriend that he had found a happier hunting ground. She would not be hearing from him. So I was the courier of the sad news. She was heartbroken and teary-eyed for several days. To my knowledge, she did not start any more relationships with GIs.

The prisoners that I held in custody ranged across the span. Some were mild offenders, and others were real criminals. Perhaps one of the worst offenders was a GI who was AWOL. He stayed in a GI uniform and assumed the rank of a Lieutenant. He made his living stealing army vehicles, particularly trucks. One of his routines was to call a motor pool and request a two-and-a-half- ton truck to meet a train with soldiers that were coming in. He fabricated an authoritative story. He came in advance of his men. He arranged to have the truck pick him up before going to the railway station. The Lieutenant, truck and driver would then proceed to the railway station. Well, they waited, but their train would not come. So the bandit Lieutenant would finally excuse himself and go get himself a cup of coffee. Upon returning to the truck, the two would wait some more. Well, the bandit Lieutenant would finally let the driver go and get himself a cup of coffee while the Lieutenant would stay with the truck. The bandit Lieutenant not only stayed with the truck, but he took off with it. He had stolen some thirteen or fifteen trucks this way. He was also credited with stealing several other vehicles. He did not just operate in one place, but he moved around to conduct his stealing trade.

After being taken captive, he was able to tell where he had sold some of the trucks. The Army was able to repossess a number of them. These had been repainted and modified so that their identity was not so obvious.

The bandit Lieutenant carried a 45-caliber US Army pistol in a shoulder or vest holster. A closer examination showed that the pistol was cocked and on safety. The dust and dirt on the pistol showed that it had been carried in that condition for a long time. Here was an adult male who looked respectable, clean and honest, but on the inside he was crooked, sly, dishonest, unloyal, dangerous and unworthy of any trust. I shudder to think what kind of life the man was building for himself.

On the milder side, some GIs were brought in simply for disorderly conduct. They had gone out on the town, drank too much and then lost control of themselves. Some of our own MPs (while off duty) were even brought in. One GI from our platoon sat in the cell for several days. He could not stand the isolation. He pleaded with me to get his shoe polish because the leather in his shoes was cracking. I believe he was released before I was able to get the polish to him.

Sometimes the jail population dwindled to just a few occupants, and then suddenly it was overflowing, perhaps sixteen to twenty prisoners. There was only one bunk per cell, but there were times when I had five prisoners in such a small room. One day I had such a loaded cell with five German PWs with various other detainees in the other cells. I took them all to dinner, then to the latrine and back to their cells. After leaving the latrine, they all filed back into their rooms. Then I counted the people in each cell to make sure they were all there. After that I closed the door and latched it with the sliding bar on the outside. I did this one evening and had closed three cells. As I peered into the fourth, there were four prisoners standing in front of the bunk. "Where is the fifth?" I asked. *"Ach er liegt hier!"* (Oh, he is lying here!) The two PWs in the center stepped sideways apart to show me. I accepted their answer, slammed the door shut and latched it with the sliding bolt. After checking in all the prisoners and latching all the doors, I left for the evening.

Well, the next morning I was short five German PWs, one cell door was open, and the Captain's jeep was missing! I was in trouble! The afternoon before the five German PWs built themselves a dummy out of coats and blankets on their bunk. After dinner, one

PW stayed in the latrine while I locked up the other four. That night, the fifth PW was nice and opened only the cell with his buddies. He could have opened the rest of the cell doors, but he did not. Close to the jail exit was the Captain's jeep, which they were able to wire up and make it run. That night I was not guarding the jail, and neither was I posted at the entry gate. So my prisoners made the most of it by making a clean getaway. Well, within the day, our MP patrols were able to pick up five German PWs driving a stolen jeep. I never saw our Captain but was told that his home was in San Antonio, Texas. I was hoping that a Captain from Texas would be easy on me. He was. I got "off the hook" without getting a severe reprimand. In our modern day, a worker with my duties would probably claim an "overload."

Our own GIs often gave the MPs a difficult time by resisting arrest and then continuing with disorderly conduct. The MPs usually worked in pairs. I do not know what all an apprehended GI may have done to the MPs, but I do know that the MPs worked over several GIs after they reached our compound. Then they turned their captive over to me for detention. In most cases, both the apprehended GI and the MPs were civil and orderly.

After being in our quarters for a month or more, the routines were well established, and the off duty GIs were able to take in the town. They knew the place. Their patrols took them to any part of town. The place became a home for us. A Latin GI became one of my best friends. He was such a kind and warm-hearted person. He was very friendly, and I began to appreciate him as a person. However, I soon found that he would drink more booze than he could handle. Then when he came in at night over imbibed, he would look me up. He would want to visit with me. But there was nothing I could do or say that would please him. The more we conversed, the more aggravated he became. I never found a good solution to the problem. After sobering up, he worked to be my friend again. He seemingly was completely unaware of our unpleasant encounters during periods when he was intoxicated. Needless to say, I put as much distance between us as I could.

Although things settled down and became somewhat routine, they never became stable. GIs were going home as they accumulated enough points. Therefore, we were living in a mode of change. When I first arrived at Namur, all German PWs were processed and shipped out. This was true for other detainees also. The Belgian women began to help in our kitchen. Other Belgian females were going on patrol with our MPs. The number of German PWs being picked up was decreasing. Our service and repair shop GIs were going home, so other skilled people were needed. These skilled individuals were soon found among the new German PWs that were picked up. Instead of being processed, they were put to work in our motor pool service and repair shop.

I do not know what machines and tools we had in the shop. I never had reason to visit it. But the PWs were not there very long before they were making little aluminum bracelets, rings to wear on a finger and other similar trinkets or jewelry. The rings even had various insets on their tops. They sold them at a very cheap price, but they were earning themselves a little money. Also they were keeping themselves busy. They continued to work in our motor pool shop and were still working when I shipped out of Namur. I still have two of such rings and a bracelet.

Since my assignments did not include patrol duty, I had little reason to leave the compound. But one day I was given the opportunity to go on patrol with two of our MPs. They had no particular assignment other than to patrol. This gave me an opportunity to take some pictures of the country side. I could take pictures but there were limited services to develop them.

We passed by a large beautiful chateau in which General Eisenhower had spent some time (Fig. 21). We checked in at a station on the Meuse River. A teenage Belgian boy (Fig. 22) operated a motorboat there. He wore GI clothes but was not a GI himself. He could understand English but did not speak it. If our MPs needed water transportation, he would provide it. We took a short tour on the river just to see what was around on the shore. There were no incidents while I was an observer with the MPs on patrol. After perhaps two hours of patrolling, they delivered me back to the compound. I really appreciated the opportunity to see some of the sights, sounds and landscape around Namur.

Fig. 21. A chateau located on the outskirts of Namur,
Belgium. It was within the patrol area of our MP Unit.
The information was that General Eisenhower spent one or
more nights there. It had not been damaged by the war.

Fig. 22. A young Belgian boy who operated a motor boat
on the Meuse River for our MPs. I believe that he was
available as needed and was not necessarily a part of our
routine patrol. He took us for a ride on the river.

213

With the passage of time, new opportunities continued to evolve. One day a GI came around to tell us that a vehicle was going to Brussels to purchase chocolate bars, perfumes and other items for which there was a demand. Items that were available were limited. I was not anticipating such an opportunity and needed nothing that someone else would purchase for me. After about two weeks, the opportunity presented itself again. This time I ordered a bottle of Chanel No. 5 perfume. It was costly and the bottle was small, but there were nearly no goods to buy. I had no use for the perfume but carried it to the States. After going through four years of college for a Bachelor of Science degree and another year for a Master's degree, I married and presented the bottle of perfume to my lovely wife.

As the months passed, our lives loosened up, and we were given a little more slack. The opportunity developed for the unit to run a truckload of GIs to Brussels with just an evening pass. The distance was about fifty kilometers. We loaded up late one afternoon and made the run. We reached Brussels after dark. I knew nothing about the city, and little could be seen out of a covered truck. At best, a person saw where he had just been. Our group unloaded, and we were given a time when the truck would reload for the return trip. The streets were clean, but dark, with little evidence of the war. The most telling evidence was the lack of lights in the streets. The buildings were essentially all dark. The city was dark but not dead. Many GI groups were there just as we were. We must have had a guide of some sort. After roaming the dark streets for some time, we came to a street corner scene that was dimly lit. There we saw the attraction of the city! It was the statue of "Manneken-Pis," a legendary figure in Brussels. There in a dim light was a young male boy urinating in an endless stream. Legend has it that a rich entrepreneur lost his only son during festivities in the area. After five days of searching, he was found on that street corner doing what he is still doing today. The statue of the young boy was first ordered in 1619, and he has been a city attraction ever since. I was learning some history that I did not know before. This was one of the highlights of the evening.

Our group then continued to seemingly roam the streets but we were probably being led by someone. Soon we came to an open square that seemed to be in the middle of the city. The square was filled with GIs that were just milling around. We wound ourselves through the other groups. After drifting around for awhile, we detected an aroma with which we were familiar but we had not sensed it in years. We were down-wind from its source and everyone was ready to track it down. As we moved forward the aroma became stronger and we soon saw what it was. We lined up not only to smell but to taste what we were smelling. A Belgian entrepreneur had set up a little stand and was cooking French fries (potatoes). What a treat!!! We could spend some money and actually get something for it. We never had such a delicious treat prepared for us by our army kitchen. After more than two years, these fries were "out of this world." We really enjoyed them. They were so fresh, hot, crisp and great that I will never forget the moment and the taste! What a welcome surprise! This was just like home. Only now we were four thousand miles away.

We then roamed the open square for awhile. There were a few dimly lit shops that may have had some chocolate bars in them. But the shops were closed. The open square was surrounded by some tall buildings that could hardly be seen in the darkness of the night. We soon made our way back to the loading station where we boarded our truck and started back to Namur. In a war-torn area there are no home or street lights. My memory recalls a dark city, Manneken-Pis and some delightful, most welcome, fresh, hot, just out of the kettle French fries.

In 2001, as we (a group of veterans and their family members) retraced the path of the Seventy-Sixth Division across Germany, we flew into Brussels, Belgium. After freshening up a little, we went out on the town for the rest of the day and evening. This time we had a tour guide. The first place that we visited was an open square in front of a big hall. There were stores and markets surrounding the square. The hall was clean and attractive; a magnificent building with impressive spires at each corner and a central spire with multiple levels of little spires around it that just kept on reaching up into the sky. This was Town Hall in the Grand Place. The central spire is 330 feet high; it is finally crowned with a sixteen-foot gilded copper statue of St. Michael. The Gothic structure was erected during the period of 1402–1454. The area was cool and clean, and the air was so fresh. The famous mammoth chocolate bars could be bought in many of the shops. After being there for a few moments, I remembered that I had been there before. It was in 1946 or fifty-five years earlier. At that time, I ate French fried potatoes in this square. This time my wife, Alice, and two of our sons, Allen and Charles, were with me. As they admired the scenery and the architecture for the first time, I stood there in awe realizing all that I did not see that night over a half-century ago. In 1946, we could see only the silhouettes of the buildings. This time the Grand Place was visible to us in all of its magnificent splendor. We admired the Gothic architecture of the structures along with the other tourists that were there.

Then our guide took us down a street a few blocks, and there on the street corner was "Manneken-Pis" still doing what he has done so well for nearly four centuries. Indeed I had seen all of this before, but that was in a dark and ghostly city. This time the city was alive, vibrant, free and reenergized.

Everyone on our tour (2001) enjoyed the sights and scenes so much that we went back that evening. First we ate a delicious meal on a side street, and then we proceeded to the Grand Place with the Town Hall. The open square was dimly lit, but the Town Hall was illuminated with bands of colored light that slowly moved up the structure to the tips of the spires. What a breathtaking sight! A brass band was playing in the open patio with people sitting and eating in the open square area. What a grand place to reminisce! What a difference fifty-five years made! The place was magnificent, relaxing and peaceful. This is the life and freedom that we fought for. The people there were able to enjoy that freedom with us. How do we thank and tell the people who sacrificed their lives and paid the ultimate price for us to have, enjoy and keep that freedom?

My time in Europe was accumulating day by day, week by week and month by month. The "Points" for me to go home were increasing while the points required for this event were decreasing. I was about to accrue the magic number. I did not retain much of my earnings, but with nothing to buy, I was carrying more money than needed for my trip home. Consequently, one day I sent most of my money home. I kept only as much as might be needed for my journey. Surely my name had to be near the top of the "going home" list.

In another day or two, my name was called. It was not for my journey home, but rather I was now eligible for a furlough to Switzerland. I had waited for more than a year for this opportunity, but it never came. I was now without travel money and felt certain that my tour of duty in Europe was about to end. I was on the next list to go home.

Now I had the opportunity to unpack all of my goods and decide what to take and what to leave. We were not restricted to a certain number of pounds. The deciding factor was "How many pounds could I physically carry?" Over the months, I had accumulated a radio, a six-shooter pistol, a German swastika flag, stainless steel 50-caliber machine gun shells and other items.

The radio was unique because it had a rheostat at the end of its input line. It could be set for a number of input voltages. As we moved from Germany to France to Belgium, the secondary electrical service voltages differed or changed. All I had to do was to find the magnitude of the service voltage, then set this on my rheostat and the radio would have the proper voltage. It was not fancy but it was convenient. The electrical alternating current frequency in Europe was 50 hertz. The radio served me well for several months. I sold it or nearly gave it away to a GI friend who was still waiting.

The stainless steel 50-caliber shells were used by the German army for repair and maintenance of their guns. The swastika flag was big enough to hang from a room ceiling to its floor. It could have adorned a street as it may have hung from a standard adjacent to a window on one of Hitler's parade routes. I finally limited myself to what I could stuff into my duffel bag and the weight that I could carry. Even today I still have a large and a small "First Aid" box as the medics carried. I was allowed to carry them with me.

21

Return Trip Home

Then one morning in July, I was picked up with others by truck and transported on what was probably the "Red Ball Express" highway from the vicinity of Namur, Belgium, to Le Havre, France. There we dismounted the truck and marched up the ramp onto a small Liberty ship, the SS *Alhambra Victory*. This was similar to the ship on which we had crossed the English Channel from Weymouth to Le Havre nearly a year and a half before. We loaded but stayed in dock.

The SS *Alhambra Victory* was a VC-2 model ship built for Cargo (SS *Alhambra Echo*, 1946). It was 455 feet long and 62 feet wide and had a draft of twenty-eight feet when fully loaded. Its dead weight was 11,000 tons and had a convoy speed of sixteen knots with a capacity of 4,561 tons. It was powered by a 6,000 horsepower super-heated steam turbine with an oil-fueled boiler. The ship could carry 1,500 troops. For proper flotation, the ship carried 1,050 tons of sand and 250 tons of cement as ballasts.

After boarding, we could not leave the ship. Instead the ship was our home in harbor. The port was not especially clean, and the odor of the port and ocean was quite strong and nauseating. Several GIs threw their meals over the ship's rails before we left the port. We could see ocean traffic come and leave. On the ramp next to us was what seemed to be a shipload of mail bags (Fig. 23). They made me wonder how many letters were en route to me when I was now going home? Also, if there was a letter for me, I wonder who could find it?

Fig. 23. These mail bags were on the dock at the port in Le Havre, France. What else could come in bags like that? Our ship, the SS *Alhambra Victory*, was docked nearby.

The harbor itself still showed the ravages of war. Perhaps 150 yards behind us was a ship lying on its side (Fig. 24). It could have been a victory ship about the size of the one that we were on. Several warehouses had been erected or rebuilt but the reconstruction had just begun. Only my imagination can suggest what all happened to make the area that which the picture shows. Many of the docks in the port were still in ruins. Those which could be used had been cleaned up and were busy with ship traffic. Most of the original dock and port facilities had been destroyed. What was there now seemed to be temporary make-shift facilities. They were serving the purpose until something better could be constructed. It was a key facility, however, because I both entered and left Europe through it.

Fig. 24. This is a general view of the port facilities at Le
Havre, France, in July 1946. There was now a lot of activity
in the port while much of the facility was still in ruins.
Note the capsized ship's hull in the middle of the picture.
What all happened here to create a scene like this?

After we were on board for more than a day, the SS *Alhambra Victory* pulled out of harbor. We were leaving Europe!!! Every day on board, we received a little newsletter, *The Alhambra Echo*. Its mast head contained the following information: Tr. Commander, Capt. E. Seymour; S. S. O., Lt. N. M. Glasgow; Editor, Mr. M. Ackerman; Ed. Staff, Lt. R. Maguire with several typists, an artist and a mimeograph operator.

The voyage back was a slow and relaxing one. The ship was not big enough to have lookout ports below the deck. It had a single smoke or exhaust stack. When below deck, a person could see nothing outside. While going to Europe, my room and bunk were right on the water line. We had a lookout port that was always in and out of the ocean water. That porthole was about sixteen to eighteen inches in diameter. On our return voyage, we spent much of our time on deck watching the ship plow through the waves. The ocean was never tranquil. The weather, as well as the Atlantic Ocean, was different from one day to the next. When a wind was blowing, there were some waves that we plowed through. When there was only a breeze, the ocean would seem to heave and wane; a mound of water would heave up, only to be followed by a hallow depression at the same spot. For a person who loved to have his feet on the ground, the wave dynamics were most interesting.

Now, seventeen months after our voyage to Europe, our trip across England, crossing of the Channel, landing in Le Havre and our "forty or eight" ride to Metz, France, there were about three GIs with familiar faces that I recognized as old friends. They also recognized me. We could tell each other very similar stories. However, as we accumulated points at the same rate and had similar recent backgrounds, we served in very different outfits and took different paths across Europe. But now we met once more on the same ship that was taking us back to the States. We were grateful and happy survivors. Each of us left friends behind who paid the ultimate price or who were less fortunate and were shipped back home as wounded and disabled soldiers.

En route to Europe, we probably had several thousand men on board the USS *West Point*. I saw only a few hundred of them and made a brief acquaintance with some of the ones who had a personality similar to mine that were quartered with me. The mood then was one of being calm, deliberate and determined. Making friends was incidental and not the focus at that time. Now to see the same friendly face with exuberant expectations was a real joy. We could enjoy the morning sunrise together and knew that tomorrow's sunrise would be even better.

We seemed to be alone, but unafraid, in the vast expanse of the Atlantic Ocean. We never met or saw another ship, there were no B-24 bombers or destroyers escorting us. We were going to a place that we were somewhat reluctant to leave, but were happy and grateful for the opportunity to make the return trip.

Many GIs spent their time on deck during the day. At night, we were sleeping well so we really were not short on rest. The ocean with all of its sights was most interesting. After a day or more out, we found an interesting personality on board—a WAC (Women's Army Corp). She was well dressed. I do not believe that she wore bars on her shoulders. Her uniform was sharp and impeccable. She ventured out on the ship's deck and stopped at its railing while admiring the ocean as we did. She seemed to be by herself when there was so much male company around.

The thing for us to do was to walk the deck and stop at the railing close to her. If she wanted to talk to us she could, and we might even have the opportunity to talk to her. We made the move. She had a little Chihuahua dog in a harness on a leash. She soon sensed our presence and pulled up on her dog's leash with the directive, "Come on Shacky, let's go." Seemingly she knew the army slang and used it to name her dog. Her few words answered many of our questions. She disappeared and I never saw her again. If she had acquaintances on board ship, they were not in our group.

We saw no officers on board and the ship's officers did not show themselves. The ship's newspaper listed officers in its masthead. They probably operated in some area of the ship but we really did not need them.

Edition No. 8 of the SS *Alhambra Echo* was a "Souvenir" issue dated July 14, 1946. (See Appendix D.) The cover page showed a ship steaming into New York harbor with the words beneath it "YOUR MESS KIT DAYS ARE ALMOST OVER." The first article in the paper was entitled "WHAT DO YOU THINK?" The question was "In what ways has your army career been beneficial to you as an individual?" Among numerous responses, some were from a First Lieutenant, Infantry Platoon Leader; a First Scout of the Thirty-Sixth Infantry Division; a Corporal in a Heavy Weapons Company in the Ninth Infantry Division; a T/5 Dispatcher of the 3708 Quartermaster Truck Company; a Pfc. Rifleman in the Sixty-Ninth Infantry Division; a T/3 Chief Clerk in the G-4 Section of the Third Army Headquarters and numerous others. Their comments were most interesting and ranged across the board. For example, "I have learned to get along with all classes of people"; "A chance to see more of the world"; "Makes a man out of a boy"; "A sight-seeing tour of Europe"; "I haven't learned anything in the Army"; "It has satisfied my lust for travel. Now I'm perfectly satisfied to stay in the States for the rest of my life"; and others.

On the eighth day we docked at Pier 11, Staten Island, New York, before proceeding to Pier 15 where the troops debarked. We took a ferry and passed behind the Statue of Liberty—the Statue of Liberty!!! What a jolt!! What has she meant to me? What does she mean to me now? I have seen so much hardship, distress, suffering, death and destruction. These are not the symbols of "freedom and liberty" that I know. The Statue of Liberty! She deserves a big hug of gratitude. She embodies all of the virtues for which I fought. She has held and preserved these virtues while I was gone. She now manifests and exhibits my pride for a job well done. She still proclaims "Liberty and Justice for All." She is now returning those virtues back to me!! Every generation has the responsibility to pass this virtue on. What a sobering thought.

FREEDOM IS NOT FREE!!!

We were en route to a railroad station on the New Jersey side of the Hudson River. From there we took a train to the Port of Debarkation at Camp Kilmer, New Jersey, where I received my train tickets to San Antonio, Texas, the place where I was inducted.

My thoughts were of home, and I do not remember the route which the train took to get me there. After perhaps a day of travel, we reached Texas. The names of the towns began to have a familiar ring. After some hours, they became even more familiar. I tracked the successive towns with increased interest. Giddings, a town nine miles from my home, had railroad tracks that ran north and south as well as east and west. It began to appear that we could be on the north-south tracks. I claimed a seat at a window and was watching closely. The train began to slow down and suddenly the scenery became very familiar as we slowly pulled into Giddings. As I remember the train did not stop but it had to travel slowly because of street and high-way crossings (Highway 290 from Houston to Austin). This highway was the main street in Giddings. As we crossed it, I saw not only Giddings, but also my Father's red Ford, flatbed, one-ton truck. It

223

was parked at the curb of the street. I did not know that he would be in town and he did not know that I was coming through. The train never stopped and we lumbered on to Fort Sam Houston in San Antonio.

The most dramatic vision that remains with me in San Antonio is that of an officer sitting at a desk with a typewriter. He was looking at my records while asking me questions and then he would type something. After a little while, he started to hand the paper to me with the comment "Here is your Honorable Discharge Certificate." I hesitated for a moment, and he said, "Would you also like to have this document in wallet-size sealed in plastic?" "Yes" was my reply. In another few moments, I had my discharge paper and my certificate encased in plastic (Fig. 25). The backside of the Discharge Certificate contained my "Enlisted Record and Report of Separation" (Fig. 26). After seventy-three years, it is still mine, and I become more proud of it with time.

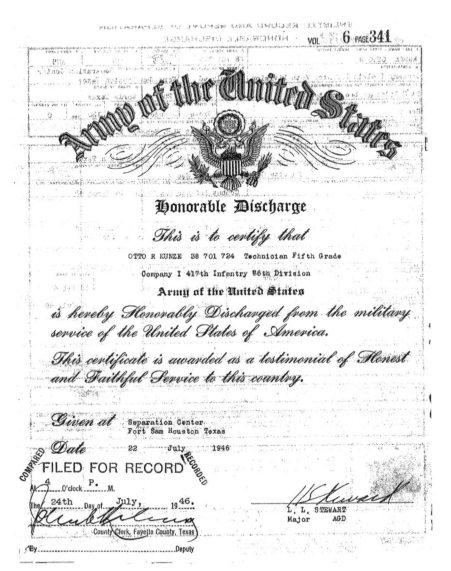

Fig. 25. The Honorable Discharge Certificate
for T/5 Otto R. Kunze, SN 38701724.

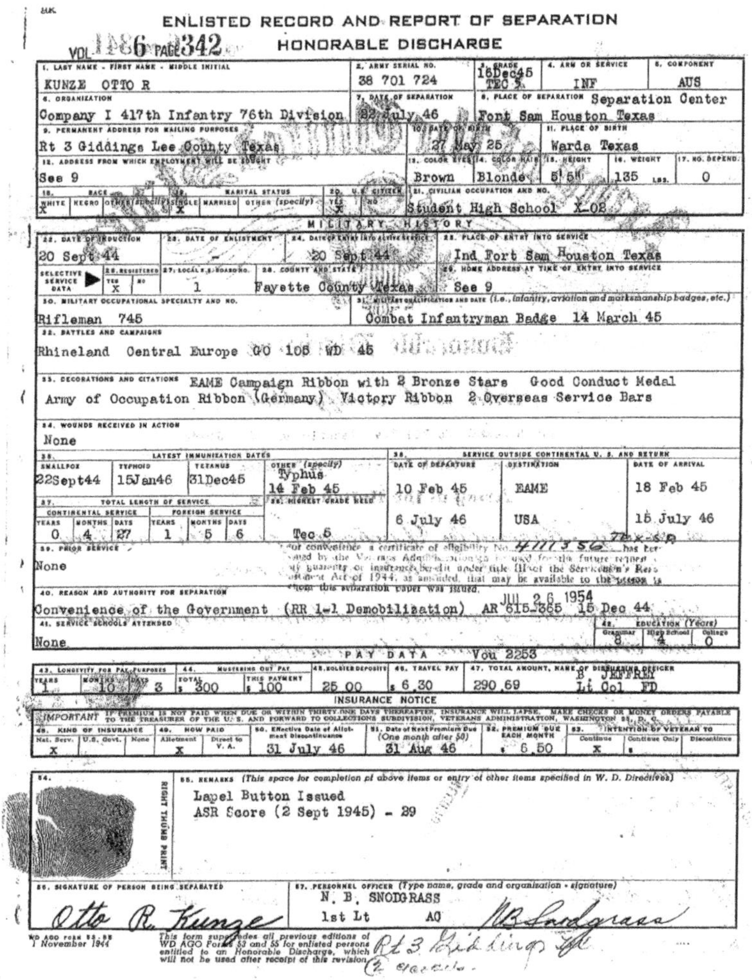

ENLISTED RECORD AND REPORT OF SEPARATION
HONORABLE DISCHARGE

VOL 1486 PAGE 342

1. LAST NAME - FIRST NAME - MIDDLE INITIAL: KUNZE OTTO R
2. ARMY SERIAL NO.: 38 701 724
3. GRADE: TEC 5 (16Dec45)
4. ARM OR SERVICE: INF
5. COMPONENT: AUS
6. ORGANIZATION: Company I 417th Infantry 76th Division
7. DATE OF SEPARATION: 22 July 46
8. PLACE OF SEPARATION: Separation Center Fort Sam Houston Texas
9. PERMANENT ADDRESS FOR MAILING PURPOSES: Rt 3 Giddings Lee County Texas
10. DATE OF BIRTH: 27 May 25
11. PLACE OF BIRTH: Warda Texas
12. ADDRESS FROM WHICH EMPLOYMENT WILL BE SOUGHT: See 9
13. COLOR EYES: Brown
14. COLOR HAIR: Blonde
15. HEIGHT: 5' 5"
16. WEIGHT: 135 LBS.
17. NO. DEPEND.: 0
18. RACE: WHITE X
19. MARITAL STATUS: SINGLE X
20. U.S. CITIZEN: YES X
21. CIVILIAN OCCUPATION AND NO.: Student High School X-02

MILITARY HISTORY

22. DATE OF INDUCTION: 20 Sept 44
23. DATE OF ENLISTMENT: -
24. DATE OF ENTRY INTO ACTIVE SERVICE: 20 Sept 44
25. PLACE OF ENTRY INTO SERVICE: Ind Fort Sam Houston Texas
SELECTIVE SERVICE DATA: 26. REGISTERED: YES X
27. LOCAL S.S. BOARD NO.: 1
28. COUNTY AND STATE: Fayette County Texas
29. HOME ADDRESS AT TIME OF ENTRY INTO SERVICE: See 9
30. MILITARY OCCUPATIONAL SPECIALTY AND NO.: Rifleman 745
31. MILITARY QUALIFICATION AND DATE (i.e., infantry, aviation and marksmanship badges, etc.): Combat Infantryman Badge 14 March 45
32. BATTLES AND CAMPAIGNS: Rhineland Central Europe GO 105 WD 45
33. DECORATIONS AND CITATIONS: EAME Campaign Ribbon with 2 Bronze Stars Good Conduct Medal Army of Occupation Ribbon (Germany) Victory Ribbon 2 Overseas Service Bars
34. WOUNDS RECEIVED IN ACTION: None

35. LATEST IMMUNIZATION DATES

SMALLPOX	TYPHOID	TETANUS	OTHER (specify)
22Sept44	15Jan46	31Dec45	Typhus 14 Feb 45

36. SERVICE OUTSIDE CONTINENTAL U.S. AND RETURN

DATE OF DEPARTURE	DESTINATION	DATE OF ARRIVAL
10 Feb 45	EAME	18 Feb 45
6 July 46	USA	15 July 46

37. TOTAL LENGTH OF SERVICE

CONTINENTAL SERVICE YEARS	MONTHS	DAYS	FOREIGN SERVICE YEARS	MONTHS	DAYS
0	4	27	1	5	6

38. HIGHEST GRADE HELD: Tec 5
39. PRIOR SERVICE: None

For convenience a certificate of eligibility No. 4111356 has been issued by the Veterans Administration to be used for the future request of any guaranty or insurance benefit under title III of the Servicemen's Readjustment Act of 1944, as amended, that may be available to the person to whom this separation paper was issued.
JUL 26 1954

40. REASON AND AUTHORITY FOR SEPARATION: Convenience of the Government (RR 1-1 Demobilization) AR 615-365 15 Dec 44
41. SERVICE SCHOOLS ATTENDED: None
42. EDUCATION (Years): Grammar 8 High School 4 College 0

PAY DATA Vou 2253

43. LONGEVITY FOR PAY PURPOSES: YEARS 1 MONTHS 10 DAYS 3
44. MUSTERING OUT PAY: TOTAL $ 300 THIS PAYMENT $ 100
45. SOLDIER DEPOSITS: 25 00
46. TRAVEL PAY: $ 6 30
47. TOTAL AMOUNT, NAME OF DISBURSING OFFICER: 290 69 B. JEFFREY Lt Col FD

INSURANCE NOTICE

IMPORTANT: IF PREMIUM IS NOT PAID WHEN DUE OR WITHIN THIRTY-ONE DAYS THEREAFTER, INSURANCE WILL LAPSE. MAKE CHECKS OR MONEY ORDERS PAYABLE TO THE TREASURER OF THE U.S. AND FORWARD TO COLLECTIONS SUBDIVISION, VETERANS ADMINISTRATION, WASHINGTON 25, D. C.

48. KIND OF INSURANCE: Nat. Serv. X
49. HOW PAID: Allotment X
50. Effective Date of Allotment Discontinuance: 31 July 46
51. Date of Next Premium Due (One month after 50): 31 Aug 46
52. PREMIUM DUE EACH MONTH: $ 6.50
53. INTENTION OF VETERAN TO: Continue X

54. RIGHT THUMB PRINT
55. REMARKS (This space for completion of above items or entry of other items specified in W. D. Directives): Lapel Button Issued; ASR Score (2 Sept 1945) - 39
56. SIGNATURE OF PERSON BEING SEPARATED: Otto R. Kunze
57. PERSONNEL OFFICER (Type name, grade and organization - signature): N. B. SNODGRASS 1st Lt AG

WD AGO FORM 53-55, 1 November 1944. This form supersedes all previous editions of WD AGO Forms 53 and 55 for enlisted persons entitled to an Honorable Discharge, which will not be used after receipt of this revision.

Fig. 26. Enlisted Record and Report of Separation for T/5 Otto R. Kunze.

A few months later, I received a Presidential Citation (Fig. 27) through the mail from Harry S. Truman, then President of the United States. It expresses the gratitude and appreciation of a grateful Nation for the leadership and services rendered in World War II. The personal qualities that served the Country so well in war were now to be used to further exalt our Country in peace.

TEC 5 OTTO R. KUNZE 38701724

To you who answered the call of your country and served in its Armed Forces to bring about the total defeat of the enemy, I extend the heartfelt thanks of a grateful Nation. As one of the Nation's finest, you undertook the most severe task one can be called upon to perform. Because you demonstrated the fortitude, resourcefulness and calm judgment necessary to carry out that task, we now look to you for leadership and example in further exalting our country in peace.

Harry Truman

THE WHITE HOUSE

Fig. 27. A Presidential Citation from Harry S. Truman, then President of the United States, to Tec. 5 Otto R. Kunze 38701724 expressing the appreciation of a grateful Nation for the leadership and services rendered in World War II. The personal qualities that served the country so well in war were now to be used to further exalt our country in peace.

Just recently I had my Ford 150 pickup truck serviced at a local dealership. A woman came into the waiting room to check the coffee. She spoke with an accent, so I addressed her in German. She came back with the comment "No compree, I speak French." After a few more remarks, I found that she was Belgian and had grown up in Brussels. A brief conversation followed in which I told her of my participation in World War II. Her eyes beamed with surprise, and she burst out with "You liberated my Country!" It was not very long, and she had told nearly every employee in the place "He liberated my Country." Her Father worked in the Belgian Stock Exchange and was shot by the Nazis. She really made me feel that I had fought for a cause, and she expressed her gratitude for my efforts to everyone in sight.

I had been in the military service for twenty-two months. My health was excellent. During my service period, I had no tooth-aches, no teeth filled and saw dentists only at physical checkups. My Immunization Register shows that I received vaccinations as follows: one for smallpox, three for typhoid, three for tetanus, two for typhus and several others that are not readable. I made no special trips to first aid stations and carried no medications with me. The journey was a little frightening because I did not feel to be adequately pre-pared for little physical ailments. My most memorable need for assis-tance was for the body lice that I picked up in Paris, France, while traveling from Le Mans to Namur, Belgium. I was able to fulfill all the assignments given to me on the duty roster.

I was processed out of the army and given bus tickets to Giddings, Texas. The trip was made with only one bus change. There were no direct buses to Giddings. From Giddings, I had to "thumb" my way to Warda, my home. A stranger picked me up and dropped me off on Highway 77 about three hundred yards from my home. I slung the duffel bag strap across my shoulder one last time and made my final march with it. I was greeted by my Mother, and we shed some tears of happiness and joy together. What a blessing from God to have brought me back safe, well and alive. My Dad soon came in from the fields and also welcomed me home.

The next morning, we had a home cooked breakfast of bacon and eggs, which I thoroughly enjoyed. After returning thanks and a moment of silence, my Dad said, "Well, I'm going to fix fence today." I nodded my approval with an okay and then sat around the house all day waiting for someone to tell me what to do. The next morning, we had another excellent breakfast. After returning thanks, my Dad said, "I will continue fixing fence today." I nodded my approval and said, "That's fine." I spent the day at home waiting for a duty call, but none came. On the third morning, my Mother served another delightful breakfast. After returning thanks, my Father quietly said, "I'm going to repair more fence today." My reply was "Dad, I'm going with you."

Postscript

After being discharged from the army, Otto Kunze entered Texas A&M University in the fall of 1946. His choice of disciplines was Agricultural Engineering. In 1950, he graduated with a Bachelor of Science Degree as an outstanding student in the College of Agriculture. He proceeded to Iowa State College (now Iowa State University) to earn a Master of Science Degree in the same discipline. The GI Bill for Veterans paid for most of this education. In the fall of 1961, he proceeded to Michigan State University to earn a PhD degree. His savings bonds, purchased during the war, helped to finance his doctoral program. He did his PhD research on rice grains. In the year 2000, the American Society of Agricultural Engineers recognized his research as one of the "Outstanding Agricultural Engineering Achievements of the 20th Century."

After receiving his MS degree from Iowa State University in the spring of 1951, Otto married Alice Ruth Eifert, a local girl, in his home community. The marriage was blessed with four children: Glenn, Allen, Charles and Karen. In the fall of 1971, Glenn was called into the military service. He proceeded through basic training before he was shipped overseas to Europe. He was stationed at a missile base near Neubrücke, Germany. Glenn was the third-generation Kunze to follow in his Father's and Grandfather's footsteps to do military service in Europe. Glenn's Great Great, Grandfather left Germany because his area of residence was always engaged in war.

References Cited

A Veteran's Presentation (Televised), Memorial Day Program, Anonymous, 2004. Washington D. C.

Buchenwald Memorial (Leaflet) 2000. Text by Ursula Haertl; Photographics by Gabriele Krynitzki, Naomi Tereza Salmon; Graphics by Hinz&Kunz. Published by Buch- und Kunstdruckerei Kessler GmbH, Weimer, Germany.

World War II—A Personal History, 76th Infantry Division. Bye, Bill Sgt. 2005. pp 207–211 in *417th Infantry Regiment WW-II Historical Events* by Jay Martin Hamilton Lt. C. (Retired). Published by Mike's Copy, 924 South Central, Medford, Oregon, 97501.

Encyclopedia Britannica, 1965. William Benton—Publisher, Volume 3. Warren E. Preece - Editor; Howard E. Kasch – Managing Editor. Chicago, USA.

417th Infantry Regiment WW-II, Historical Events. Hamilton, Jay Martin, Lt. C. (Retired). Primary Author and Editor. 2005. Published by Mike's Copy, 924 South Central, Medford, Oregon 97501.

We Ripened Fast; The Unofficial History of the Seventy-Sixth Infantry Division. Hutnik, Joseph J., 1st Lt., 1946. Board of Directors of the Seventy-Sixth Infantry Division Officers Association. Copyright 56-32410, Baltimore, Maryland.

Kittleson, Carl J. 2005. As reported in a tape transcription in *417 Infantry Regiment WW-II Historical Events*, pp 213-218. Published by Mike's Copy, 924 South Central, Medford, Oregon 97501. See Appendix C.

Knight, James R. http://76thdivision.com/jrknight417L.html. Company L, 4l7th Regiment by James Richard Knight. See Appendix B.

Loreley-Lied. Brentano, Clemens – 1800, originated character; Heine, Heinrich – 1822, poems author; Silcher, Fredrich – 1837, wrote music. Reprinted from http://www.tyskopgaver.dk/lorelei1.htm. Mark Twain translation. Reprinted from http://www.loreley.de/loreley/marctwai.htm. See Appendix A.

Moes, Eberhard, (undated), Taschen Atlas, Kraft durch Freude, Amt für Reisen, Wandern und Urlaub, Berlin; Gesamtherstellung: Georg Westermann, Braunschweig, Deutsches Reich.

SS *Alhambra Echo*—Souvenir Edition, 1946. Published on board the SS *Alhambra Victory* while en route to the United States. Editor: Mr. M. Ackerman, Edition No. 8, July 14. See Appendix D.

Service Prayer Book, Weber, Edmund W. (Editor), 1941. Authorized by the Army and Navy Commission, Evangelical Lutheran Synod of Missouri, Ohio and Other States. Columbia Printing Co., Chicago.

Appendix A

Loreley-Lied (The Loreley)

Loreley-Lied von Heinrich Heine und Friedrich Silcher -
Ich weiß nicht was soll es bedeuten

Ich weiß nicht was soll es bedeuten
Dass ich so traurig bin;
Ein Märchen aus alten Zeiten,
Das kommt mir nicht aus dem Sinn.

Die Luft ist kühl und es dunkelt,
Und ruhig fließt der Rhein;
Der Gipfel des Berges funkelt
Im Abendsonnenschein.

Die schönste Jungfrau sitzet
Dort oben wunderbar;
Ihr goldnes Geschmeide blitzet,
Sie kämmt ihr goldenes Haar.

Sie kämmt es mit goldenem Kamme
Und singt ein Lied dabei;
Das hat eine wundersame,
Gewaltige Melodei.

Den Schiffer im kleinen Schiffe
Ergreift es mit wildem Weh;
Er schaut nicht die Felsenriffe,
Er schaut nur hinauf in die Höh'.

Ich glaube, die Wellen verschlingen
Am Ende Schiffer und Kahn;
Und das hat mit ihrem Singen
Die Lore-Ley getan.

The Loreley

I cannot divine what it meaneth
This haunting nameless pain:
A tale of the bygone ages
Weeps brooding through my brain.
The faint air cools in the gloaming,
And peaceful flows the Rhine,
The thirsty summits are drinking
The sunset's flooding wine.

The loviest maiden is sitting
High-thrones in yon blue air,
Her golden jewels are shining
She combs her golden hair;
She combs with a comb that is golden,
And sings a weerd refrain;
That steeps in a deadly enchantment
The listener's ravished brain.

The doomed in his drifting shallop
Is tranced with the sad sweet tone,
He sees not the yawning breakers.
He sees but the maid alone.
The pittiless billows engulf him!
So perish sailor and bark,
And this, with her baleful singing,
Is the Loreley's gruesome work.

Translated by Mark Twain

Reprinted from http//www.loreley.de/loreley/marctwai.htm

Appendix B

Company L, 417ᵗʰ Regiment
By James Richard Knight

I went overseas as a BAR man with the 76ᵗʰ infantry Division, 417th regiment, Company L. Of all of the actions in which we took part, two are indelibly etched in my memory. The first is our assault crossing of the Sauer River and the second is the action which resulted in my capture.

We had just finished up in the Bulge when we were trucked south to Echternach, Luxembourg. This city is on the bank of the Sauer River which separates Luxembourg from Germany. The Siegfried Line starts just across the river so we faced not only crossing a swift flowing river at flood tide, but also the ferocious defense provided by camouflaged pill boxes and fortresses.

We met flat-bed trucks about a mile west of the river. These trucks carried wooden scow-like boats that were stacked on the trucks, one nested into the other. Each squad carried its own clumsy, heavy boat to the edge of the river cliff.

By this time it was dusk and we could barely see the river which was several hundred yards below us. But we could see the opposing German cliff which loomed even higher above the river. I suppose this was supposed to be a surprise assault, but we started receiving artillery fire even before we started our descent, which turned out to be a terrible fiasco.

Our company, and I suppose, other companies to either side, started down but didn't get very far before boats broke loose, banging into trees, with guys run over by boats, crushed into trees by boats, screams, star shells (flares) turning dusk into day. It was a scene out of Dante. Many were wounded.

By this time I was officially the assistant squad leader, but since the squad leader had just shot himself (S. I. W.), the boat was mine. Somehow, my squad got to the water's edge with only bumps and bruises but now we're faced with crossing this river, under fire, with flares that made us feel naked, and with no one who knew anything about boats. I saw that the river was moving fast from left to right. The boat came equipped with six oars so I put four on the left side and two on the right to somehow keep the boat from being turned to the right and heading down stream.

We shoved off and paddled through a hellish scene. Boats went by us overturned, guys in the water yelling. German 20 MM automatic weapons rounds flying everywhere (and exploding on contact).

I could see that we were moving much faster to the right than forward but our boat front was pretty much pointed towards the far shore.

As we got closer I saw that there were bushes in the water close to shore and I told the two guys in front of the boat to grab them and hold on. One held on but the other jumped over the front to pull us in. Sadly, these bushes turned out to be tree tops, and I had my first casualty of the action - The river was at flood stage.

The boats were so dispersed that only our boat and one other (from another company) were close when we landed. As is usual, we had been given no plan or other instructions so we were on our own.

Enemy fire was heavy and now included small arms fire. I could barely make out a draw to our left and I had my squad to go in that direction. We had no more casualties until we hit mines about halfway up the draw. One of my guys was beyond help and several were hit but remained ambulatory. The mine explosions told Jerry where we were which resulted in our being pinned down for quite some time.

We eventually reached the crest of the cliff, found a position with some defilade and stayed there for the balance of the night. At dawn we found other elements of our company and prepared to deal with the Siegfried Line.

For the first few days our company attacked pill boxes during daylight hours -with heavy casualties, too heavy to continue in this fashion. We had crossed the river with full platoons which were now decimated. The pill boxes and fortresses had connecting and cross fires. We were hit by everything the enemy had and from multiple directions.

We were forced to hold up during the day and try to advance at night. This worked much better and we fought our way to the Prum River but casualties continued to take their toll and our Battalion was finally relieved because there were too few of us left to be an effective force. At the end of the action the entire platoon numbered eleven men. Our regiment received a Presidential Citation for this action. (see copy enclosed). *(Original citation reprinted from alternate source on the following page.)*

GO 19

GENERAL ORDERS} No. 19

WAR DEPARTMENT
WASHINGTON 25, D. C., 10 February 1947

	Section
TERRE HAUTE ORDNANCE DEPOT, TERRE HAUTE, INDIANA—Section V, WD General Orders 146, 1946, rescinded_____	I
BATTLE HONORS—Citation of unit_____	II

I__TERRE HAUTE ORDNANCE DEPOT, TERRE HAUTE, INDIANA.—Section V, WD General Orders 146, 1946, is rescinded.
[AG 680.1 (26 Dec 46)]

II__BATTLE HONORS.—As authorized by Executive Order 9396 (sec. I, WD Bul. 22, 1943), superseding Executive Order 9075 (sec. III, WD Bul. 11, 1942), the following unit is cited by the War Department under the provisions of section IV, WD Circular 333, 1943, in the name of the President of the United States as public evidence of deserved honor and distinction. The citation reads as follows:

The *417th Regimental Combat Team*, consisting of the 417th Infantry Regiment, 901st Field Artillery Battalion; Company C, 801st Engineer Combat Battalion; Company C, 801st Medical Battalion; and Company B, 160th Engineer Combat Battalion, is cited for outstanding performance of duty in action against the enemy from 7 to 12 February 1945 in the vicinity of Echternach, Luxembourg. Members of this combat team led an assault across the swollen Sauer River into one of the deepest portions of the Siegfried Line. The river was at flood stage, the current so swift that attempts by engineers to erect a footbridge proved futile, and the crossing had to be made in assault boats. The alerted enemy covered the area with heavy artillery, mortar, and machine-gun fire. Many of the boats were overturned before reaching the far shore and heavy casualties were suffered. Despite all difficulties, the major portion of the 1st Battalion, 417th Infantry Regiment, succeeded in making the crossing on the first night. Under heavy fire, members of this battalion scaled the muddy, steep, pillbox infested cliffs, whose every approach was heavily sown with mine fields, and succeeded in capturing the high wooded ground near the river bank. Two strong infantry counterattacks, supported by armor, were launched by the enemy, but both were repulsed after bitter encounters. Although this was the combat team's first engagement in combat, the 1st Battalion was the only unit in this vicinity to reach its objective on its initial assault and hold the ground gained. By similar aggressive action, the remainder of the 417th Infantry Regiment made the river crossing on the second and third nights and established contact with the initial force. The swiftly flowing river prevented supplies being crossed by boat and it became necessary to supply isolated groups by air. Despite violent enemy attempts to dislodge it, the combat team held tenaciously to the bridgehead it had wrested within the Siegfried Line and secured a strong foothold, which facilitated the movement of other forces across the river and insured the success of an operation of major importance. In its initial appearance in combat and in the face of conditions which at times appeared prohibitive, the *417th Regimental Combat Team* displayed outstanding heroism, determination, and an indomitable fighting spirit, which reflect great credit on all participants and are in keeping with the highest traditions of the armed forces of the United States.

BY ORDER OF THE SECRETARY OF WAR:

OFFICIAL:
EDWARD F. WITSELL
Major General
The Adjutant General
AGO 1658B—Feb. 716118°—47

DWIGHT D. EISENHOWER
Chief of Staff

U. S. GOVERNMENT PRINTING OFFICE: 1947

A month or so later, we were dug in on a ridge line, having pushed Jerry and company off the same ridge line the previous night with only desultory fire and no casualties in my squad.

Word came down that we were moving to another sector, and indeed another company from our battalion came to replace us.

We slogged along a couple miles to the south and then turned east on a road that ran through a valley with high hills on each side. Pretty soon we came upon some blown up jeeps and a few half trucks from the 10th Armored Division, and we all smelled trouble.

L Company dug in on a wood line to the left of the road. Facing us about 500 yards down the hill was a town that turned out to be Schmitten. There was no defilade between the wood line and the first house so I was amazed when L Company was told to "march fire" down the hill and into the town. I told my squad to handle the rifle fire but hit the ground as soon as the first MG42 opened up - and then to get back to the wood line as best they could. Needless to say, the attack never really got off the ground, but still L Company took a number of casualties.

By now anybody with half a mind should have known by the 10th armored vehicles and the intensity of the fire when we tried to "march fire," that the enemy was sizeable and stubborn. It turned out that it was an SS battalion fighting an organized retreat while inflicting as many casualties as they could.

Nevertheless, the second platoon of L Company, my platoon, was told to circle around Schmitten through the hills and take the town on the same road, beyond Schmitten, which turned out to be Dorfweil.

Two noisy tanks were sent with us so the element of surprise was gone. But still we took Dorfweil with light casualties because the town was lightly defended and being used principally for their casualties and supplies.

By the time I got my second squad dug in on the right side of the road on the approaches to town it was pitch dark. Another squad was on the other side of the road and the third squad was in the buildings behind us. About one hour later, all hell broke loose. A couple of light artillery pieces opened up, beyond rifle range, and the hills both left and right poured small arms fire down at us.

We started taking casualties right away so I pulled my squad into the house directly behind us as did the squad on the other side of the road. From that point on, it was a wild melee of shooting from windows, jumping fences into the next yard - at one point, my assistant squad leader and I were lying on the steps leading to a basement and firing at shadows appearing over the fence. I particularly remember that position for a couple of reasons. First, a grenade landed between us, exploded, blew us out of the stairwell but otherwise did no damage to us. It was evidently a concussion grenade. And secondly, I remember believing that I hit a couple of heads coming over the fence on my left and sadly it turned out that one of them was our own medic. I found this out after we were captured and we were told to pick up the bodies, both theirs and ours.

I kept my squad together as best I could. Seven of us and four or five from other squads ended up in the last house on our side of the road. Some of this group were wounded and four of my guys didn't make it to the last house. In any event, they surrounded the house and told us to come out, which we did.

When they got us all out of the houses, they lined us up against a wall. This was shortly after Malmedy and I was ready to bolt if that guy nursing the MG42 started looking serious. But the moment passed and we were marched east under guard for several hours. From that day, we could hear the firing a little west of us but whenever it got closer, we were marched to the next town east.

After almost two weeks of this, someone forgot to tell our guards to move us. Incoming artillery fire drove our guards, only four of them inside the building with us, so we made quiet plans to jump them when small arms fire indicated that our troops closed in. We accomplished this, took our guards prisoner and got back to our own lines.

Here are three names of those captured with me.

Timothy Gleason -Atlanta, Georgia
Charles Albert -Queens, New York
Andrew Rochina -Canaisie, New York

Our Lieutenant was a raw replacement and was not a factor in this incident.

The two tanks were also captured, one was completely disabled and the other was taken over and used by the SS troops.

It goes without saying that I was extremely lucky, receiving only scratches from enemy fire several times, easily patched up by the company medic.

However, after my discharge I immediately began to lose a lot of weight and have stomach pain which I toughed out for some months before turning myself into Hines Veteran Hospital where over a period of some weeks with many tests, I was diagnosed with ulcerative colitis. I attributed this to the sudden absence of danger after living through it daily for such a long period of time.

James Richard Knight
852 Talcott
Lemont, Illinois 60439
(630) 243-6195
Reprinted from
http://www.76thdivision.com/jrknight417L.html

Appendix C

Company I,
417th Infantry Regiment,
76th Infantry Division, US Army
By Carl J. Kittleson

Carl J. Kittleson, 37298297, Co I, 417th Inf Regt
76th Inf Div, US Army
Tape Transcription

"Those last couple of years at Mankato (Teacher's College) were kind of stressful, because of what was happening in the world. The war in Europe was getting worse all the time, and a lot of my classmates volunteered and a lot of us were drafted. We were concerned about that a great deal. A group of us had meetings regularly with some faculty members and some ministers locally, to discuss what we should do. All of us had really serious objections to learning how to kill somebody, but I was the only one in that group that stood by my belief as a conscientious objector, and went into the service as a conscientious objector. The others all got commissions, and good deals in the service but more about that when we come to the Army segment of these annals.

The summer after my senior year, I was scheduled to be drafted in August. I was playing in a group called the Cleats Cavaliers; this was Cletus Fredricks from Madison Lake. Don Olson played bass and accordion with that group, and every Saturday night we played a job at the Bloody Bucket nightclub in St. James. This was kind of a rowdy place, and bootleggers were there regularly, but we never had any problems. It was a regular job, playing every Saturday night. The three of us, Don Olson, Buck Wearig from Madison Lake, and myself decided that before we were drafted we would take a trip together. So we took off right after the job one night and we toured the west in Don's Ford. We went to the Black Hills, the Badlands, to Yellowstone, and Denver. Then we headed back, and we got back to St. James just in time to start the job, on time, the next Saturday night. That was quite a week; we covered a lot of ground in a week. And shortly after that, on August 20th I was drafted. So, we'll talk about the Army next.

I forgot to tell you that before Anita left for California, we became engaged. I remember I saved up and spent $32 for the engagement ring. It doesn't sound like much, but it was more then than it is now (more about that later). You have to remember that when I was drafted, I was drafted as a Conscientious Objector. And to be classified that way, you had to submit a lot of paperwork, and I did that. It wasn't easy for a while, I was sent to basic training with a quartermaster unit, which basically is a non-combatant unit. There were several CO's in that group, David Landmark and others. One night they called an alert, and we were all supposed to go down to the Company Headquarters and draw out a rifle, and take a post somewhere and we refused to draw out a rifle, and they didn't understand. They didn't know what to do with us. But I have to give them credit. They made a real effort to understand our point of view, and nobody was harsh or belligerent about it, except maybe some of our colleagues. After basic training in the quartermaster corps, during which I never did qualify on a rifle, I was assigned to Special Services at Camp Lee, Virginia, which is where I did my Basic Training. I had a real cushy job, I should have just stayed with it. I put on a Sunday afternoon musical for visitors in the service club. And I conducted a men's glee club (it never got over 10 guys) and I copied instrumental parts for a radio show band that we had. I tried out for a Chaplains Assistant job, which meant I had to play the organ for the hymns. I played the organ one Sunday, and I couldn't play them fast enough for the Chaplain that was leading the Service. He got kind of angry with me, and I never did make Chaplain's Assistant. I had a friend who was a Chaplain's Assistant, George Anderson; we went out to dinner frequently in Petersburg, VA. As more and more of my college friends were being killed in action, or killed in training accidents, the more I felt guilty about this Conscientious Objector thing. Besides, I wasn't using my education much. So I applied to the Secretary of War to change my status from CO to 1A. He did that, and I was almost immediately transferred to the infantry at Ft. Jackson, South Carolina. I trained with the Infantry for a long time. I earned Sergeant's stripes during that time. I had a buddy, Bob House, was his name, and he later became an official in the National MENC (Music Educator's National Conference). He was a cello player. When we were in Camp Lee, he used to play the cello afternoons for the Sunday afternoon musical that I put on. We'd get together nights after training. We'd meet at the PX, get a pint of ice cream and a bottle of Coke, sit there and talk. He later applied for the Army band director's school, which he made. Before he left there he wanted to get married. I forgot to tell you, before I left Camp Lee I got a "Dear John" letter from Anita, and she was going to marry that pilot that was out there flying the planes that she was building. Isn't that romantic? So I sold my engagement ring to Bob House for $32, and he was married while we were at Ft. Jackson.

I trained in Ft. Jackson with the 106th Division, it was an infantry division. The training was tough. Endless hours taking the rifle apart, and putting it back together, long marches in the heat. A guy with a truck load of watermelons would follow our column. And we'd take a break and he'd sell a bunch of watermelons while we were taking our break. These long, long hikes. I remember a guy in our outfit. He was the slowest guy in the outfit, and his name was "quick". He was a Tennessee hillbilly. He'd have a terrible time on these long walks. Sarge would come up to him and say, "how ya doin' quick?" And quick would say "Oh Sarge I think I could make it if I could take my shoes off." But of course that was forebodden. While I was in South Carolina I often went to Columbia, SC, which was the closest town to Ft. Jackson, and I often went there for Sunday evening services and became very friendly with a gal by the name of Marge Baker. Her folks were missionaries in Brazil. She spoke Portuguese, but she spoke good English too. But, we became quite close.

The more I slogged it out with the 106th Division, the more I thought that I was not using my College education for anything, and I ought to apply for Officer School or something else that would use it (but I didn't want to be an Infantry Officer, oh Lord!) So I applied to the Air Force, and was admitted, surprisingly enough. They sent me to Miami Beach for assignment; it was a sort of reception center. I remember right outside of my hotel room there was banana tree. It must have been out of season, I never saw any good bananas on it. Having come from hot South Carolina to Miami Beach, there was no great change; it was still a lot warmer than it is in Minnesota. I was in Miami Beach from Thanksgiving to just after New Years. I remember on Christmas Eve, or mebey it was New Years Eve, I had KP duty. So by the time I got off KP everybody else was in town already having a good time. But I went downtown anyway, by myself, went to a little bar, and they had a piano in the bar. I sat down and started to play the piano. (I had some good piano lessons from Ed Eckley at Mankato State and I knew a few tunes so I sat down and played). A couple that was there enjoyed it I guess, and they bought me a drink, and that was the extent of my celebration. Then they sent us to Morningside College in Sioux City, Iowa for our college training. This was the first phase of Air Force training for flying personnel. So, I was back in college. The training in Sioux City was quite rigorous. We had physical training every morning, but it was a pretty spirited group. We sang when we marched anywhere from one class to another, morale was very high. The classes were kind of tough, meteorology and quite a bit of math, it wasn't easy. They had a little band there and the conductor, Jerry was strictly an amateur, and he knew that I had more training than him so he turned the band over to me, and I conducted a concert while we were there. That was as close as I had been to Mankato since I went into the service so I got home quite often. Weekends sometimes we'd stay in Sioux City. They had a nice ballroom there, Kay Kaiser played there one night, some of the big bands came through. But it wasn't to be, I guess. This was in 1944, it was at a point in the war where the War Department decided that they didn't really need new Air Force personnel, what they needed was more ground troops. So, all of us who had transferred from ground troops to the Air Force were sent back to the kind of outfit that we came from. It was a terrible blow. Gosh. I was sent back to the infantry, to the 76th Division, which was training in LaCrosse. When I joined them, they had just returned from winter maneuvers in northern Michigan, but they weren't leaving for overseas (I forgot to mention that the day that the word came down that we were all going back was April Fool's Day, how appropriate). When I got to the 76th Division, they didn't quite know what to do with me, because I had a Buck Sergeant's rating, and they already had their rating's assigned – their table of organization was all filled up, and I was just an extra burden for them to carry. They tried to demote me several times, but they were unsuccessful because the Colonel, the Regimental Commander, liked the band that we had. The band that we had, the Special Service non-com was Pete Seizinger, not important except that he later became director of the Guthrie Theater for quite a few years. But he wanted to start a band, so he started a band and I got my horns sent from home (I guess I picked them up on a weekend pass). But we had a little band. It started out with 6-8 guys. It grew, gradually, until we had a full dance band. We had 4 saxes, 3 trumpets, 2 trombones, guitar, bass, drums and keyboard, so it was a big band. We used to play USO dances in surrounding towns, LaCrosse, Sparta. But the Colonel heard us on several occasions, and he really liked the band, so he would never let them strip me of my Sergeant stripes. We played for a lot of Company parties, and USO dances, it was a lot of fun. We had an arranger that was a big time arranger, a professional arranger, Don Brown was his name. I think he arranged for Les Brown. He wrote some beautiful arrangements for us. But, it was more foot slogging, long hikes, maneuvers, bivouacs. We played for retreat ceremonies every night, and dances on the weekends, so it wasn't all that bad.

We were slated to go overseas late fall of that year, 1944. The last furlough that I had before I went overseas I fell in love. Madly in love with a gal by the name of Vie Westerburgh. I proposed to her, and she turned me down. She didn't want to wait for a guy that was going to get killed in the war, I guess. I was heartbroken. We shipped out. We went to Ft. Dix, and then we were shipped out from New York on a troop ship. I was seasick and broken-hearted; it was a miserable trip over. Guys kept telling me to get off my knees. It was Thanksgiving Day when we shipped out, so we were in Southern England for the Holidays.

We were there for a couple months, and the band played for some parties. I went to a USO dance, and I met Pauline. I took her home after the dance, and we got to know each other a little bit. She was a very religious person, I didn't know it then, but she was a member of the Jehovah's Witnesses, but I knew that she was a very sincere Christian gal and I thought "she would never treat me like that gal at home", and we kept up a relationship as long as I was in England, and then we wrote letters back and forth while I was in and out of action. I think it was February when we shipped out and went to Belgium. We had to spend a night or two in an open field, huddled around a bonfire before they had any accommodations for us. We went on patrols, but there weren't any German's around and we didn't have any confrontations until we went to Luxembourg. In Luxembourg we went to the town of Echternach. Echternach was a village on the Sauer river, which was the border between Luxembourg and Germany, and the Germans had built fortifications along the German side of the river, concrete pill-boxes, and had been sitting there for years. As soon as they knew we were coming they zeroed in with their 88's, which were a frightening kind of artillery. They made a screaming sound when they came in – it was really frightening. We came to Echternach in the afternoon, and we dug foxholes in a hillside that was between us and the riverbank, which protected us there. But that night was the most terrifying night of my life. It was awful. They were really ready for us, and we had to cross the river in boats. The engineers brought the boats down to the riverbank and our platoon sergeant would load the guys into the boats and send us across. Well, half the time, the artillery would hit the boats, and he would have dead and wounded all around him. By the time we came down to get into the boats, he lost his mind completely. He had gone berserk, and just ran screaming toward the rear. I don't know what ever happened to him, but he was mad a hatter that night. Our boat got across alright, I had about half of my squad with me, and we started up a hill. It was terribly eerie. Shells would explode, you'd have flashes light lightning, once in a while a phosphorus shell would go off and light up the sky. It was a weary, pale kind of light. We found a trail, and started up a hill toward what seemed like a cabin ahead of us. When we got to the cabin, there were dead bodies stretched out on a big table-some of our guys that had gone in front had evidently run into landmines, which exploded about waist high, exploding all the shells in their ammunition belts and they were literally cut in two. It is hard to talk about this. But we eventually found the rest of my company in an abandoned farm house. We spent the rest of the night there. A couple of patrols went out, but didn't come back. In the ensuing days we captured several concrete pill-boxes. They were manned by demoralized troops that must have been foreign captive soldiers. They were ready to give up. We would holler for the German's to come out, and usually they would come out with hands up. One time our BAR man (Browning automatic rifle – it was built like a rifle, but shot like a machine gun) was standing next to a foxhole outside one of the pill-boxes. When we hollered for the German's to surrender, a German soldier popped out of the foxhole right next to him and scared him. He fell over backwards right on top of the German soldier. I don't know which one was more scared. But that same night, we underwent some sniper attacks. I dived into a bomb crater; it was about as big as a kitchen, and 7-8 feet deep. When it started to get dark, and I wasn't sure whether the company had taken the pillbox in front of me, or the one behind me, so I didn't know which way to go. So I poked my head up to see if I could tell what to do, and the German sniper shot a tracer bullet right over my head, so I ducked down again. Every time I stuck my head up to take a look, there was a sniper bullet passing overhead. So I waited until it got dark, then I ran as fast as I could, and found my company.

We were isolated because the engineers were not able to put a bridge across the river yet to get tanks and mechanized equipment across the river. So we existed on K-rations for almost two weeks. They had to drop K-rations to us from a light plane that was used for artillery observations normally, and they would drop big bags of food in a big open field. The problem was, we were on one side of that big open field and the Germans were on the other side, and sometimes it was questionable who was going to get that food. Some of us survived, a lot of us didn't. It took us 13 days to move ahead 1 mile, then we were relieved. It was such a relief to see those tanks come across the river and come up to relieve us. We went to a rest area, and were quartered in a barn with straw mattresses. It was alright, it was warm. They took us by truck to a captured school building that had showers, so we had our first bath in weeks. During the rest periods I was writing letters to Pauline, and she would write to me. I asked her to marry me, and she agreed, so we went to work on all the paperwork that was necessary.

Most of our action after that time was to follow Patton's armored column. We were maybe a day or so behind his troops cleaning up leftover pockets that he left behind. I remember in one small town we really had it made. We took over a nice house, and the guy had a Hi-Fi record player, they didn't have stereo yet, but they had a Hi-Fi record player with some nice Brahms recordings, and a box of cigars, so we had a nice evening. One of the pockets that we ran into was a small village that contained a German officer training school. Our Colonel didn't want the town messed up too much, because he wanted it to become his Regimental Headquarters, but there were a few diehards left in town. They had a mortar set up and a machine gun set up to the only road going into town. We were fired on, and we crouched in a ditch, and then went ahead one by one, but an awful lot of the guys were hit by the fire. By the time I ran into town, I was running over dead bodies and wounded guys, but I made it into town. On the way into town, I received my only wound of the war. A machine gun bullet hit my M-1 rifle as I was carrying it at the ready position on the hip. It hit the M-1 rifle (which has a lot of wood on it), and all the wood was splintered off, and I got a sliver in my finger. Anyway, I got into town safely. This was the only time in the entire war that I shot at an individual that I could see. He was crawling up a hill a long way away, 3-400 yards away. I am sure I never hit him.

The rest of the war was mostly long walks all day long behind tanks. Once in a while we'd get strafed by a lone airplane that the Luftwaffe had left. We wound up in Heartmannsdorf, which is in Bavaria not too far from Leipzig. Our main job right then (the fighting was over but the refugees were coming through in our direction to escape the oncoming Russian Army) was to monitor the columns of escapees. It was during this period that we started the band again. They sent a truck with two of us band members back to France to pick-up the instruments that had been stored there. They assigned us two houses for the band members to live in. We rehearsed in there, and began to play company parties, officer parties, various types of parties, but they started to send guys back to the states en-route to Japan, because the Japanese war was still continuing. So our band became smaller and smaller, so we wound up with a Dixieland band. It was a lot of fun, because every time we played a company party, the host company would make sure there was a bottle of cognac under every chair, so we were never hurting for good times. One night we came home feeling pretty good, and we decided to go out the window and have a jam session in the apple tree that was alongside the house. So we got out our horns, climbed into the apple tree and played jazz (I don't think the neighbors were too happy about that). This was a time when I was able to use some of the techniques I learned from my mothers raising canaries. The master bedroom was occupied by the trumpet player and the bass player, we came home one night and there was a bird flying around their room. We couldn't get him to fly out, but I remembered what my mother did; get him wet so he can't fly, and you can set him free. So we didn't have a hose, but we had containers and buckets, so we were in their bedroom throwing buckets of water around trying to wet down the bird so he couldn't fly. We eventually did. In the meantime, Pauline and I had completed all the paperwork to get permission to get married over there. The time came that they were reassigning me to Japan, so we were married. I only had a couple of days for our honeymoon, and then was shipped back to the states, Pauline would come later. I went back on the Queen Elizabeth II, which was quite a boat. Sammy Kaye's band was on the dock in New York to play for us when we docked. By this time, the Japanese war had ended, so instead of going to Japan, I went to Ft. Snelling to be discharged. What a relief it was to be out of the Army, but I was sorry that Pauline couldn't have come home with me.

This was in November that I was discharged. I celebrated a little, and looked at some teaching jobs that hadn't been filled in November, but they looked so bad, so miserable. The band rooms were wrecks, nobody in his right mind would want to teach there. So I decided to go back to school. I applied at Eastman, but they had so many returning vets that were graduates from there that they referred me to Minnesota. So I went to the University of Minnesota. I enrolled there in January 1946, and worked on my Master's degree. One friend that was wounded in that first action we had at Echternach, he was in my Company, Al Iverson was his name, he got me a conducting job with the choir at Wesley Methodist Church in Minneapolis, next to the University. It was sometime after the first of the next year that Pauline was given transportation on a British "warbrides" boat and I met her train in Chicago. We were able to find an apartment near the University, and she secured a job at Dayton's at the cosmetic counter.

Gary Kittleson family, Gary, Fran, Joshua, Caroline and Caleb Gary's youngest

S Sgt Carl J. Kittleson 37 298 297
Born 10/25/20 US Army 8/20/42 to
10 Nov 45 I Co 417th Inf Regt, 76
Infantry Division

Sons of Carl J. Kittleson, Left Gary Right Carl J. Jr

Army of the United States

Honorable Discharge

This is to certify that

Carl J. Littleson 37 298 297 Staff Sergeant
Company I 417th Infantry

Army of the United States

is hereby Honorably Discharged from the Military Service of the United States of America
This Certificate is awarded as a testimonial of Honest and Faithful Service to this country

Given at Separation Center Camp McCoy, Wisconsin

Date 20 November 1945

Arthur M. Schmitz
Arthur M. Schmitz Major Sig C

ENLISTED RECORD AND REPORT OF SEPARATION—HONORABLE DISCHARGE

Littleson, Carl J	37 298 297	S-Sgt Inf AUS	
Co I 417th Inf	10 Nov 46	Camp McCoy Wis	
635 Wall St Mankato Minn	26 Oct 20	Lk Mankato Minn	
Des 9	Blue Brown 5-3 146 lbs		
3	X X	Teacher Music 2-5A-21	

MILITARY HISTORY

	20 Aug 42	Ft Snelling Minn	
	Nicollet Inn Dec 2		
Band Leader 022	Carbine-85 Rifle-M1		

Africa, Sicily, Central Europe

None Wounds received in action

None

American Theater Service Ribbon, European African Middle Eastern Theater
Service Ribbon, Good Conduct Medal

Jul 44 Sep 44 Sep 44	Typhus Nov 44	25 Nov 44	270	4 Dec 44
8 11 0 9 4-Jul	Unknown	USA	7 Aug 45

None

Conv of the Govt, No 1 (Demobilization) AR 615-365 15 Dec 44

PAY DATA

3 4	300 100	None	110.45	Oldenburg Maj FC

IMPORTANT Von G18081

Inactive Service (ERC) Fr 7 Aug 42 to 19 Aug 42
ASR score (2 Sep 45) 61
One (1) Overseas Service Bar
No Time Lost Under AW 107
Lapel Button Issued

Carl J. Littleson Marie E. Ehler
Marie H. Ehler 1st Lt WAC
Assistant Adjutant

16th -216- November AD 1945

970883

Appendix D

Souvenir Issue
SS Victory *Alhambra Echo*
July 14, 1946

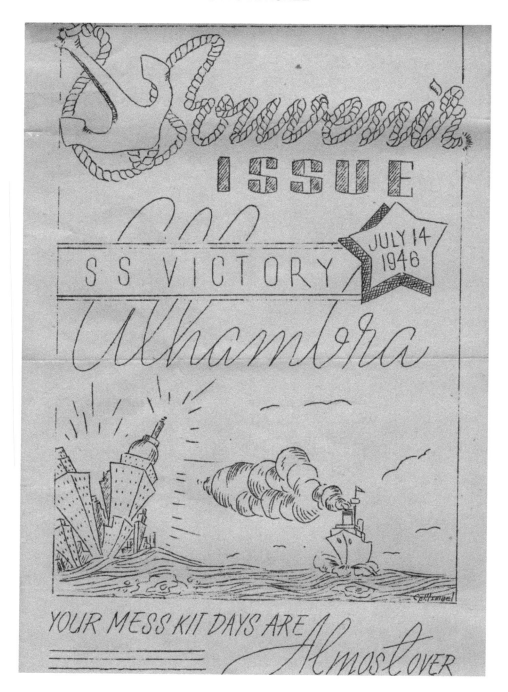

THE ALHAMBRA ECHO

Published daily aboard the S.S. Alhambra Victory under the auspices of the Special Service Office. This Publication uses Camp Newspaper Service material. Republication of credited matter prohibited without permission of CNS, 205 E. 42nd St., N. Y. C. 17.

Tr. Commander......... Capt. E. Seymour
S. S. O................ Lt. N.M. Glasgow
Editor................. Mr. M. Ackerman
Ed. Staff.............. Lt. R. Maguire
.... T/3 W. Mulford
Sports................. Sgt. S. Shapiro
.... T/5 D. James
Artist................. Cpl. J. Ysmael
Mimeograph............. T/4 K. Myers

No. 8   14 July 1946
        SOUVENIR EDITION

        *   *   *

        WHAT DO YOU THINK?

Today's question: In what ways has your Army career been beneficial to you as an individual?

1st. Lt. GEORGE P. PUSEY, Marseilles, Ill. (37 months of Service) -- Infantry Platoon Leader.

My Army service has taught me a great deal more about humanity and countries other than my own. I consider the three years in the Army definitely worthwhile.

Mr. Marshall Ackerman, Mt. Vernon, N.Y. (36 months of service) -- 1st. Scout, 36th Inf. Div.

The most important thing is that I have learned how to get along with all classes of people. It has satisfied my lust for travel - now I'm perfectly satisfied to stay in the States for the rest of my life. It has given me a finer appreciation of the things I left behind when I entered the Service.

T/Sgt. Grover Newman, Boise, Iowa. (16 months service) Section Chief Chem. Warfare Gas Dump.

The greatest benefit that I have received in the Army is the experience of meeting all nationalities and types of people and the chance to travel -- an opportunity that I wouldn't have had otherwise.

Cpl. W. D. Harrison, Greenville, Ala. (20 months service) Driver, Heavy Weapons Company, 9th Inf. Div.

Service in the Army has created for me a

chance to see more of the world than I otherwise would have. It certainly makes a man out of a boy, quickly.

T/5 Carmen Giammattei, Southington, Conn. (14 months service) Dispatcher, 3708 QM Truck Co.

The primary benefit is that I have received is sight-seeing tour of Europe.

Sgt. Robert Jones, Claymont, Del. (24 months of service) Aircraft loading tech., Orley Field (Paris).

The service in the Army has taught me a lot of things about life. The time hasn't been wasted, but I wouldn't want to do it over again.

Pfc. James Heffernan, Akron, Ohio. (22 months of service) Rifleman, 69th Inf Div.

Time in the Army has smartened me up in more ways than one, although I wouldn't want to go through it again - it hasn't been so bad as a whole.

Pfc. Edward Armanini, Springfield, Mass. (24 months service) Rifleman, 80th Inf Div

I haven't learned anything in the Army. I've enjoyed myself but it has been so much wasted time.

1st. Lt. Hubert D. Shurtz, Kinkneyville, Ill. (39 months service) S-3, 508 MP Bn.

I gained one year of college education - ASTP and Service overseas in Europe has been an education in itself. I have had and opportunity to visit the famous European spots that I have heard about but didn't understand. Also read a couple volumes of Frank Harris.

T/3 Francis Buckley, Baltimore, Md. (14 months service) Chief Clerk, Military Communities, G-4 Section, Third Army Hqs.

One of the most beneficial things has been basic training's physical fitness program, it helps make a man. Being overseas has given me the opportunity to actually see the deplorable conditions which exist in foreign countries which I had not previously believed actually existed. The American policy of occupation isn't constructive in that it doesn't try to educate the 14 year old and under German children to democratic policies. I think that some sort of Boy and Girl Scout organization should be formed to guide these future leaders of Germany.

        *   *   *

Farewell FROM THE CHAPLAIN

This is the Farewell Edition of the ALHAMBRA ECHO. Tomorrow we say farewell to the Steamship Alhambra itself. Indeed, it seems that this is a time of farewells to a number of things - farewell to many ship-board acquaintances, farewell to our many experiences in France, Germany, Austria and other countries in Europe, farewell at least for most of us to the Army, it's rules and regulations, it's uniforms and it's chow. Farewells that make us happy and perhaps some farewells that make us a bit sad.

But what happens when all the farewells have been said? Why, then we say "hello! Hello Statute of Liberty, hello America, hello Mom, hello Dad, hello baby(keep your mind on the right baby, and you know which is the right one, because this is the Chaplain that's doing the writing).

Anyway, these are some great hellos, aren't they men. Then let's add a few words to them. Hello Statute of Liberty, you can count on me just the same as ever because I'll never let you down. Hello America, I'm home again, so stop worrying. Hello Mom, gee you look good, gosh but I love you. Hello baby - oh well, fill this in yourself, if you want to.

And look men, let's say one more hello. Hello God - Thanks.

> JAMES W. CURRIE
> Ship's Chaplain

As Transport Commander, I wish to extend my thanks to all aboard for their cooperation and help in trying to make this a pleasant trip home.

May you find everything in the States as you hoped it would be. Here's wishing everyone a speedy trip from Camp Kilmer to his own Home Sweet Home.

> ERNEST H. SEYMOUR
> CAPTAIN, TC
> Transport Commander

"KUNZE UP FRONT!"

A NOTE OF THANKS

In this, the last issue of the ALHAMBRA ECHO for this trip, I wish to extend my heartfelt appreciation to several men aboard the S. S. Alhambra Victory without whom this newspaper would never have been published.

First, thanks to 1st Lt. RAYMER MAGUIRE for some swell inquiring reporter colums and all the poop on what makes the ship go. Ray, you really helped fill a gap in the paper.

Thanks to T/3 WILL MULFORD who fiddled with the radio most of the day and managed to eke some swell sports copy out of the miscellaneous code and aerial heiroglyphics spouted by the receiver. Will did a particularly super job on the All-Star game.

Thanks to SGT. SID SHAPIRO and T/5 DALLAS JAMES who literally beat out the ECHO, turning in some beautifully cut stencils in double time. They really earned their passage aboard this ship!

Merci to CPL. JOE YSMAEL who was responsible for all the art work in the paper, with the exception of one feeble attempt on the part of your editor. Joe, you did wonders with those stencils and our one measly little stylus.

Gracias, too, to T/4 KEN MYERS who must have a sore arm from grinding out so many copies of the paper. Ken is about the most expert mimeograph operator on board and he gave unstintingly of his labors to the cause.

Danke to 1st Lt. STEVE FAZEKAS, who may not play the best game of bridge in the world, but who tries hard, and can draw some nice straight lines. My appreciation also to the two ship's chaplains for their cooperation, and a special bow to 1st Lt. NORMAN GLASGOW, the Alhambra's fiery little Special Service Officer, who made this daily rag possible by showing me how to glue Camp Newspaper Service cartoons to the stencil.

And a big orchid to all the fellows who so cheerfully volunteered to come up to the Newspaper Office and staple the paper together each day. These men remain anonymous, but they deserve a vote of thanks for helping out.

So I take my hat off to the aforementioned group, who waged and won a battle against a regiment of gremlins who continually pushed the typewriter off the desk, inked the mimeograph roller, lost our copy before we put it to press, and in general, tried their best to sabotage the ECHO.

MARSHALL ACKERMAN
THE EDITOR

H-HOUR IS ALMOST HERE

We're on the last leg today -- the last leg of our journey home. No matter how rough the sea was or how often we got KP, just thinking about sailing past the Statue of Liberty made the trip a pleasant and a memorable one.

Just thinking of home meant quite a bit. As we made plans for our first few weeks over and over again in our heads, the Alhambra couldn't keep pace with our wonderful thoughts. It hasn't been a bad ship, though. We owe a lot to the ship and its crew for some mighty "smooth" sailing (most of the time).

Now, on the eve of our debarkation in the States, and our return to the schools, businesses, cities, villages and farms of America, we can already begin to look back with fond recollections of Army and ETO life. Don't jump down my throat so soon. I don't say that you'll all be reenlisting next week. But few can honestly regret their stay in the service -- all the swell friendships made, all the interesting places seen and more important, all the things learned in the past couple of years.

Most of the knowledge we have gained has consisted of small insignificant items -- how to make a bed, how to blend Vitalis and coke into a smooth drink, the culinary art of preparing K-Ration pork loaf, and maybe even a few phrases of Deutsch or Francais. But when we add all these things together, they spell an army career, and several years of our lives. Who can say these years have been wasted?

When we get back into the swing of things, people who sweated out the war on the Home Front will want our opinions of vital economic and political problems of the day. True, we aren't the first overseas veterans to return home, but our thoughts will still be welcomed and carefully weighed. The folks will want to know "was ist loess" with the army of occupation, and they'll expect us to give them the lowdown and give it sensibly.

Are you prepared to act as a spokesman for the occupational forces? Have you thought about America's part in keeping fascism under a democratic heel in Europe? And what about Russia? People will want to know these things and it's up to us to let them know the score.

We can do what a lot of men are doing -- those who return with a bitter outlook on everything and everyone. We can say the French are no good, the British are trying to milk us dry, the Russians are playing us for suckers, all officers get the gravy in Germany, etc. I don't profess to know the answers to the questions back home, but I suggest that we all use our heads in giving opinions of European and army problems. Don't sound like an empty-headed fool when you get home! Keep quiet until you have something to say, and then say it!

And conversely, don't go home bitter about the rise in prices, the industrial chaos and the consumer shortage. The world doesn't owe you a living. We all had a job to do and we all did our part creditably. Now, let's resume our places in society normally. It may be a little rough getting oriented at first. As a matter of fact, I expect that it will take me at least ten seconds to get back into the swing of things. How about you?

                                        THE EDITOR

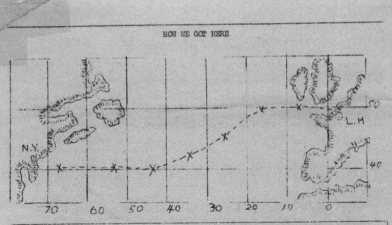

HOW WE GOT HERE

Day	Date	Latitude	Longitude	Distance Last Day	Distance Traveled	Distance To Go	Average Speed
Sat.	6th	49°30'N	0° 15'E	-	-	3160	-
Sun.	7th	49°48'N	06°40'W	265 mi	265 mi	2845	17.5 knots
Mon.	8th	49°00'N	17°42'W	431 mi	696 mi	2464	17.2 knots
Tue.	9th	45°53'N	27°05'W	418 mi	1114 mi	2048	16.7 knots
Wed.	10th	42°37'N	35°56'W	422 mi	1536 mi	1760	16.9 knots
Thur.	11th	40°26'N	44°15'W	402 mi	1958 mi	1358	16.7 knots
Fri.	12th	40°21'N	53°12'W	406 mi	2344 mi	952	16.2 knots
Sat.	13th	40°22'N	61°15'W	365 mi	2699 mi	587	14.7 knots
Sun.	14th	40°13'N	67°47'W	335 mi	3034 mi	273	14.0 knots

DOPE ON DOCKING

The S. S. Alhambra Victory will arrive at the Ambrose Light Vessel tomorrow morning, Monday, 15 July, at 0500 hours. It will proceed immediately to Pier 11, Staten Island, New York, and drop anchor.

Our final destination is Pier 15. The troops will debark, cross the pier and take the Staten Island Ferry which steams past that glorious lady, the Statute of Liberty, on the way to the railhead on the New Jersey side of the Hudson River.

We will then board trains for the Port of Debarkation at Camp Kilmer, N.J. After as short a stay there as possible, we will proceed to our respective separation centers for that little white slip of paper that we have been sweating out for the past few years. Here's wishing all a swell trip home.

MORE BOUQUETS

It seems as though we are doing nothing but thanking people in this issue of the paper, but there are a few people still to be mentioned to whom we owe our thanks.

First, the mess attendants, cooks, food handlers and KP's who made our mealtimes so pleasant. The food throughout the trip was really tops.

We must extend our thanks to Capt. Seymour for handling the difficult task of Transport Commander so ably. And also the skipper and all the officers and men of the crew for getting us home safely and quickly. The Ship's Surgeon and his staff also deserve our appreciation for tending to our ills and dishing out the welcome motion sickness preventative at the right times. Thanks also to the permanent party men, the projectionists and all the rest who made our voyage so "bon".

VICTORY SHIPS
IN WAR AND PEACE

The SS ALHAMBRA VICTORY is one of the VC-2 model ships built as a cargo vessel during the War. 455.25 feet long, 62 feet wide at midship, draft 28 feet when fully loaded, dead weight of 11,000 tons, with a convoy speed of 16 knots, and a cargo capacity of 4561 tons, she has proved to be one of the finest type of cargo vessels ever built.

In the opinion of our Skipper, Captain Arthur Dowell, the Victory ships make an excellent peace time cargo vessel. Its large holds with the smaller booms capable of lifting 5 tons, a 50 ton boom foreward of #3 hold and a 30ton boom aft of #4 hold make the Victory model ship ideal for any type of civilian cargo. Its sixteen knot speed, supplied by a 6000 horsepower super-heated steam turbine make this oil-fueled ship an economical one, in the world's fast-cargo-vessel class.

The war-time ships built by the United States mark the first time that all-welded ships received a complete trial. No definite decision has been reached, as yet, to the overall merits of all-welded ships, as the Victory-model-ship is, but apparently this type of construction has been very successful.

After V-J Day, more of the Victory model ships were converted to troop transport than any other type of U.S. Cargo vessel. In the opinion of many shipping authorities, this conversion created the finest accommodations for troops, including the large passenger liners.

The conversion of a Victory takes forty days, and makes major changes of the interior of the vessel. Large ventilation systems have to be installed, as well as plumbing and personnel entrance hatch-ways. Part of the ship's fuel bunkers are diverted to fresh water bunkers to supply the 1500 troop capacity with neccessary fresh water. Unseen by the passengers is the 1050 tons of sand and 250 tons of cement blocks used as ballast.

These transports, owned by the United States War Shipping Administration are consigned to private shipping companies for operation, and are chartered to the Army for the exclusive use of transporting its personnel to the Zone of the Interior. The company which operates the SS Alhambra Victory is the American Mail Line Limited.

THE RABBIT HUTCH

"This is the Radio Voice of the S.S. Alhambra Victory serving you with transcriptions from the Armed Forces Radio Service."

Most of us aboard ship got to know that phrase pretty well during our eight day voyage. And we appreciate the services of the two "Rabbit Hutchers" who gave us the daily entertainment.

1st Lt. Guss King Babb of Tulsa, Okla., is one member of the duet that jockeys the disks so handily. Guss was with the 83rd Infantry Division in combat and just left Salzburg, where he was a POM inspector. He plans to return to school at Oklahoma University after a restful summer at home. Guss started working in the radio game in his high school days back in Tulsa and Oklahoma City.

The versatile second party of the team is 2nd Lt. Phil Sterling, of Philadelphia, Pa. Phil has been stationed with the 39th Regiment of the 9th Infantry Division in Prien, Germany. He was a rifle platoon leader, a job he plans to give up for good now that he is almost home. His plans are indefinite after he finishes a refresher course at the University of Pennsylvania. Phil's radio experience includes service with several independent Philadelphia outlets.

Before the Rabbit Hutch sighns off for the last time, the staff of the ALHAMBRA ECHO, self-appointed spokesmen for the passengers and crew of the ship, say to the "Turntable Twins," thanks and good luck.

RADIO NEWS

CIVVY STREET

"Just got back from what war?"

"- - - TENSH - - HUT!"

"Why aren't you in civilian clothes?"

WASHINGTON -- Secretary Byrnes is expected to confer with President Truman shortly after his return from Paris today, and will make a radio broadcast to the nation, subsequently, concerning progress made by the Foreign Ministers at Paris.

TOKYO -- General MacArthur's May report to the President praised the Japanese acceptance of democratic processes. The General especially complimented the Japanese on the legal and democratic selection of a new Premier, sharply contrasted to the old secret election method.

WASHINGTON -- The House passed the British Loan yesterday and the bill now goes to the White House for the President's signature.

WASHINGTON -- Paul Porter, successor to Chester Bowles in the presently defunct OPA, forecast inflation far more serious than that which followed the last war if price controls are not promptly restored.

WASHINGTON -- Overseas air service is still disrupted as a result of the recent C.A.A. grounding of all aircraft. C.A.A. will conduct an open inquiry on the training-flight crash in Pennsylvania and a Congressional investigation may follow.

NEW YORK -- In a third memorandum to the United Nations Atomic Energy Control Committee, Bernard Baruch outlined the United State's position on atomic control. The memorandum insists that decisions on violations of the Atomic Control rulings of the U.N. not be subject to veto by one of the four powers.

*   *   *

A PLEA TO YOU

This special souvenir edition of the ALHAMBRA ECHO is being published for everyone on board the ship. Please take only one copy so that each passenger may receive this souvenir issue.

*   *   *

TODAY'S POEM

"Your teeth are like the stars," he said,
And pressed her hand so white.
He spoke the truth for like the stars,
Her teeth come out at night.

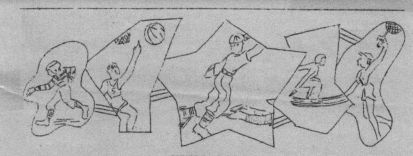

GREETING TO SPORT

Emergency restrictions of one nature or another were curtailing the American sports program at the time most of us departed from the "land of plenty." But tomorrow we return to the world's greatest sports arena, once again in full swing.

England has its cricket, Scotland its bowling-on-the-green, Norway its winter sports, Spain its bullfights; France has its bike races, Switzerland its curling matches, Greece its marathons, and Cuba its cockfights.

But where can the spectator find as many sports as your Uncle Sammy offers: football, basketball, volley ball, baseball, hockey, boxing, wrestling, track, tennis, golf, horse racing, motor-boat racing, sailing, canoeing, ice-boating, polo, swimming, water-polo, badminton, handball, ping-pong, to mention but a few.

One has a choice of the Kentucky Derby, a Joe Louis fight, the National Open, or the World Series; the Poughkeepsie Regatta, the Rose Bowl game, a Stanley Cup match, or a Salinas rodeo; the Indianapolis races, the Davis Cup play, a "Garden" basketball double-header, or a Billy Rose Aquacade.

If you want something as satisfying, but less strenuous, you may watch a billiards match, or one of horseshoes or quoits, a skeet-shooting contest, or a swimming meet (especially one with Esther Williams).

For the unusual, you can take in a log-rolling melee, a sculling championship, or a slalom event. For a real side-show try a wrestling match, and you'll get all the theatricals. Or for violent sports...some "African" golf.

It's strictly a matter of personal choice whether a Yankee Stadium double-header wows you more than a Notre Dame football classic, an Indiana basketball thriller or some wild-west bronc riding.

Perhaps you'd rather see Leo Durocher sassing the umps than Sammy Baugh tossing a touchdown pass. Maybe you'd prefer a Golden Gloves challenger flattening his opponent. Or maybe you'd even choose Crosby and Hope in a benefit golf match. You've got a world of freedom in your choice!

And whether with ice-cold-coke or foaming beer, we ALL enjoy America's universal indoor sport - second guessing (some call it Monday Morning quarterbacking) at the 19th Hole, where we argue till the wee hours over the greatest sports array in this wide world.

G I - ing THE SITUATION

INFORMATION ABOUT GOVT. BENEFITS FOR OVERSEAS VETS OF WORLD WAR II

BENEFIT	REQUIREMENTS	WHEN TO APPLY	DURATION OF BENEFIT	LENGTH OF TRAINING	MONEY BENEFITS ALLOWANCES, ETC
MUSTERING - OUT PAY.	*		Three (3) payments.		$300 in installments of $100
GI BILL OF RIGHTS EDUCATION.	Under 25 when entered service or education interrupted. (everyone gets 1 year) * *	Within 2 yrs after discharge or 2 yrs after end of war.	Courses must be completed by 7 yrs after end of war.	Up to 4 school yrs. depending on length of service. Army schooling taken off G I Bill time when Army Credits are used for civilian credits.	Free tuition, books, plus $50 a month. ($75 a month if you have dependent. Less if you have job).
LOANS.	Used for home, farm, business. Prove you are good risk. Max. interest - 4%**	Same as for education. (above)	Repaid within 20 years		Govt. guarantees 50% on loans up to $4000.
EMPLOYMENT OLD JOB.	Old job must have been "other than temporary" * *	Within 90 days after discharge.	Can't be fired for 1 yr. unless "misconduct".		Entitled to all accrued increments.
NEW JOB.	Registered with USES. * *	Anytime.		Varies with course.	
FEDERAL CIVIL SERVICE.	Take required exam. (some jobs are for Vets only)	Anytime.			5 points added to score. 10 if disabled.
READJUSTMENT ALlowances. (unemployment compensation).	Register with USES, be available for "suitable" work or for free training. * *	Within 2 yrs after discharge or end of war.	52 weeks (maximum)		$20 a week if unemployed. Diff. between wages & $23 if partially employed.
GI INSURANCE.	Present term policy may be converted after 1 yr and before 8 yrs from date of issue.* * *		In case of disability for over 6 months. Payment of premiums suspended for duration of disability		Death benefits in monthly installments to beneficiary. Face value of policy from $1000 to $10,000.
PENSIONS SERVICE CONNECTED DISABILITY	Disability incurred in or aggravated by service. * *	Anytime. Use VA Form 526.	For duration of disability (subject to exam by VA at any time)		From $11.50 to $265.00 per month.
NON-SERVICE CONNECTED DISABILITY.	Permanent disability; income less than $1000 ($2500 if married or have minor children.) * *	Anytime.	For duration of disability		$50 per month (increased to $60 after 10 yrs or at age 65).
VOCATIONAL REHABILITATION.	Pensionable disability incurred or aggravated by service. * *	See next column.	Training to be completed within 6 yrs after end of war	Up to four (4) years.	At least $92 a month, plus additional amounts for dependents.
MATERNITY AND INFANT CARE.	Wife of EM in 4 lowest pay grade (below grade of S/Sgt.) @	As soon as wife discovers pregnancy.	During pregnancy, child-birth and infant care for 1 year.		Doctor and hospital fees.

* HONORABLE DISCHARGE
** OTHER THAN DISHONORABLE DISCHARGE
*** UNSPECIFIED
@ MUST BE STILL IN ACTIVE SERVICE AT TIME OF APPLICATION FOR THESE BENEFITS.

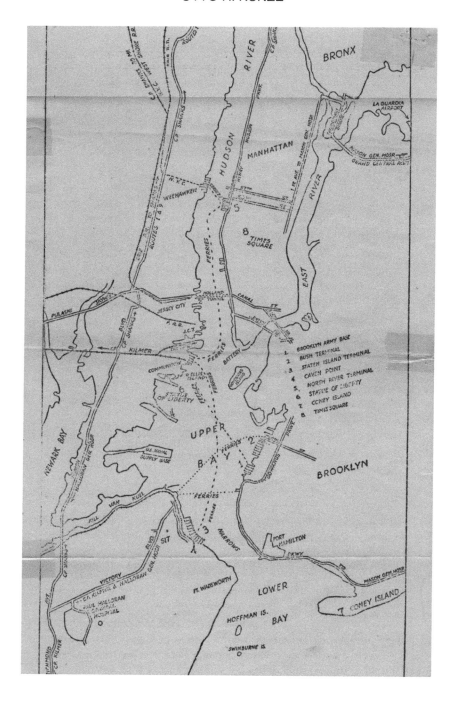

About the Author

Otto Kunze is of German ancestry and was reared in the small German community of Warda in central Texas, USA. He learned English in grade school. He graduated from high school in 1943 before being inducted for service in WWII. He fought as an infantryman in the German theater. After being discharged from the Army, he proceeded to Texas A&M University (TAMU) where he earned a BS degree in 1950. He earned an MS degree from Iowa State University in 1951 and a PhD degree from Michigan State University in 1964. All degrees were in Agricultural Engineering. His PhD research was in rice technology. He became a Professor at TAMU where he taught and did research for thirty-five years. His research garnered worldwide attention and was recognized as an Outstanding Agriculture Engineering Achievement of the 20th Century. He served as a Rice Process Consultant in India, China, Hungary, Czechoslovakia, Germany, Japan, Philippines, Taiwan,

Thailand and Puerto Rico. He also served eleven years on the Texas Air Control Board with appointments by two Governors of the State. He retired to his family farm in central Texas where he raises cattle, pursues his rice research and writes.